DEMOCRACY
&
DIPLOMACY

THE AMERICAN MOMENT

Stanley I. Kutler, Series Editor

DEMOCRACY & DIPLOMACY

The Impact of Domestic Politics on U.S. Foreign Policy, 1789–1994

Melvin Small

The Johns Hopkins University Press
Baltimore and London

To Jordan Matthew Small
and his generation, who must continue to monitor our
democracy's foreign relations in the twenty-first century

The Johns Hopkins University Press
2715 North Charles Street
Baltimore, Maryland 21218-4319
The Johns Hopkins Press Ltd., London

Material from "The Politics of Foreign Policy," a chapter
in Stanley I. Kutler (ed.), *The Encyclopedia of the United States*
in the Twentieth Century, appears with permission of Charles
Scribner's Sons, a division of Macmillan Library Reference USA,
a Simon & Schuster Company.

Library of Congress Cataloging-in-Publication Data and a list of books
in the American Moment series will be found at the end of this book.
A catalog record for this book is available from the British Library.

ISBN 0-8018-5177-7
ISBN 0-8018-5178-5 pbk.

Contents

Series Editor's Foreword

SCHOLARS, DIPLOMATS, and foreign policy practitioners regularly decry the role and influence of domestic politics on foreign policy, but they cannot wish it away. Twenty years after the Vietnam War ended, skirmishes over that war continue in the United States. The President's draft record, the fate of alleged POWs, and the normalization of relations between Vietnam and the United States resonate in domestic politics. Just when it seemed that we had an ideological consensus agreeing that the POW/MIA issue was settled, the new Republican Chairman of the House International Relations Committee attacked President Clinton for having "broken trust" with the American people as he agreed to the exchange of low-level envoys between the United States and Vietnam. Practicality, however, has reigned in this matter as American business interests, anxious to pursue the Vietnamese market potential, have been able to work their will. But the force of domestic politics stifled any real progress or initiative on Vietnam normalization for those two decades.

The role of the mass media has made the situation worse. Instant reporting about casualties and events in Somalia, for example, unleashed a tidal wave of complaint against a national policy of "nation-building" and produced pressures for the prompt withdrawal of American troops. Political groups seized the opportunity for opposition, no matter that their own president initiated the policy. Our four-year cycle of presidential elections is no longer something on the distant horizon but is always with us as political forces maneuver for some momentary advantage.

Dean Acheson, Harry Truman's Secretary of State from 1949 to 1953, found himself regularly pilloried by a Congress and a public confused, indeed terrified, by the prospects of the Cold War. Exasperated and frustrated by the vehemence of the attacks, Acheson later expressed his fear that "the limitation imposed by democratic political practices makes it difficult to conduct our foreign affairs in the national interest." That judgment is about as old as the republic itself. Alexis de Tocqueville worried that American democracy would impose passion, not prudence, on our foreign policy. Henry Kissinger and others have complained that it is impossible to effectively carry out foreign policy in an open society, beneath the glare of public scrutiny.

Melvin Small examines the influence of domestic policies on American foreign policy in this engaging, thoughtful book. While a variety of variables are important ingredients for making foreign policy—including bureaucratic politics, the philosophies of individual leaders, and, of course, rational self-interested security concerns—domestic politics may well be the most influential and difficult to understand. Ethnic Americans and their loyalty to their "roots," no matter how far removed they may be, have certainly been a powerful voice in foreign policy considerations.

But is the influence of domestic events necessarily bad, Small asks? A careful student of the interrelationship between domestic politics and foreign policy, Small questions whether the assumption about the tension between a democratic society and the conduct of foreign policy is necessarily true. Despite complaints from time to time, foreign powers have learned to live with the vagaries of American foreign policy, influenced and conditioned as it has been by frequent elections, a probing media, the sensitivities of ethnic groups, and an independent legislative branch. Using examples throughout American history, Small argues that American foreign policy makers more often blundered when they operated secretly and in an undemocratic manner than when they worked with interested groups, outside the government's institutional apparatus. Such efforts, Small suggests, were more likely to produce consensual agreements that retained public backing.

Stanley I. Kutler
Madison, Wisconsin

Acknowledgments

THIS BOOK BEGAN as an essay for *The Encyclopedia of the United States in the Twentieth Century*, edited by Stanley I. Kutler of the University of Wisconsin. After I became intrigued with the subject about which there is no book-length treatment, Kutler encouraged me to prepare one for his American Moment series. During both projects, I received invaluable advice and direction from this indefatigable natural resource in our profession. I am grateful as well to Charles Scribner's Sons for permitting me to use portions of the essay in this book.

Colleagues to whom I am indebted for reading all or part of the manuscript are Alexander DeConde, University of California–Santa Barbara; Robert A. Divine, University of Texas; Lloyd Gardner, Rutgers University; Rhodri Jeffreys-Jones, University of Edinburgh; Ralph Levering, Davidson University; Keith Nelson, University of California–Irvine; Bradford Perkins, University of Michigan; Geoffrey Smith, Queen's University; and Athan Theoharis, Marquette University.

The efficient staff of the history department of Wayne State University, Ginny Corbin, Gayle McCreedy, Delinda Neal, and Amanda Rayha, all assisted me in a variety of ways. The university granted me a sabbatical, during which time I worked on the manuscript. Helpful, as well, were the people at the Johns Hopkins University Press: Henry Tom, Barbara Lamb, and Therese Boyd. Most of all, as usual, I am indebted to my wife and best friend, Sarajane Miller-Small, who was an invaluable editor and proofreader through the book's several stages.

Introduction

WHEN ALEXIS DE TOCQUEVILLE visited the United States in the 1830s, he saw much to admire in the distinctive political system that was barely a half-century old. He expressed concern, however, about the potential for disaster in the way foreign policy had been conducted in the new republic.

> Foreign policies demand scarcely any of those qualities which a democracy possesses; and they require, on the contrary, the perfect use of almost all of those faculties in which it is deficient. . . . It cannot combine measures of secrecy, and it will not await their consequences with patience. . . . Democracies . . . obey the impulse of passion rather than the suggestions of prudence . . . and abandon a mature design for the gratification of a momentary caprice.

Tocqueville was not the first observer to worry about the abilities of democratic polities to conduct effective foreign policies. Over 2,000 years earlier, Thucydides expressed similar concerns about leaders in the Greek city-states who permitted domestic political considerations to affect questions of national security. He regretted how post-Periclean Athenians "by committing even the conduct of state affairs to the whims of the multitude . . . produced a host of blunders, and amongst them the Sicilian expedition."

To be sure, domestic political considerations affect leaders in authoritarian societies as well. They, too, must worry about how their policies will impact upon internal economic and political developments even in their tightly controlled states. History is replete with despots who sought to allay domestic discontent by fabricating external crises or by launching expansionist binges that were not in their nations' interests.

Nevertheless, leaders of authoritarian regimes are far better able to conduct diplomacy in secret than are their democratic counterparts. They do not have to worry about the vigorous press in a free society that often foils attempts by presidents to shield their foreign policies from public view. One of the hallmarks of a democratic society is supposed universal access to information about the nation's business. But such openness just does not work in the international sphere where diplomats hold their cards close to their vests. Woodrow Wilson himself realized the folly of trying to negotiate "open covenants, openly arrived at" once he began operating in the real world of international politics.

Even more important, autocratic rulers are not compelled to stand for freely contested elections during which time often uninformed or jingoistic voters evaluate their foreign policies. For American presidents, this means that during their first term, after spending six to nine months learning the job, they have a year and a half at most to fashion bold or controversial foreign initiatives before they have to begin running on their record sometime prior to their fourth year in office. During that year, because almost everything that presidents do or say in the international arena affects election prospects, they tread cautiously, or pander to popular nationalist sentiments in ways that are not always defensible in terms of the national interest. The situation does not improve appreciably during presidents' second term because they are seen by foreigners as lame ducks with waning powers whose policies will be changed by their successors.

Moreover, candidates often use foreign policy issues demogogically in ways that could ultimately affect national security. On one occasion in 1969, National Security Advisor Henry Kissinger warned the Soviet ambassador not to pay attention "to separate critical statements by the president on one Eastern European country or another, since this is only tribute to some layers of the U.S. population which play a role in American elections."

During election years, the opposition party, as well as other nations, rightly suspect that presidential foreign policy initiatives are geared, more than usual, to currying favor with voters and not necessarily to protecting the national interest of those voters. For that reason, the president's opponents in Congress are often reluctant to endorse initiatives that might be perceived as "victories" in the election campaign.

Whether in election years or not, presidents often feel compelled to cloak narrow, realistic policies in sweeping moralistic pronouncements in order to obtain support from a public allegedly too uninformed to understand the nature of international politics. Such oversimplification and overselling, which might transform an issue of *Realpolitik* into a crusade to protect freedom, can often come home to haunt a president who wants to retreat from the brink of war with a compromise settlement or even to end a war short of unconditional surrender.

Introduction

A prying free press, the requirement to stand for reelection, and the need to obtain popular endorsement for foreign policies are not the only disadvantages that democratic leaders face in the construction and conduct of foreign policy. They also find it more difficult than their undemocratic counterparts to finance their military and national security establishments, particularly in peacetime. Until the Cold War, Americans resisted allocating resources to enhance such allegedly needless—and dangerous—institutions as an army and a navy and even a diplomatic service. Indeed, this is one of the reasons why the United States, along with other democracies, was ill-prepared to confront its better-armed adversaries in the two world wars. This point also explains why the United States, more than most other nations, has been forced to rely on wealthy amateur diplomats to run embassies in major capitals.

Writing in *Why England Slept* twenty-two years before he became president, John F. Kennedy, while granting that "democracy is the superior form of government" in the long run, noted that "when it competes with a system of government . . . built primarily for war, it is at a disadvantage. . . . The weight of public opinion in the dictatorship . . . will not be of decisive importance. The dictator is able to know exactly how much democracy is bluffing because of the free press, radio, and so forth."

The pluralistic United States, with its decentralized governmental system, is weakened further in the international sphere by the relative independence of branches of the executive department, each backed by its own powerful constituency groups. For example, the Department of Labor often calls for protectionist foreign policies, while the Department of Commerce usually advocates freer trade. Similarly, when it comes to military policy, the armed services often quibble among themselves over defense appropriations, concerned about their own bailiwicks and not necessarily the national interest.

Although presidents must defend the national interest, they are not omnipotent, even in their own households when confronting entrenched and permanent bureaucracies and their related interest groups and lobbies. Discussing prospects for freer trade in the 1950s, Pres. Dwight David Eisenhower complained,

> The almond growers of California, the manufacturers of band instruments from coast to coast . . . all these and hundreds of others have added their voices to the powerful pleas of lead and zinc and of oil and coal. . . . We had an issue where the good of the United States as a whole was pitted against the power of influential lobbies.

Even societies with freely elected parliaments have been spared some of the problems in the American system created by the inherent conflict between an independent executive and an independent legislature, each of which has overlapping, constitutionally prescribed responsibilities. According to political scientist Edwin S. Corwin, the often vague and ambiguous Constitution "is an invitation to struggle for the privilege of directing American foreign policy."

Who makes American foreign policy? The president is commander-in-chief of the armed forces, but Congress declares war. Presidents execute foreign policy but Congress pays the bills. Presidents negotiate treaties but they must be approved by the Senate, and so on. Indeed, six of the eighteen powers delegated to Congress in the Constitution relate to foreign affairs. And it is not merely overlapping responsibilities that cause problems. Considering the requirements for effective diplomacy in the modern world, political scientist Robert A. Dahl found Congress, the president's partner, "remarkably ill-suited to exercise a wise control over the nation's foreign policies." The situation is exacerbated by the fact that almost all senators and representatives are elected largely on local issues related to their districts and states.

The American system is unique. For much of the nation's history, no other major international actor has divided responsibilities for foreign affairs between the executive and legislative branches of government. In Great Britain and Canada, for example, the government, led by a prime minister who enjoys a parliamentary majority, speaks with one voice when she or he announces a program. Further, American political parties in Congress exhibit far less discipline than their British and Canadian cousins.

On the other hand, with a two-party character, congressional politics are somewhat more predictable and stable in the United States than in countries such as Germany, France, and Israel. In multiparty legislatures, governments are often cobbled together from groups of disparate parties, each of which, no matter how small, might exercise a veto over the prime minister's foreign policies. All the same, when the prime ministers of countries such as Germany, France, and Israel do finally announce a program, they generally do so with one authoritative voice.

These problems distress not only Americans. Other governments complain about the lack of continuity in America's foreign relations. Presidents, who change every four or eight years, often abruptly announce new programs and emphases in the international sphere. This has become common in the post–World War II era, when seemingly intractable and controversial domestic problems drive presidents to concentrate on foreign relations where they think they can make a name for themselves. Tocqueville also anticipated this possibility when he noted that "it is chiefly in its foreign affairs that the executive power of a nation finds occasion to exert its skill and strength. If the existence of the union were perpetually threatened . . . the executive government would assume an increased importance."

In addition, because of the Senate's responsibility to reject or amend treaties, America's diplomatic partners cannot be certain that senators will endorse agreements initialed by presidents. More often than not, senators look at treaties in terms of what is in it for their regions or parties, not the nation as a whole. One post–Civil War secretary of state labeled the Senate's treaty veto the "irreparable mistake of the Constitution." Later, concerned about his ability to conduct an effective diplomacy, Secretary of State John Hay complained that a "third of the Senate was always to be found on the blackguard side of any question." He exaggerated, of course. From 1789 to 1988, of the 1,476 treaties submitted to the Senate for advice and consent, only 20 were voted down, and of those, only two since 1945. On the other hand, 15 percent were amended and many simply were not submitted because presidents knew they would flounder in the Senate. Advocates of a major role for the legislature in the treaty-making process wanted to keep the then–splendidly isolated nation's international obligations to a minimum. As Gouverneur Morris noted, "The more difficulty in making treaties, the more value will be set upon them."

Presidents have been able to circumvent the Senate through executive agreements. During the first 200 years of the union, they concluded 12,778 such agreements, with more than 10,000 coming after 1950. Many important agreements could just as well have been treaties had presidents dared submit them to the Senate.

On occasion, the mere existence of the Senate waiting to eviscerate any treaty or other agreement can play a convenient role for the president's negotiators. When in 1956, for example, Secretary of State John Foster Dulles told the Egyptians that the United States had decided to withdraw its offer to finance the Aswan Dam, he claimed that Congress made him do it. Actually, the withdrawal came at an executive initiative, largely reflecting the secretary's personal pique at Egyptian leader Gamal Abdul Nasser.

Cataloguing America's weaknesses in the foreign sphere, Tocqueville did not foresee the problem of dual loyalties in a multi-ethnic nation. Gouverneur Morris was more prescient than the French observer when, in 1787, he called for a long residency period for eligibility to stand for the Senate because "admit a Frenchman into your Senate, and he will study to increase the commerce of France; an Englishman, he will feel an equal bias in favor of that of England."

When Tocqueville visited the United States a half-century later, most white Americans were "Anglo-Americans," as he called them. After massive Irish immigration in the 1840s and 1850s, as well as the arrival of representatives of other nationalities through the decades such as Germans and Jews, ethnic minority groups became an important factor in the determination of certain foreign policies.

To be sure, many other states contain such unassimilated groups. Currently, only seven members of the international system—Denmark, Iceland, Japan, Luxembourg, the Netherlands, Norway, and Portugal—can be classified as ethnically homogeneous states without cross-border irredentist problems. Only one of them, Japan, is a major power. All of the other major powers over the past two centuries have had to contend with ethnic minorities. But the democratic United States has been the only one among them that lacks the ability to suppress the cacophony of voices from electorally powerful ethnic groups.

One of the twentieth century's most rigid isolationists, Sen. William E. Borah (R-Idaho), adopted his position in part because "this country has within her boundary people from almost every land under the sun, still conscious under certain conditions of the 'mystic chords of memory,'" which, he contended, could "transfer the racial antipathies . . . and controversies of the Old World into our very midst."

There is no reason why ethnic, economic, and political groups cannot contribute to an effective foreign policy in a democratic system. If the goal of foreign policy is to defend national security on the bases of the best interests of the entire country, however, those and other groups would have to participate in the debate over foreign policy with their own interests subservient to the national interest. This would mean, for example, that those who support Israel should urge Washington to support the Arab position when that is in the national interest, or that nineteenth-century New England fishermen should have ignored what they perceived to be British provocations when Washington determined that London was behaving in a manner consistent with international law, or that in election years opposition political parties should support a president's diplomatic initiatives that enhance national security even though they also improve his or her electoral prospects.

Unfortunately, most of the time in American history things have not worked out that way. Many U.S. foreign policies have reflected the power of strong domestic groups or lobbies, which, at least in hindsight, did not always have the national security interests of the whole at heart. The same thing has happened on domestic issues, but there the outcome of the self-interested hauling and mauling was seldom lethal. In the international sphere, Walter Lippmann found that democratic public opinion was "a dangerous master of decisions when the stakes are life and death." Here he echoed Alexander Hamilton, who wrote in the *Federalist Papers* that "the cries of the nation and the importunities of their representatives have . . . dragged monarchs into war, or continued them . . . sometimes contrary to the real interests of the state."

Because of such concerns, many political theorists from the seventeenth through nineteenth centuries consciously distinguished between the domestic and foreign spheres in their treatises about the nature of democracy. Writing in 1690, John Locke contended that foreign policy "must be left in great part to the prudence of those who have this power committed to them, to be managed to the best of their skill for the advantage of the commonwealth."

"The people" should become involved in foreign affairs in a democracy, as one idealized solution to the problem puts it, by setting broad goals for presidents to implement through the means of their choice. The people participate in the definition of broad strategy, the presidents are responsible for tactics and implementation. But the division of responsibility rarely works out so neatly. For example, during the Cold War, Americans wanted their leaders to protect them from perceived Soviet aggression but not to blow up the world or spend too much money doing it. At the start of the Vietnam War, most Americans approved the broad strategy of saving South Vietnam from communism. However, when Pres. Lyndon Johnson decided in 1965 to bomb North Vietnam to achieve that *strategic* goal, a growing minority of citizens demanded participation in the decisionmaking dealing with military *tactics*.

FROM 1789 through most of the nineteenth century, few worried about these difficult—and in many ways unprecedented—problems. The United States, secure behind its oceanic barriers, was not an important player in the Eurocentric international system. In addition, electronic media, with the capability of bringing the world live into each citizen's living room, did not yet exist. Nevertheless, even during its first 100 years, the unique nation-state became involved in many major foreign crises. In all of them, domestic political considerations figured prominently in the development of strategies to meet external threats.

In the discussion that follows, I look briefly at some celebrated cases of the influence of domestic politics on the foreign policies of the United States during the early years and then turn to the twentieth century for a more detailed analysis of this complex relationship. Despite the concentration here on domestic political variables, one should bear in mind that other sets of variables, including external events, bureaucratic politics, and the philosophies and psychologies of individual leaders, help to explain the contours of all nations' foreign relations. Above all, rational, self-interested security concerns figure in decisionmaking much of the time.

The analysis of domestic issues, which were often unrelated to national security interests, will call for a good deal of second-guessing. In making those judgments, I begin from the premise that one can generally define, at least from hindsight, national security interests in terms of the defense of the nation's territory, economy, political status, or even moral position from foreign assault. Ideally, the process by which threats to the national interest were identified and policies to meet those threats were fashioned should have been little affected by narrow domestic political issues. Presidents, Congress, and lobbies all have claimed to have only the broadest national security interests in mind when they supported or opposed certain foreign policies. We shall see.

There are those, of course, who claim that one domestic variable in particular—the economic needs of the nation-state—explain not just American foreign relations but all nations' foreign relations. They suggest that one can account for the general thrust—as well as perturbations—in a nation's foreign policies on the bases of the state of its economy. There is evidence, for example, that democratic states are most likely to engage in war or threatening international behavior during difficult economic times.

Further, in the case of the United States, the people who run its diplomatic and military establishments are more likely to be temporary appointees who come from the corporate and legal communities than career bureaucrats, as is the case in many other countries. In the period since World War II, prominent secretaries of defense have come from General Motors, Ford, Procter and Gamble, and the Bechtel Corporation, while prominent secretaries of state have come from major law firms such as Covington and Burling, Sullivan and Cromwell, and Simpson, Thacher, and Bartlett. With constant traffic from Wall Street and corporate boardrooms to Washington and back, no wonder that one secretary of defense could say that what was good for General Motors was good for the country and vice versa.

Although I discuss a variety of economic issues in this survey, including general economic health, the defense budget, tariffs and trade, fisheries, the environment, and immigration and nationalization, I also examine many other domestic matters. In addition, despite my main concern with the impact of domestic politics on foreign politics, I consider as well the impact of foreign politics on domestic politics.

Ultimately though, any analysis of the relationship between American domestic and foreign politics must remain incomplete. Domestic components lurk behind virtually every American international interaction. Consequently, I will highlight only the most celebrated cases as well as those that illustrate general themes in this area. Furthermore, as I concentrate on Washington, I will have to ignore other capitals where domestic political problems proved sometimes as central to the foreign policymaking process as they were in the United States. This will become more of an issue as we move through the twentieth century. When the United States entered world politics in 1776, however, no other nation practiced a democratic foreign policy.

DEMOCRACY & DIPLOMACY

ONE

Establishing a Tradition,
1789–1895

FROM THE START, domestic politics influenced American foreign policies—and especially vice versa. Foreign policy issues were central to the process that led those in charge of the government under the Articles of Confederation to reconfigure the American political system with a new Constitution. In no area was the Confederation so weak as in the international sphere. Congress could not solve serious boundary and economic problems with its two chief antagonists, England and Spain, in good measure because of its ineffective political apparatus.

Lacking any central diplomatic authority, the thirteen states were free to conduct their own foreign affairs in a chaotic system that frustrated other nations' attempts to establish a stable relationship with the geographical entity calling itself the United States of America. Whatever emerged from the deliberations in 1787, all delegates to the constitutional convention agreed that something had to be done to improve the way the republic handled its external affairs.

When George Washington assumed office in 1789 as the nation's first president, he had to interpret the often vague and ambiguous new Constitution in an ad hoc manner as foreign problems arose. Each action he took set a precedent for the way Congress and the president would interact in the future.

For example, while his agents were involved in treaty negotiations with southern Indians in August 1789, Washington appeared before the Senate to accept its advice and consent as required by the Constitution. He asked the Senate seven questions relating to the negotiations and followed each with "Do you advise and consent?" When the Senate moved to refer his questions to committee, Washington angrily responded, "This defeats every purpose of my coming here." He wanted immediate action. From that point, presidents generally presented completed treaties to the Senate for action, although some learned that prior consultations with legislators could smooth the way for eventual consent.

Washington established another important precedent in 1789 when he appointed Gouverneur Morris special agent to negotiate a commercial treaty with Great Britain. Circumventing the secretary of state, who was already on a short leash because of Congress's oversight responsibilities for cabinet officers, the first president discovered quickly the value of employing personal emissaries to handle diplomatic problems. Three years later, his postmaster-general negotiated an agreement on international postal regulations. This "treaty," which was not submitted to the Senate, was the first of nearly 13,000 executive agreements authorized by American presidents.

The new Constitution, which apparently gave the president the potential to become more powerful than Congress in developing and executing foreign policy, did not alter the crucial role that domestic politics continued to play in that area. When the emerging Federalist and Democratic-Republican factions adopted opposing positions on the French Revolution in the early 1790s, many who chose sides did so for partisan reasons. Indeed, the development of the American two-party system itself was both cause and effect of the positions taken on this issue by members of the government. Washington, Alexander Hamilton, and their crowd—the Federalists, or "British bootlickers" as critics called them—were less sympathetic to the French revolutionaries and more sympathetic to the British than Thomas Jefferson, James Madison, and their faction of "Gallic jackals" who became Republicans.

Hamilton, the secretary of the treasury, was convinced that the route to solvency lay through rapprochement with Great Britain. The maintenance of a healthy Anglo-American trade link was central to that endeavor. He was so concerned about the alleged Anglophobia and Francophilia of Jefferson, the secretary of state, that he operated his own secret foreign policy, often undercutting Jefferson by revealing American strategies to British agents and even advising them on postures to assume with American diplomats. In 1791, fearful that Congress would begin discriminating against British ships and goods, Hamilton advised London how to head off the crisis. Three years later, he again worked under the table with the British to avert another round of discriminatory legislation. On that occasion, Congress threatened Hamilton's programs with a bill to cut off trade with Great Britain which failed in the Senate only after Vice-President John Adams cast the tie-breaking vote.

Hamilton's behavior was less treasonous than it seems, considering the many different actors in the American government directly interested in international matters. From the treasury secretary's perspective, he had to be deeply involved with foreign affairs, particularly those dealing with trade policy. Nevertheless, the secretary of state was supposed to be preeminent in the international sphere. Jefferson was not the last secretary of state to confront this problem. Although few of his successors leaked strategies to foreign agents in the Hamiltonian manner, many cabinet officers, personal representatives of presidents, and later, national security advisors undercut the authority of secretaries of state, often with the approval of the chief executives. Jefferson resigned in late 1793, in part because he felt that Hamilton directed American foreign policy.

More than economic reasons drove Hamilton to challenge Jefferson for control of that policy. In aligning with French democrats or British conservatives, Americans also symbolically registered their views on the kind of domestic society and institutions they preferred. At no time in the nation's history after this point were domestic and diplomatic issues so intertwined, except perhaps during the Cold War when Americans fought communism and radicalism at home and abroad.

The activities of French agents in the United States also contributed to the epochal schism that led to the American party system. This was not the first time the French had meddled in American politics. During the Revolutionary period, their agents bribed or otherwise paid off congressmen and journalists to affect the outcome of foreign policy debates in their ally's Congress—and sometimes succeeded.

The problems began again in 1793 when Citizen Edmond Genêt arrived from France to enlist support for his country. He toured the nation, outfitting privateers to make war from American ports upon the British merchant marine, and tried to organize private armies to strike at British possessions near the United States. A majority of Americans were enthusiastic about the French Revolutionary government and its cause in the war that had just begun with Great Britain and its allies. Without thinking about the economic, political, and even military repercussions, some wanted to help France defeat their old enemy once again. Unwilling to become carried away by the romanticization of the link between the two democratic republics, Washington and his cabinet, including the allegedly Francophilic Jefferson, strongly opposed Genêt's meddling and announced a neutrality policy for the United States. This marked the first time that the young government adopted a major policy against the apparent wishes of a majority of the citizens. Some in Congress, and Jefferson himself, also evinced concern about the propriety of the president's unilateral proclamation of neutrality. Washington made amends later in the year when he consulted with Congress on the neutrality issue and admitted, "It rests with the wisdom of Congress to correct, improve, or enforce this plan of procedure."

Following Washington's putatively anti-French démarche, the atmosphere in the then-capital Philadelphia was tense, as mobs of Genêt supporters appeared daily on the streets to call for the president's removal from office. John Adams wrote about those dangerous times "when ten thousand people in the streets of Philadelphia, day after day, threatened to drag Washington out of his house and effect a revolution in the government."

Ultimately this potentially violent opposition backfired and embarrassed Jefferson. But the French did not learn from the experience. In 1796, their minister to the United States interfered directly in the presidential election, urging Americans who loved liberty and France to vote for Jefferson over John Adams and warning that an Adams victory would bring war.

The French schemes were counterproductive. Most Americans, including those who generally approved of French foreign policies, became so antagonistic to their meddling that this was the first and last time another nation tried to shape the outcome of an American election so blatantly. Such a reaction to foreign intervention in one's political processes is not just an American phenomenon. During the Cold War, Americans were occasionally caught trying to influence elections in developing nations; they, too, paid a comparable price when anti-American candidates often rode a tide of nationalist outrage to victory.

The meddling French agents worried about the American rapprochement with Great Britain symbolized by the Jay Treaty, which was approved by the Senate in 1795 by the narrowest of margins. In an early example of the difficulty caused by overlapping responsibilities for foreign affairs, even after President Washington proclaimed the treaty as law in 1796, Republicans in the House of Representatives, the branch of the legislature with presumably few responsibilities in foreign affairs, were almost successful in killing it. Their opposition to the bill to provide the funds necessary to implement the treaty fell short by three votes after a bitter partisan struggle, during which House chairman Frederick Muhlenberg (R.-Pa.) broke ranks with fellow Republicans to accept the bill. For his "treason" to the cause, he not only lost his next election but was stabbed by his Republican brother-in-law. Washington was quite disturbed by the affair, which he viewed as an unconstitutional attempt by the House to involve itself in the treaty-making process. He was also privately distressed by the rancor surrounding the debate over the Jay Treaty. Because of their support for the treaty, John Jay had been burned in effigy and Alexander Hamilton faced a stone-throwing mob.

This was not the only time that the House tried to circumvent the Constitution in the treaty-consenting process. In 1825, in part because some representatives were angered by what they claimed was Pres. John Quincy Adams's theft of the 1824 election, the House delayed so long in appropriating funds to send two delegates to the Panama Conference of newly independent Latin American states that the Americans did not reach the conference in time to participate. Their absence helped the British consolidate their position as the major foreign power in the region. In addition, in 1868 the Russian minister to the United States had to bribe House members in order to come up with enough votes in that chamber to fund the Alaskan purchase, as necessitated by the Senate-approved treaty. And, as we shall see, during the Cold War Congress frequently attached crippling amendments to foreign aid bills that affected presidential foreign policies.

Presidents have been able to circumvent what they perceive to be extraconstitutional House meddling by artful bookkeeping (as was the case during the Vietnam War) or by refusing to spend funds appropriated by Congress. All the same, the House's attempt to worm its way into the treaty-making process clearly violated the spirit of the Constitution, which separates the responsibility of the two chambers in that arena.

Broadsides in party-related American newspapers increased the intensity of partisan conflict over issues relating to the French Revolution and the world war that began in 1793. On occasion, their reports inflamed the population in ways that forced Washington's hand. He sent Jay to England to ameliorate Anglo-American problems in part because of popular pressures fanned by the press for an aggressive response to the illegal seizures of American vessels and property by the British navy during the first two years of its war against France. To make matters worse, when the treaty was completed and still held in secrecy, the *Philadelphia Aurora,* an opposition newspaper, obtained a copy and published it. This was one of the first in a long series of major leaks of state secrets that bedevil American diplomats to the present day.

Other nations soon confronted comparable problems. As they adopted democratic institutions, their playing fields with the United States began to level out; their state secrets also became fair game for enterprising journalists and partisan leakers. Sometimes, government officials themselves leaked information to the Fourth Estate either to affect diplomatic processes or to launch trial balloons. On one occasion in 1965, Lyndon Johnson became outraged about a diplomatic secret that appeared in the press. He called for an investigation to find and punish the traitor in his midst. His aides calmed him down when they reminded him that he himself was responsible for the purposeful leak. Most of the time, however, American—and other Western—politicians have been embarrassed and inconvenienced by premature revelations of their diplomatic strategies. In a more tightly controlled society with only an official press, authoritarian leaders may clamp a tighter lid on inflammatory stories or prevent security breaches.

Moreover, throughout American history, the free press has often propelled presidents into places they might not have selected to be on their own. One wonders, for example, whether American troops ever would have been dispatched to Somalia in 1992 had it not been for the "feeding frenzy" of journalists covering the story with heart-rending pictures of starving children. After all, just as many children were starving in the Sudan during the same period, but few newspeople were present to record those horrors.

Conversely, presidents are often more than equal to the task of competing for popular support with the press. George Washington was so distressed with the partisanship that dominated the debate over national security in Congress and the newspapers that he felt compelled to defend his policy in his Farewell Address, which he sent to a Philadelphia newspaper in September 1796. This was not a true "farewell" since he was not scheduled to leave office until March the following year. His address, including the famous admonition against "entangling alliances" that affected generations of Americans, was, in part, a political broadside to help John Adams against Jefferson in the upcoming election and a defense of the Jay Treaty, which had become a central issue in the campaign. The power of the president to compete with the press for public attention and, especially, to set the news agenda increased exponentially with the development of electronic media in the 1930s. One wonders how American history might have been altered had Washington, Madison, Lincoln, or Wilson been able to appeal directly to their constituents on radio or television.

INTERNATIONAL PROBLEMS did not go away when Adams assumed the presidency. The second president worried about the way "the difference between France and England occasions the differences here. This is to me a frightful consideration." As Anglo-American relations warmed during the last years of the eighteenth century, Franco-American relations deteriorated until they reached the stage of an undeclared, or naval "quasi-war" in 1798. This first undeclared war established an important precedent. (Washington had gone to war against Native American tribes but they were not considered nation-states.) In response to the president's order to the Navy to take action against the French on the high seas, Congress established the Navy Department, reestablished the Marine Corps, ordered the construction of twenty-four new vessels, enlarged the standing army, and authorized the Navy to capture French vessels. But it never declared war. Three years later, Thomas Jefferson initiated another undeclared naval war against the North African state of Tripoli, which he accused of state piracy. He, too, received authorization from Congress to protect American seamen from the North Africans. In this instance, Jefferson justified his actions by noting that the Pasha had already declared war against the United States. Congress has declared war five times in American history. Presidents have sent naval and military forces into battle on at least 200 other occasions, and not always with congressional approval.

Adams's war with France did not escalate beyond a relatively bloodless affair limited to periodic naval battles. In 1800, when he confronted the prospect of expanding the war or accepting a compromise peace, he had to consider the impact of his choice on his chances for reelection. Most likely, he could have helped himself by escalating rather than de-escalating in 1800, but in an unusual gesture of statesmanship he opted for a peaceful resolution of the dispute, a solution that proved unpopular with bellicose members of his party. His purge of high Federalists in government who opposed his approach to France may have sealed his fate in the presidential election. Adams later referred to his compromise peace program as the "most disinterested and meritorious action of my life." In comparable situations during reelection campaigns, not all presidents have behaved in such an apparently selfless manner.

The Federalist-Republican or Hamilton-Jefferson conflict over Anglo-American and Franco-American relations revealed several difficulties in the operation of a democratic foreign policy. In the most general sense, Jefferson and Madison argued time and again for the establishment of a new diplomacy based more upon morality and the principles of the revolutionary Model Treaty of 1776. This treaty suggested that the United States would break away from the existing international system as a neutral nation that would not employ Machiavellian principles in its diplomacy and that would promulgate new commercial principles for itself and like-minded neutrals. The Republicans' more realistic opponents, while giving lip service to democratic ideals, were prepared to operate within the existing system according to the amoral rules of international intercourse. Theoretically, with Jefferson's election in 1800, the issue appeared to be settled. But that was not the case.

The Federalists and Republicans clashed as well on defense policy. The bumptious Republicans, who talked more imprudently of war with Great Britain during the 1790s than did the Federalists of war with France, opposed large standing peacetime armies and navies. To play on the famous words of a later bumptious president, they talked loudly and carried no sticks. From the Republican perspective, and indeed from the perspective of a majority of Americans until the late 1940s, a standing army was not only costly but antithetical to a democratic system. In such a polity, when the republic was in peril, patriotic yeomen would drop their ploughs and take up arms to defend their sacred soil. Such volunteer soldiers, who could shoot the eye from a squirrel at 100 paces, would be more than a match for professional soldiers who fought only for money paid by despotic rulers—and as myth suggested, the American Revolution demonstrated. Republicans also feared that Federalists might use a standing army to suppress popular dissent. Thus, when the Republicans ultimately led the country into war in 1812, the nation was woefully unprepared because of the party's nondefense policy.

The election of 1800 was perhaps the first in which an ethnic minority group played a role by backing a candidate who promised to do the most for its homeland. Indeed, in some states citizens of foreign countries could even vote. Jefferson, who was perceived to be more Anglophobic than Adams, received a significant number of votes from Irish-Americans in New York and Pennsylvania, two key states he needed to win. Some ethnic groups also turned against the Federalists because of the harsh alien laws the Federalist-dominated Congress had passed in 1798 during the quasi-war with France. The sedition laws passed during that same year, which imposed fines and imprisonment for those "hindering the operation of the government," upset other Americans who feared that legitimate dissent had been muzzled. Thus, passionate democratic opposition to the alien and sedition acts, passed in presumed response to the need to maintain unity and security during an undeclared war, contributed to Jefferson's victory margin.

Party politics again became a factor during consideration of the Louisiana Purchase in 1803. Americans in areas bordering the Spanish and then French territory long had clamored for assistance from Washington to obtain free access to the Mississippi and certain commercial activities in New Orleans. In response to their pleas, Federalists had introduced and passed in Congress aggressive resolutions calling upon the president to protect American rights against the French in the area. When Jefferson obtained Louisiana, many Federalists turned around and opposed the windfall on partisan grounds, national security interests to the contrary notwithstanding. That is, if Jefferson is for it, we are against it, especially since the new states of the territory would most likely support Republican policies.

To be sure, one did not have to be a narrow partisan to express concern about the Louisiana Purchase. John Quincy Adams, who possessed a national vision, felt that taking the territory was "greater in itself and more comprehensive in its consequences than all the assumptions of implied power in the years of the Washington and Adams administrations." Jefferson himself was concerned about the constitutionality of his actions. A strict constructionist, he privately doubted whether he had the power to purchase the territory and make its inhabitants citizens of the United States. But abstract philosophical arguments paled in the face of the need to expand the country to maintain its agrarian nature. He was convinced that the unique democracy being developed in the United States could best be preserved by increasing the demographic dominance of the yeoman farmer. A smaller United States could eventually be dominated by a commercial- and urban-oriented majority less likely to perpetuate the values of the Revolution. The United States, therefore, had to expand in order to preserve its national character.

Through the first half of the nineteenth century such expansion was linked as well to another domestic issue—slavery. Given the delicate balance between slave and free states, whenever expansion became an issue, whether it involved dreams of annexing Canada or grabbing parts of the Mexican southwest, the indigenous populations' stance on slavery became as important a consideration as the diplomatic and martial strategies employed to obtain the territories.

ALTHOUGH FEDERALISTS were strongest in New England, more than just partisan issues provoked their opposition to Jefferson's economic war against England. Whatever the wisdom of his ill-fated embargo of 1807, Jefferson's measure was a self-denying program that struck hardest at the pocketbooks in one section of the country. That section's reaction demonstrated the difficulty of convincing people worried about their livelihoods to see beyond regional concerns. In the debates over terminating the policy, one Virginia representative asked in 1808, "Are the great interests of the country to be given up, because one class of people would receive relief from it?" Opponents of the embargo might respond that as New Englanders went so went the rest of the nation. Hence their position was principled and not selfish. But all particular economic groups could make similar cases over any issue that concerned them. Moreover, it was one thing to oppose the embargo in political debate; it was quite another for the affected states to refuse to enforce its provisions. This resistance led Jefferson, a presumed champion of states' rights, to send federal agents to New England to make certain that the law of the land was being observed.

Trying to make the best of an unpopular program forced upon him by the British, Jefferson claimed that his embargo would encourage the development of a more autarkic economy. By cutting off trade with Great Britain, the nascent American commercial sector would begin to thrive.

Jefferson rammed his embargo through Congress in frustration over his inability to obtain a general settlement with London following the *Chesapeake* affair. The clearly illegal attack by a British vessel against the American frigate *Chesapeake,* resulting in the death of three sailors, had incensed Americans more than any single incident during the decade prior to the War of 1812. Citizens of Virginia were so enraged that the governor had to call out the militia to keep order. Jefferson could have obtained a declaration of war against the British had he asked for one at that point. Moreover, in 1807, because of the *Chesapeake* outrage, the country was far more unified than it would be in 1812. Of course, given the Republicans' nondefense policy, the nation was ill-prepared to do battle with the British empire in 1807. Thus, the president wisely decided to ignore the impassioned pleas for war from large segments of the public.

James Madison's policies toward Great Britain, which led ultimately to the War of 1812, were also shaped by domestic politics, with, for one thing, the 1812 election weighing heavily upon him as he decided for war in the spring of that year. From 1805 through 1812, the Republicans failed to resolve their many disputes with Great Britain. Even though no new crises had arisen in 1811 and early 1812, Madison felt that time was running out and that he had to take forceful action to defend national security—and his party's political security. His opponents in the fast-fading Federalist party helped keep alive their slim hopes of a return to power through an incessant attack on the failures of every measure the Republicans had introduced to protect national

Democracy and Diplomacy

security over the previous two administrations. The importance of the election in the war–no war decision becomes even more salient when one considers that this was the only one of America's major wars until Vietnam that was not precipitated by a specific *casus belli*—Mexican soldiers shot at Americans in 1846, the *Maine* sank in 1898, the Germans declared unlimited submarine warfare in 1917, the Japanese attacked Pearl Harbor in 1941, and North Koreans crossed the 38th parallel in 1950. What was the *casus belli* in the spring of 1812? Two of the five grievances presented by Madison in his war message to Congress, impressment and the British-backed Indian menace on the frontier, were no longer serious problems by 1812. Two others, British "hovering" outside the three-mile limit and the alleged insulting behavior of a British minister in 1809, were minor matters. The most important grievance, the British Orders in Council, which mandated their obnoxious practices on the high seas, had been amended before the United States went to war. Of course, owing to the time it took for that news to reach Madison during that cableless period, he was unaware of London's démarche when he asked Congress for a declaration of war.

Republicans might rationalize their apparent partisan need to go to war before the election of 1812 in national security terms. Some maintained that the resurgence of an elitist Federalism could lead to the destruction of democratic institutions and thus the nation. But all parties could make similar self-serving claims about any election.

The heated arguments over entry into war and its prosecution clearly reflected the way localized economic interests often came into conflict with the presumed national interest. One of the main reasons for getting into war was the defense of America's neutral rights on the high seas. Madison's last economic weapon, Macon's Bill No. 2, while reopening trade with the belligerents on a provisional basis, failed to bring Great Britain to heel. His bluff was called when France apparently agreed to its terms and Great Britain did not. The nation allegedly could not tolerate the continual affronts to its sovereignty committed by the imperious British navy. Yet most of those directly affected by those affronts, shipowners and merchants from New England, were willing to grin and bear them as just another business cost—as long as they could maintain their lucrative trade with Great Britain and other European customers. Some were so distressed by the economic impact of what they called "Mr. Madison's War" that they threatened to secede from the Union. Pleased about that prospect, the British looked the other way when New Englanders traded with their cousins in British North America during the war. When two other American wars produced strong partisan opposition, they, too, were personified derisively as "Mr. Polk's War" and "Lyndon Johnson's War." Few people called World War II "Mr. Roosevelt's War."

Among Madison's supporters both for war entry and for his prosecution of the war were southerners and westerners who seemingly had less to lose from British attacks on American vessels than New Englanders. But they were in the throes of a depression in 1811 and early 1812, a depression they blamed, to some degree incorrectly, on British interference with their ability to ship their goods to market. Like their northern compatriots, they, too, viewed the war in part in terms of their economic self-interest. In this case, that self-interest did not conflict with the presumed national interest as interpreted by the Republicans.

The alleged Indian menace, one of the five reasons Madison gave for going to war, was another regional issue that ultimately affected the entire nation. Among those same westerners who suffered depression in 1811 were expansionists who often violated Indian rights, against federal policy, with relentless land-grabbing beyond their borders. Indian outrages, allegedly incited by the British, could be interpreted as legitimate defensive actions against the wild men of the western waters who operated an independent foreign policy. Throughout the first three-quarters of the nineteenth century, the actions of expansionist frontiersmen often embroiled the United States in conflict with Native Americans and foreign countries. Much of the time they acted on their own, in violation of solemn U.S. treaty commitments.

Whether or not Madison presented a good case to the legislators, this was the only time Congress held a lengthy debate before declaring war. The other four war declarations were preceded by rather perfunctory deliberations, in part because of a perceived need to act with dispatch.

ALTHOUGH THE WAR of 1812 ended more or less in a tie, it did produce a military hero, Andrew Jackson, who led American forces to victory at the Battle of New Orleans, albeit after the peace had been signed at Ghent on Christmas Eve in 1814. For a nation opposed to military institutions, it is surprising how many presidents and presidential candidates owed their celebrity to wartime exploits. Beginning with George Washington, of course, and Jackson, among war heroes who became presidents were William Henry Harrison (the Tippecanoe in "Tippecanoe and Tyler too"), Zachary Taylor, Franklin Pierce, U. S. Grant, Rutherford B. Hayes, James A. Garfield, Benjamin Harrison, Theodore Roosevelt, and Dwight David Eisenhower, with others, including Winfield Scott, John C. Fremont, George McClellan, and

Winfield Hancock, running on losing tickets. In all countries, particularly before the advent of electronic media capable of creating a wide variety of "heroes" from Michael Jackson to Michael Jordan, military heroes became the most popular and best known of all citizens.

Andrew Jackson added to his popularity with his victorious campaign in Florida in 1818, which led to crises with Great Britain and Spain. Jackson, who was ordered to protect American borders from incursions by Indians under Spanish control, decided that the best way to accomplish that feat was to eject Spain from all of Florida. Upon Jackson's triumphant return to Washington, Congress investigated his activities during a twenty-seven-day inquiry, the longest in the nation's history up to that point. That inquiry was orchestrated by Henry Clay who was motivated not only by the fact that the increasingly popular general had abused his authority in Florida but also because he was the ambitious senator's major political rival in the west. Furthermore, Clay was still fuming because he had not been appointed secretary of state. Had Congress rebuked Jackson, Clay might have been able to stake an exclusive claim to his region's loyalties in future presidential campaigns. Another future presidential candidate, Secretary of State John Quincy Adams, took Jackson's part even though he privately disapproved of the general's unauthorized actions. Against a majority in Monroe's cabinet, he supported the general to keep the pressure on the Spanish to sell Florida and to defend national honor against the British who were angered because Jackson had two of their citizens executed for helping the Indians.

Five years later, many of these same figures were involved in the complicated politics surrounding Pres. James Monroe's enunciation of his epochal doctrine. Here Henry Clay and John Quincy Adams clashed again, this time over whether to accept Great Britain's offer of cooperation in Latin America and whether to extend support to Greek revolutionaries in their war for liberation from the Ottoman Empire. To be sure, they and other presidential contenders such as Secretary of War John C. Calhoun approached those issues with an eye to their international ramifications. Nonetheless, as they considered their positions in the fall of 1823, they had to be aware of the domestic political ramifications as well. At the least, the way they ultimately responded to the problems made a good deal of sense in terms of the constituencies to whom they were trying to appeal for political support in the wide-open campaign of 1824.

The domestic minicrisis produced by the British offer of cooperation in Latin America was not the last Anglo-American crisis of the century. Most of the United States' nineteenth-century conflicts and crises involved Great

Britain, often over issues unresolved by the American Revolution. Almost all were fraught with significant domestic implications. For example, John Quincy Adams's failure to obtain a West Indies commercial treaty with the British hurt him in the 1828 election.

The fisheries issue was more important. Fishermen from New England periodically broke British laws regulating their limited rights to fish off the coast of British North America. Acting independently of the government, they were concerned about their livelihood. That understandable but parochial economic concern brought the United States and Great Britain to the brink of war on several occasions and led to moves and countermoves involving issues such as disputed boundaries and trade. Characteristic of the relationship was the opportunistic manner in which the British suddenly began to enforce fishery laws in 1852 in order to obtain limited reciprocal trade for Canada, something they accomplished in the Marcy-Elgin Treaty two years later.

Anglo-American problems in the Northeast along the Canadian border during the late 1830s and early 1840s illustrated the way state enforcement authorities, militias, and judges in the U.S. federal system could propel the central government into serious crises. New York State, for example, insisted on its right to try Alexander McLeod, a Canadian charged with murder in conjunction with the 1837 raid on the *Caroline,* a vessel assisting Canadian insurrectionists. London claimed that McLeod, a deputy sheriff from Upper Canada, had been engaged in a legitimate military action for his government and thus was not subject to civil murder charges.

Secretary of State Daniel Webster agreed with the British that international law supported their arguments concerning the illegality of McLeod's prosecution, but he contended that the federal government could not interfere with New York's judicial system. Webster's principled stance and delicate diplomacy with the British, who threatened to go to war if McLeod was executed, was unpopular with many jingoes in Congress. As one legislator exclaimed floridly about the *Caroline* incident, "Sir—The waves of Niagara have extinguished the fires of that vessel. They have silenced forever the agonizing shrieks of her remaining crew—but the cry for vengeance still comes up from her deep and agitated bosom, in tones louder than the thunder of her own mighty cataract."

McLeod, who was found not guilty in a New York court, escaped such vengeance. The incident led Congress to pass a law giving federal courts jurisdiction in similar cases.

Along that same international border, thousands of Americans joined

Hunters' Lodges, martial societies pledged "never to rest till all tyrants of Britain cease to have any dominion or footing whatever in North America." Their armed forays into Canada exacerbated tensions in Anglo-American relations until Gen. Winfield Scott arrived late in 1838 to clamp a lid on the illegal activities.

Similarly, in a boundary dispute between Maine and New Brunswick in 1838–39, local militia engaged in a few bloodless skirmishes in the comic-opera Aroostook "War," which again led to another Anglo-American mini-crisis revolving around the cutting of lumber in an area that had been contested since the Peace of Paris. Pres. Martin Van Buren again had to dispatch Scott to mediate a truce between the contending parties.

Few other countries, then and now, have had to contend with the problems caused by states—or provinces—taking independent and legal political, economic, or even military actions against a foreign government. As with America's other unique features, after a few such crises like the *Caroline* and the Aroostook War, other nations began to understand the nature of the federal system. Nevertheless, as we shall see, this did not always mean that they accepted the situation with good humor.

In 1841, in a fourth Anglo-American crisis during the same period, the British seized the American-owned *Creole,* a vessel engaged in the slave trade. Although the United States had outlawed the trade in 1808, it continued illegally on ships like the *Creole.* All nations, with the exception of the United States, accepted the British role as the enforcer of the international antislave-trade regime. American unwillingness to permit the British navy the right of search and seizure involved national pride, as well as the influence of the South in such matters.

The tension in Anglo-American relations produced by these incidents, as well as several others, eased with the consummation of the Webster-Ashburton Treaty in 1842. Reflecting a compromise on many issues, its approval by the Senate was by no means a certainty. President Tyler allocated secret funds to "sell" the treaty through propaganda and public-relations campaigns in newspapers and legislatures. Moreover, Secretary of State Webster engaged in a bit of chicanery when he employed the so-called Sparks map, whose authenticity he knew to be dubious, to convince people in Maine and Massachusetts that the boundary compromise he had arranged was favorable to the United States. Interestingly, three years later, when Lord Aberdeen prepared to accept a comparable compromise on the Oregon boundary issue, which struck some in his country as a sellout, he also engaged in a newspaper propaganda campaign to convince his public of the wisdom of retreat from its maximum demands. Although Great Britain was somewhat less of a democratic nation than the United States, gone were the days when a British prime minister could merely sign a treaty and assume public support or indifference.

Democratic populaces that have been appealed to by jingoistic politicians during a crisis often find it more difficult to tolerate a compromise settlement than less-empowered populaces. Such was the case with the surprisingly passionate opposition to the Webster-Ashburton Treaty that, in fact, not only offered a relatively fair solution to several problems but headed off the prospect of a more dangerous international crisis.

FOREIGN POLICIES have rarely played the paramount role in elections at any time in American history. They were, however, a factor on occasion in the nineteenth century, with each party accusing the other of not being nationalistic enough or of truckling to foreign enemies. Sometimes this overheated campaign rhetoric affected the way the winning candidate structured his relations with the outside world.

Characteristic was the 1844 election, when Democratic candidate James Knox Polk's claims to all of the Oregon country up to the 54°40' line and his call for the annexation of Texas stirred up jingoes. His party's campaign rhetoric made it more difficult for him to accept the reasonable compromise of the 49th parallel (which he favored) and, with some "help" from a bumbling British envoy, almost led to war with Great Britain before the crisis was resolved in 1846. Fortunately, even though such exaggerated rhetoric could exacerbate international tensions during and after elections, foreign powers learned to discount the bellicosity and xenophobia they experienced every four years. They also learned that as presidential elections approached they had to exercise extreme caution in their dealings with the American government.

On the Oregon Treaty itself, Polk returned to an earlier interpretation of the Constitution in terms of the advice-and-consent clause. After Washington's problems with the advice part, presidents submitted completed treaties to the Senate for its consent only. In this case, since the controversial Oregon Treaty could have become embarrassing for Polk had it been associated with him alone, he submitted a draft to the Senate without endorsing it. Thus, when and if the retreat from the 54°40' line became an issue, both the executive and the legislature would have to share the blame.

Polk also promised in the 1844 campaign to reannex Texas, that most American of states, which was an independent nation from 1836 to 1845.

The United States did not annex Texas earlier because Mexico, claiming sovereignty, threatened war if it did so and, more important, because of domestic politics—Texas would have entered as one or more slave states and upset the delicate balance between the North and the South. This was the central issue in American politics during the first half of the nineteenth century. For example, in 1836 Andrew Jackson delayed recognizing the independence of Texas, a republic that permitted slavery, because he feared that such a démarche would hurt the chances of his protégé, Martin Van Buren, in the upcoming election. In 1844, an annexation resolution failed in Congress by a two-to-one margin, in good measure because of the slavery issue. Similarly, several years later, presidents Franklin Pierce and James Buchanan were frustrated in their attempts to buy Cuba because of that issue. Much of the debate over expansion in the antebellum United States revolved around the different economic and political interests of the North and the South.

The Democrats' final foreign policy goal during the 1844 campaign was to obtain California from the Mexicans. American interest in California had little to do with direct threats to national security, although a modest case was made about French and British designs on that Mexican state. Americans wanted California primarily for its ports. Indeed, many antiwar Whigs went along with Polk's request for war because of their constituents' interest in securing the ports of San Francisco and San Diego, which would improve their abilities to engage in commerce with the East. Similarly, in their negotiations with London, Americans were insistent about obtaining the port area around present-day Seattle because the configuration of the mouth of the Columbia River further south precluded the possibility of making Astoria into a suitable port.

In the Mexican War, as well as the War of 1812, the Korean War, and the Vietnam War—all limited wars—Americans quickly began to tire of their commitments and to argue among themselves about ultimate goals. Polk's request for war had carried by a whopping 174–14 vote in the House and 40–2 vote in the Senate after only a two-day debate. (The debate over war in 1812 consumed seventeen days.) In 1846, it was difficult to vote against war or even to consider the issue at a leisurely pace since "American blood had been shed on American soil" and American boys faced Mexican guns. In a demonstration of the president's power to "declare" war as commander-in-chief, Polk placed those boys in harm's way when he ordered the Army into the disputed territory between the Nueces and the Rio Grande rivers. When he voted against the war resolution, Congressman John Quincy Adams (Ind-Mass.) noted that "it is now established as an irreversible precedent that the President of the United States has but to declare that War exists, with any nation, and the War is essentially declared." Similarly, Sen. John C. Calhoun (D-S.C.) contended that Polk "stripped Congress of the power of making war, and what is more and worse, it gave that power to every officer, nay to every subaltern commanding a corporal's guard." Later, other congressmen who had become carried away in the heat of the moment in 1846 began to have second thoughts not only about the circumstances surrounding the vote for war but the trajectories of the military campaigns as well.

The Mexican War, or "Mr. Polk's War" as the Whigs called it, was a highly politicized affair (even though some generals were prominent Whigs), especially when it became clear that the Democratic president was interested in seizing more territory than just the land between the Rio Grande and the Nueces. In January 1848, the House of Representatives narrowly passed a Whig-sponsored resolution proclaiming that the war had been "unnecessarily and unconstitutionally begun by the President of the United States." The resolution weakened Polk at home and had not State Department envoy Nicholas Trist negotiated a peace before the Mexicans could profit from American domestic disunity, they might have been inspired to fight on. One hundred and twenty-one years later, another Congress also enacted resolutions during wartime that affected another president's military and diplomatic strategies.

The opposition to Polk was led by the Whigs. On issues relating to the most important elements of national security, it is surprising to see how often members of Congress split along party lines, even when their differing ideologies did not relate to the specific issues involved. As we have seen before, and as we shall see in the discussion to come, American politicians frequently felt no compunction about seeking political advantage on issues of war and peace.

Not all Americans slaked their expansionist thirsts in the Mexican War. When he made a triumphant grand tour of the United States in 1851–52, Louis Kossuth, a leader of the failed Hungarian Revolution of 1848–49, appealed to Americans to assist his revolution. This is just the thing Alexander Hamilton earlier and Walter Lippmann later worried about—an unrealistic and emotional democratic populace becoming so carried away that it might compel its leaders to launch a dangerous quixotic crusade. As in the 1790s when they embraced the French revolutionary cause, in 1823 the Greek rebellion against Turkey, and in the 1830s the several Canadian rebellions, romantic citizens, and even some of their leaders, dreamed of supporting fellow democrats in Central Europe. Secretary of State Daniel Webster, for one, publicly endorsed Hungarian independence in an undiplomatic gesture that angered the Austro-Hungarian government. (Webster was then maneuvering for the presidential nomination.) As in those earlier periods, cooler heads prevailed in 1852. By the time the venerated old statesman Henry Clay spoke out strongly against any intervention in the revolutions in the Old World, the brief Kossuth craze had ended.

In another post–Mexican War flurry of leftover expansion, some Americans became interested again in Canadian annexation. Canadian displeasure with London's new antimercantile economic policies in the late 1840s sparked that interest and led the British to propose a free-trade or reciprocity treaty between their colony and the United States. The resulting Marcy-Elgin Treaty was so controversial that the State Department gave lobbyist Israel Andrews $118,000 under the table to buy journalists and bribe legislators. Andrews was employed by the British as well, but he only required $90,000 to smooth the way in Canada. Here was quite an unusual approach to treaty-making, indeed.

THE CIVIL WAR, the nation's most severe crisis, featured many examples of the way domestic politics impinged on foreign affairs. The fighting itself began in a manner that underscored the power of the president to "declare" war. Abraham Lincoln sent federal troops into action without Congress's approval. Congress was not in session during the crucial period. Of course, since the Confederacy, from the Union's perspective, was not an independent country, Lincoln did not launch a war; he was merely putting down a domestic insurrection. He also increased the size of the Army and Navy without congressional authorization. He claimed "as commander-in-chief . . . I suppose I have a right to take any measure which may best subdue the enemy." In the 1863 Prize Cases, the Supreme Court supported his actions, ruling that the "President was bound to meet it [civil war] in the shape it presented itself, without waiting for Congress to baptize it with a name."

Lincoln's secretary of state, William Seward, owed his position to his leadership of the Republican party, not to his foreign policy expertise. This loose cannon demonstrated his inexperience—if not incompetence—when he concocted a plot to provoke a foreign war in order to unite North and South against a common enemy. In an April 1, 1861, or "April Fools" note, he suggested France, Spain, England, or Russia as likely candidates. The president, who rejected the initiative, was not amused.

Yet Seward almost got his war when the U.S. Navy illegally removed Confederate agents from the *Trent,* a British vessel, in November 1861, and

London took extreme umbrage. With the war going badly for the Union at that point, many Northerners hailed the event and called for stiff resistance to British demands. The American minister to England, Charles Francis Adams, was upset with "the irresponsible outpourings and journalistic utterances" like the "incoherences of the inmates of an insane asylum" that made his attempts to settle the issue so difficult. The United States could ill afford to alienate a British government that was rooting for a Confederate victory and the concomitant weakening of the United States. Adams's diplomatic counterparts in London, operating in another country "burdened" with a free press, were similarly affected by strong nationalist sentiments expressed in newspapers and Parliament.

Two years later, Lincoln issued his Emancipation Proclamation, in part as an attempt to curry favor with foreign observers whose governments were tilting toward the Confederacy. Adams had advised him that the British, who had been flirting with recognizing the Confederacy, might be diverted from that action if the United States declared an end to slavery. The Confederacy itself later considered freeing the slaves in order to obtain recognition from European powers. Both the North and South were correct in their perceptions, particularly with the key power whose navy patrolled the Atlantic. Although Great Britain was not yet a nation with universal suffrage, its generally abolitionist citizens were powerful enough to serve as a brake on those in the cabinet who saw things in *Realpolitik* and not just moral terms. Interestingly, British leaders were not moved by the Emancipation Proclamation, in part because they perceived it as an opportunistic ploy. In 1861, Lincoln refused to proclaim that the war with the South was about slavery because he feared losing the support of those who saw the conflict in broader terms revolving around the illegality of secession. When Lincoln finally made slavery an issue in 1863, the British cabinet was underwhelmed.

Politically incorrect as slaveholders, Confederate statesmen thought they had one major economic card to play to obtain recognition and even support from London. In an attempt to create a depression in the British fabric manufacturing industries, Jefferson Davis embargoed cotton exports. At the start of the war, Great Britain had been importing as much as 80 percent of its cotton from the United States. Ironically, Abraham Lincoln's blockade of the South aimed in part at accomplishing the same purpose in order to cripple Richmond's economy. Like Jefferson's embargo of 1807, Davis's Civil War measures, although economically disruptive, did not bring the British to their knees. More important, they weakened the Confederacy's ability to finance its war.

Finally, in the years following the war, Irish-American Fenians produced a series of Anglo-American crises when they launched several invasions of Canada to free Ireland from British rule. They hoped to embroil the United States and Great Britain in a war that might result in Ireland's independence. Although their plan was farfetched, they did strike during a difficult period in Anglo-American relations; the United States was angered by British and Canadian behavior during the Civil War, including Confederate plots and raids launched from Canada into the United States at such places as St. Albans, Vermont. Between 1866 and 1870, the Fenians' several cross-border forays resulted in scores of casualties. The last raid, symbolically, was launched *from* St. Albans.

The Fenian issue, as well as other festering Anglo-Canadian-American problems relating to the Civil War, was resolved in the Treaty of Washington of 1871. The United States did rather well in these complicated negotiations. At the least, the Canadians were furious at the British for selling out their claims far too cheaply. Here, Pres. Ulysses S. Grant and his negotiators were aided by the tough line taken by Sen. Charles Sumner (R-Mass.), the head of the Foreign Relations Committee, and by other nationalists who defeated the Johnson-Clarendon Convention in 1869, which would have resolved, through a compromise, the ever-nettlesome fisheries dispute. American diplomats pointed to the difficulties they would again face in the Senate with the Treaty of Washington unless the British were more forthcoming at the bargaining table.

During the period from the end of the Civil War to the turn of the century, Congress was ascendant over relatively weak presidents. In part this situation reflected the temperaments and philosophies of the presidents. It was also true that the absence of a major international crisis meant that American politics revolved around domestic issues where the playing field for the contest between the executive and the legislative branches was more level. Characteristic of the strength of Congress was the way it foiled Andrew Johnson's and U. S. Grant's modest expansion programs. In Johnson's case, the Senate opposed his Caribbean project in good measure because it opposed his Reconstruction policy. In Grant's case, the personal hostility between the president and the head of the Foreign Relations Committee helps to explain much of the antiexpansionist sentiment on Capitol Hill.

In 1867, Johnson agreed to purchase the Danish West Indies. House leaders responded that they would refuse to appropriate the $7.5-million price for the islands. They never had to act on that threat since the Senate Committee on Foreign Relations, reflecting general congressional and public antiexpansionist sentiments, unanimously opposed the deal. The lobbyists the Danish government employed to buy enough senators to guarantee passage of the treaty failed in their task. Several years later, a stronger President Grant hoped to annex the Dominican Republic. However, he did not count on the leadership skills of Sumner, who organized the forces necessary to defeat the treaty.

"Twisting the Lion's tail" had been a popular political pastime in the United States throughout the nineteenth century. With Irish-Americans found primarily in the Democratic party, its politicians often supported anti-British activities of Irish liberationists, Canadian rebels, and annexationists in the United States. As late as the 1990s, prominent Democrats expressed tacit support for the Irish Republican Army's program to liberate Northern Ireland. This support for people the U.S. government labeled "terrorists" angered the British, whose civilians were often the targets of IRA bombs.

Irish-Americans and their backers did not cause all of the problems in Anglo-American relations. In 1888, in a case of unsolicited foreign interference in American domestic politics, the intemperate statements of British minister Sir Lionel Sackville-West influenced the 1888 election when he made it appear that his country supported the Democrats. The not-very-clever diplomat was duped into revealing his preference for Pres. Grover Cleveland by a Republican dirty trickster writing under a pseudonym. Anglophobes, among them Irish-Americans, had earlier flocked to Cleveland's banner when James G. Blaine uttered the unfortunate anti-Catholic, anti-Irish "Rum, Romanism, and Rebellion" phrase in 1884. In 1888, many of them voted for Cleveland's opponent, Benjamin Harrison, who won a close election. Because of the celebrated Sackville-West affair, which not only hurt Cleveland's reelection prospects but led to a crisis in Anglo-American relations when London refused to recall its minister, diplomats have been careful about revealing their favorites in American election campaigns.

The campaign of 1888 featured another Anglo-American issue as well. The perennial fisheries problem, which had reached a minicrisis point in 1887, was resolved by the Cleveland administration in the salutary Bayard-Chamberlain Treaty of 1888. The treaty, which was completed before the election, was defeated in the Senate by the Republicans. Whatever the merits of the Anglo-American compromise arrangement, one senator privately explained his rationale, noting that "we cannot allow the Democrats to take credit for settling so important a dispute." The moral of the story was, once again, beware of any major foreign policy initiative during an election year—it could be used for or against one of the two contending parties.

In that same election in which Cleveland received more popular but fewer electoral votes than Harrison, many German-Americans who had voted for Cleveland in 1884 switched to his opponent in 1888. They were concerned about what they perceived to be Cleveland's assertive diplomacy toward Germany in a dispute over Samoa. Unexpected German-American votes, along with the aforementioned Irish-American votes, contributed to Harrison's winning margin in the electoral college.

THROUGH THE United States' first hundred years, the fact that Congress made the immigration and naturalization laws little affected American diplomacy, save problems over British recognition of American naturalization procedures prior to the War of 1812. And in that case, Congress and the president saw eye to eye in defending American naturalized citizens unjustly impressed into the British navy. The main reason for the lack of conflict between the two branches of government in this area was that up to 1882, people of any nation could emigrate to the United States. In 1882, however, in the first of many racially based immigration restrictions, Chinese were excluded from entering the United States.

Major opposition to Chinese immigration came from the West, especially California, where Chinese constituted as much as 10 percent of the population. The presidents—indeed presidents during most eras—did not support racially based immigration laws because they naturally angered the countries discriminated against. Rutherford B. Hayes vetoed an earlier discriminatory bill in 1879 and Chester A. Arthur vetoed the first version of the exclusion bill in 1882. Both knew that the law violated the terms of the Burlingame Treaty of 1868 that governed relations between the United States and China. Fortunately for the United States, China was too weak to do more than lodge a formal protest about the insulting 1882 immigration restriction act. Such would not be the case two decades later when modern Chinese nationalism emerged to confront U.S. racism. Even in this earlier period, the Chinese government was able to obtain an indemnity from the United States after violent anti-Chinese riots in 1885.

Curiously, while many Americans approved of the exclusion of the Chinese, they had been developing warm feelings toward members of that nationality—as long as they stayed on their side of the Pacific. Missionaries had much to do with Americans' favorable, if paternalistic, views of the Chinese. Supported by churches, they sent back photographs and reports from the field and made periodic speaking tours in the United States to popularize their image of China and their notions of what the American government should do to protect their charges as well as themselves. The widespread missionary activity in China, which became a frequent part of services and meetings in thousands of churches over five decades, helped create the environment for a more aggressive policy to defend the Chinese in Asia—if not in the United States. American business interests supported the work of missionaries in China. Representing those interests, one of the first of the old China hands, Charles Denby, claimed that when "a semi-civilized people becomes completely civilized, new wants arise which commerce supplies" and "the missionary is the forerunner of commerce." In later years, other missionaries in Hawaii and Central America influenced foreign policy through their public-relations work in their home churches.

In 1891, another form of localized racism roiled the diplomatic waters between the United States and a foreign power. In New Orleans in March of that year, the superintendent of police was murdered. That murder had been preceded by several notable incidents of warfare between mafia factions. Citizens believed that members of the fast-growing—and resented—Italian population in that city were responsible for the superintendent's murder, and when those arrested were found not guilty, a mob rushed to the jail and lynched eleven of the accused, including three Italian citizens. Secretary of State James G. Blaine shared Rome's anguish, but he could not intervene formally in Louisiana's judicial processes.

In this context, the young solicitor general William Howard Taft commented on the "anomalous character of our Government, which makes the National Government responsible for the action of the State authorities without giving it any power to control that action." The federal government is responsible to other governments to protect their citizens in the United States but the states are responsible for law enforcement in their locales. The Italian government understood this. Nevertheless, responding angrily to Washington's relative inaction because of the demands made by its public, Rome severed diplomatic relations over the issue, which on the surface was a minor one. Of course, it was easy for citizens in an emerging democratic society such as Italy's to become impassioned about nationalism and foreign slights that its own government would have kicked under the rug. That was what concerned Tocqueville when he wrote about the *American* system.

IN THE MID-1890S, when the United States was figuratively granted membership in the major-power club, its foreign policies became more important for the entire international system. Symbolic of the change was the appointment of the first American ambassador in 1893. Up to that point, Americans made do with a lower level of diplomatic representative, the minister plenipotentiary and envoy extraordinaire, because, they contended, an ambassador represented the "person" of a "sovereign" and the United States was proud not to have a king. It was also true that the Europeans saw little reason to accord Americans the diplomatic courtesy of exchanging ambassadors because that rank was generally reserved for major powers.

This view was more than just an arcane formality. Ambassadors ranked much higher in protocol-minded Europe than did American ministers, and more important, because of their legal relationship to the sovereign, ambassadors could more easily negotiate directly with kings and prime ministers and not just their underlings.

By the time the major powers granted the United States ambassadorial rank, the dimensions of the problem posed by the role domestic politics played in American diplomacy were clear. Whether they involved elections, partisan conflict between a legislature of one party and a president of another, ethnic minority groups, the autonomy of the states, or local economic issues, diplomats in Washington and around the world had become well aware of the peculiar political system that had developed in the United States.

TWO

The Progressive Era,
1895–1920

THE 1890S WERE a watershed in the history of America's foreign relations. Until that point, its unusual system, in which domestic politics not only influenced but often determined foreign policy, little affected major international developments. Now the assertive young nation was an emerging great power, and an expansionist one at that. Thus, partisan wrangling over external affairs on Capitol Hill and parochial interests of ethnic and economic lobbies began to concern observers in world capitals.

As in the earlier period, the fashioning of U.S. trade and tariff policies always reflected the influence and power of financial and corporate interests. For example, the tariff on sugar, determined by political deals struck between American producers and legislators, both of whom were little concerned with *Weltpolitik,* affected the shape of relations with Hawaii and Cuba. Provisions of the McKinley Tariff of 1890 hurt the powerful Hawaiian sugar exporters, mostly American expatriates, so much that they launched a revolution in 1893 as a prelude, they hoped, to annexation. Similarly, the Wilson-Gorman Tariff of 1894 dealt a blow to Cuba's sugar producers and contributed to a depression, creating economic and political dislocation that led to the Cuban insurrection against Spain in 1895. After the Spanish-American War, the reciprocity treaty of 1903 with Cuba and relevant provisions of the Payne-Aldrich Tariff of 1909 had a good deal to do with determining the economic, social, and political destinies of Cuba and the Philippines, particularly in the way those laws compelled both nations to develop as virtual adjuncts of the American economy.

Expansionists and jingoes in the Republican party and the media assailed the cautious Democratic president Grover Cleveland for his refusal to accept the Hawaiian pineapple when it fell into his lap in 1893 and for his unwillingness to invoke the Monroe Doctrine when asked to do so by Nicaragua during a conflict with Great Britain in 1894 over control of the Mosquito Coast. As we have seen, it is easier for a president to operate a relatively independent foreign policy during his first two years in office than in the last two when he and his party begin to plan for the next election.

Thus, Cleveland found himself under growing pressure during his last two years to flex America's muscles or risk giving the Republicans a potent issue with which to work in the 1896 election. Increasingly, they were riding the tide of popular nationalism and the return, after fifty years, of the spirit of Manifest Destiny. When Venezuela complained in 1895 about British violations of the Monroe Doctrine in a dispute over the boundary of neighboring British Guiana, Cleveland and his secretary of state, Richard Olney, fired off an unusually intemperate message to London that came close to being an ultimatum. Venezuela's claims had been popularized in the United States by lobbyist William Scruggs whose pamphlets went through four editions. The normally patient and conservative Cleveland, who had been stung by previous partisan assaults against his alleged lack of assertiveness, was concerned about the beating the Democrats had been taking over his foreign policy.

He was clearly out of step with the mood of the times. The new spirit of Manifest Destiny had overtaken the land with businesspeople, clergy, intellectuals, and even reformers excited once again about spreading American values and products beyond their borders. The Republicans had adopted the issue as their own. Cleveland and his Democrats could not ignore this momentous development. The result was a crisis with Great Britain that could have led to war. However, occupied by even more pressing problems on the Continent and in southern Africa and facing a very powerful young Jonathan, the British backed away from confrontation over the Venezuelan boundary.

In 1896, in another example of the increasingly partisan warfare over diplomatic strategies, Republicans in Congress pushed through a resolution supporting the recognition of Cuban belligerency in their war for independence from Spain. Cleveland opposed the resolution, claiming correctly that he and not Congress was responsible for recognizing belligerency. Nevertheless, the resolution encouraged the Cubans to expect more assistance, angered the Spanish, and thus reduced Cleveland's options during his last year in office.

America's precipitation of the Spanish-American War itself, an event that symbolized its arrival on the world scene as a major player, was deeply influenced by domestic factors: the quality of its diplomacy, reactions to the severe depression that began in 1893, a related "psychic crisis," American investments in Cuba, the "Yellow Press," an active Cuban lobby, and especially, the perception that Pres. William McKinley was a weak leader.

In the first place, virtually alone among major nations to this day, American presidents often reward the party faithful with a diplomatic posting instead of filling key embassies with members of their professional foreign service. Pres. William McKinley's seventh choice for the difficult position in Madrid in 1897 was Stewart Woodford, a New York lawyer, without experience, who did not speak Spanish. Considering the fact that Spain went a long way toward meeting McKinley's prewar ultimatum in the spring of 1898, one wonders what would have happened had a more perceptive professional diplomat been on the scene.

This was neither the first nor last time that the United States would be ill-served by an amateur diplomat. It was true, of course, that the salaries for foreign service officers were so meager that many could not afford to maintain embassies in European capitals in a manner befitting an envoy from a major power. In addition, until the 1960s, conservative, sometimes racist and anti-Semitic, upper-class white male Easterners dominated the service, a "nurse for snobs" according to one critic. Since a democracy's diplomatic corps should have better reflected the nature of the society from which it came, bypassing the professionals made some sense in terms of the nation's values.

In addition to the amateur and inexperienced diplomat McKinley chose to represent the United States in Madrid, the great depression of the 1890s, the worst in the nation's history to that point, also played a role in creating the environment that led to America's entry into war and its later retention of Spanish colonies in the Philippines, Puerto Rico, and Guam. Many leaders, who considered overproduction to be the chief cause of periodic depressions, were convinced that the economy could be made permanently healthy through external expansion. In 1893, the first depression year, the *New York Herald* urged with confidence, "Today we produce of manufactures more than any two nations of Europe; of agriculture more than any three; and of minerals more than all together. The necessity for new markets is now upon us."

It was not coincidental that the search for markets dominated the program of the National Association of Manufacturers, which was founded in the depression year 1895. In order to enhance the search for new markets, Americans needed Pacific bases for coaling stations and to protect their merchant marine. In 1903, as the United States contemplated more forward movement in Asia, Sen. Henry Cabot Lodge (R-Mass.) reported that "I have had letters from Lawrence [Mass.], where some of the mills make cotton goods urging the strongest possible action." Some historians claim that this one issue, the search for markets to relieve overproduction and thus end depressions, explains almost all of American foreign policy from the taking of the Philippines to intervention in the Vietnam War.

Aside from the business community's pressing interest in markets, the so-called psychic crisis of the nineties, which was also related to the depression and its byproduct, social instability, led many Americans to embrace jingoism as a way to displace their problems. A rally around the flag against a foreign adversary could take people's minds off local issues. At the least, a public in this sort of mood would be ready to lash out against a perceived enemy. Indeed, individuals tend to be at their most aggressive when they are coming out of a depression—which was the case with Americans collectively in 1897.

A more narrow economic issue involved the impact of war on American property-holders who had $50 million invested on the island. Cuban rebels burned sugar plantations not only to destroy the local economy and destabilize the country, but also because they hoped that foreign owners would pressure their governments, particularly Washington, to do something to end the war.

American entry into war was affected as well by the new mass-circulation Yellow Press, which aroused the population with sensational accounts of Spanish barbarism and cruelty. Many of the stories were exaggerated or untrue but they sold newspapers in an increasingly competitive marketplace. For example, the reviled Spanish concentration-camp policy, which was no more brutal than American fortified hamlets during the Vietnam War, appeared in press accounts almost as a precursor of Hitler's death camps.

The most famous of the yellow pressmen, William Randolph Hearst, played an enormous part in the events preceding American entry into war. Hearst obtained a private letter in which Spanish Ambassador Enrique

Dupuy de Lôme criticized President McKinley and published it in his *New York Journal* in February 1898. American outrage at Dupuy de Lôme's critique contributed to the tense state of Spanish-American relations when the *Maine* exploded in Havana harbor only a few days later.

Slick Cuban public-relations teams, or juntas, based in key American cities fed newspapers many of the atrocity stories they published. Similar well-financed foreign propagandists representing American allies and enemies scored comparable triumphs with the media and Congress in the century to come with their printing presses—and faxes—and political contributions.

The press and the juntas reinforced the cynical position taken by many previously antiexpansionist Democrats in Congress who, like the Republicans when Cleveland was president, saw intervention in the war as a winning political issue. Had McKinley not asked Congress for a declaration of war in April 1898, the Democrats, with their eyes on the by-elections that fall, might have introduced a war resolution themselves. Although it has never happened, the Constitution certainly permits Congress to declare war without the president's approval after overriding his veto. Fearing such a development two years earlier, Cleveland had warned several legislators privately that if they declared war, he would not send the military into battle.

Republicans in Congress pressured McKinley as well, even though some were uncomfortable with the way national security had again become a political football. Senator Lodge commented in March 1898, "To threaten war for political reasons is a crime. . . . But to sacrifice a great party and bring Free Silver [a Democratic proposal] upon the country is hardly less odious." Here Lodge might have contended that his seemingly narrow partisan interest really reflected the national interest since the nation would have been ruined had a Democrat won the presidency in 1900. But all politicians can make such an argument to defend their cause, as was seen when Pres. Richard Nixon employed questionable means in 1972 to undermine the campaign of that alleged dangerous radical George McGovern.

As in earlier crises, many American leaders obviously thought it was in America's national security interests to get tough with Spain, liberate Cuba, and take colonies. But just as many were motivated by narrow partisan or economic concerns that had little to do with those interests. How else to explain the way the Democratic party abruptly changed its tune on expansion?

The colonies acquired in what John Hay called that "splendid little war" became an issue in the election of 1900 when the Democratic candidate, William Jennings Bryan, ran as an anti-imperialist against the alleged imperialist McKinley. The posture he planned to adopt in the upcoming election determined Bryan's intricate strategy in the congressional debate over the controversial expansionist peace treaty with Spain. The anti-imperialist Democrat influenced several of his party's members in the Senate to vote for the treaty, against their better judgment, because "we are now in a better position to wage a successful contest against imperialism [in the 1900 election] than we would have been had the treaty been rejected." The sticking point for many of his colleagues, and even a few Republicans, was the retention of the Philippines. Indeed, the anti-imperialist faction in the Senate resolved to set the archipelago free with dispatch in a resolution that failed passage by one vote only a week after the treaty was approved. They were joined by millions of Americans who did not want their government to assume the responsibilities that went with taking an extracontinental empire. At least 70,000 Americans from both parties joined anti-imperialist leagues in 1898, with the most prominent and influential—the Boston-based Anti-Imperialist League—playing an important role through the Progressive Era.

Anti-imperialists employed many arguments grounded in domestic politics to combat the treaty. Some feared that the taking of the Philippines would lead to competition from cheap and even contract labor. Others worried about the cost of maintaining increased military and naval forces to protect the archipelago. Still others expressed concern that the incorporation of people of color into the country could lead to a dilution of its Anglo-Saxon or at least European blood lines. Finally, there was no constitutional precedent for the taking of a colony that could not ultimately achieve statehood. The racially mixed Philippines surely would never qualify for that honor.

More than just the Philippines bothered anti-imperialists. The archipelago was not quite America's for the taking since native revolutionaries, originally supported by the United States, began to fight the new colonizers for their independence. The nasty counterrevolutionary war fought to suppress the rebels of Emilio Aguinaldo led to documented charges that the United States used brutal means, even torture, in the jungles of the Philippines. Many Americans were as distressed to read press reports of how an American officer felt that the nation should "have no scruples about exterminating this other race standing in the way of progress and enlightenment" as they would be sixty-eight years later when another officer talked about having to destroy a Vietnamese village in order to save it. The anti–Philippine War movement was so effective that President McKinley was forced to impose censorship and to institute other policies comparable to those employed by the Federalists 100 years earlier to squelch opposition to the quasi-war with France.

As successful as the anti-imperialist opposition was, as is usual in most presidential elections, domestic and partisan factors were more important than the annexing of a war in the Philippines in explaining the outcome in 1900. Whatever the issues, many Americans consistently voted for their party. The Republicans were the majority party in the United States from 1896 through 1928. All things being equal, which they were not in 1912 and 1916, Republicans were the favorites in every election during that period in much the same way that the Democrats enjoyed a similar advantage from 1932 through 1968.

Seeking to attract urban immigrant votes, Bryan also tarred the imperialist Republicans with Anglophilia for their support for England in the Boer War (1899–1902). A disgusted Secretary of State John Hay, an unabashed architect of the Anglo-American rapprochement, complained in 1900, "Whatever we do, Bryan will attack us as a slave of Great Britain. All their state conventions put on an anti-English plank in their platforms to curry favor with the Irish (whom they want to keep) and the Germans whom they want to seduce. It is too disgusting to have to deal with such sordid lies." The election of 1900 may also have been the first in which a group of African-American leaders took a stand on foreign affairs, opposing imperialism in the Philippines and the Boer revolt in South Africa.

To counter Bryan's appeal to the sizable minority of anti-imperialists in the election of 1900, although the issue was not crucial to McKinley's reelection, Republicans trumpeted the Open Door notes that Hay had issued in 1899 and 1900. The secretary of state had spoken out against new European spheres of influence in China, a country ripe for the picking after its defeat by the Japanese in 1895. To the untutored observer, Hay's anti-imperialist "paper bullets" seemed to have saved China from more foreign aggression. In reality, Hay's notes, virtually ignored by the powers, had little to do with their decisions to cease carving up the Chinese empire. Moreover, the secretary was less interested in Chinese independence than in keeping the door open to American trade and investment in a seemingly unlimited market of 500 million consumers. He and McKinley had been subjected to vigorous lobbying from such organizations as the National Association of Manufacturers to protect America's future markets in China from European competitors. The Open Door Policy, which partially explains American entry into World War II—as well as the Korean and Vietnam wars—was based primarily upon the perceived need to find markets to avert the sort of depression that had devastated the country from 1893 to 1896.

To make matters worse, John Hay, who took credit for his party for saving China, privately called his notes "mere flapdoodle." The realistic diplomat understood that the powers did not stop their plunder because of his new doctrine. He even tried to secure a naval base in China for the United States. But Republicans used his rather innocuous notes to demonstrate their anti-imperialism and successful foreign policy. Had Hay or McKinley informed Americans that the notes were not significant, they might have nipped the ultimately disastrous Open Door Policy in the bud.

Hay's second series of notes involved the Boxer Rebellion. When McKinley dispatched 2,500 troops to China in 1900 as part of an international relief force to protect westerners from the Boxers, he did so without congressional authorization, even though he was sending Americans into combat thousands of miles from the continental United States.

Interest in the China trade renewed interest in a transoceanic canal in Central America. Would-be American canal builders immediately confronted a problem that had been addressed in the Clayton-Bulwer Treaty of 1850, which implicitly mandated a joint Anglo-American operation in the area. Thus, when Congress threatened to pass a resolution calling for the building of an exclusive American canal, the venerable treaty to the contrary notwithstanding, Secretary of State Hay hurriedly negotiated the Hay-Pauncefote Treaty to accomplish that goal before Congress violated an international obligation. Critics on Capitol Hill who objected to provisions of the proposed treaty, particularly its nonfortification pledge, passed major amendments while Democrats, backed by Irish- and German-Americans, sought to make it an issue in their 1900 campaign. This powerful opposition forced Hay to withdraw the draft treaty and negotiate a second agreement. Fortunately for the United States, the British decided to cut their losses in the Western Hemisphere, curry favor with the United States, and concentrate their energies and attention on the increasingly tense European cockpit. Thus, they had to accept a second treaty less advantageous than the first. Here, one might argue that the Senate's "meddling" led to a better Hay-Pauncefote Treaty in terms of the national interest. Of course, it is unlikely that politicians on Capitol Hill gave much thought to the consequences had London refused to renegotiate the original package.

The treaty became a political football again in 1912 when Congress passed a Panama Canal tolls bill that would have given American vessels a price advantage over their rivals. Democratic presidential nominee Woodrow Wilson supported the differential toll idea, a popular issue with American nationalists ever-ready to twist the British Lion's tail. When he became president, Wilson reversed course, convinced that it would be dishonorable for the United States to violate the Hay-Pauncefote Treaty.

The debates over the location of a trans-isthmian canal offer another example of domestic business considerations determining foreign policy. Agents of the New Panama Canal Company, which owned the rights to any canal built in Panama, exercised considerable—and to some degree nefarious—influence on the congressional decision for a Panamanian instead of a Nicaraguan route. In the first place, during the election campaign of 1900, they donated the huge sum of $60,000 to the Republican party. Not surprisingly, the Republican platform endorsed the Panama route. Not being the recipients of such largess, the Democrats supported the Nicaraguan route. In comparable situations later in this century, lobbyists generally tried to buy support from both sides of the aisle.

McKinley's election in 1900, however, did not guarantee the Panama route. Confronted with the prospect of losing its entire investment in 1902 when the Nicaraguan route seemed to have the support of a congressional majority, the company arbitrarily cut its price at the eleventh hour and then engaged in successful under-the-table lobbying that resulted in legislators opting for Panama. Had the canal been built in Nicaragua, the United States would not have been forced to support a revolution bankrolled by the New Panama Canal Company in Panama (then a province of Colombia), would have owned a canal closer to its own ports, and would have avoided much of the ill will caused by the fact, as Sen. S. I. Hayakawa (R-Calif.) boasted over seventy years later, that "we stole it fair and square."

Ironically, the crisis was precipitated by the Colombian Senate's rejection of the canal treaty that John Hay had negotiated with that nation's minister in Washington. Ignoring the comparable role that the American Senate played on occasion, Theodore Roosevelt was outraged that the "Bogota lot of jack rabbits" dared reject a treaty that had apparently been acceptable to the executive branch of government.

Roosevelt, who may not have stolen the canal but who claimed that he took the canal while Congress debated when he blocked Colombian reinforcements from invading the isthmus during the Panamanian revolt, became involved in several major crises during his seven years as president. Two of the most important dealt with immigration laws that reflected the United States' anti-Asian biases.

Since 1882 Chinese people had been restricted on a temporary basis from immigrating to the United States. In 1904, Congress made the exclusion permanent. The new legislation angered many in the first generation of modern Chinese nationalists, who responded with a successful boycott of American goods and businesses in their country. Roosevelt sympathized with the Chinese, the only ethnic group excluded from immigration to the

Democracy and Diplomacy

United States, but would not challenge the popular congressional bill. When the boycott continued through 1905, the trustbuster threatened the Chinese government with punitive action unless it compelled its citizens to cease their actions in restraint of trade. This was a rather unfriendly and contradictory demand from a nation that only five years earlier had stood so proudly for Chinese independence with its much-ballyhooed Open Door Policy.

The Japanese, against whom American racism was directed one year later, were far stronger than the Chinese. When the San Francisco school board decided to segregate its schools to keep often older Japanese (and Korean and Chinese) students away from their American counterparts, the Tokyo government, fresh from a smashing triumph in the Russo-Japanese War (1904–5), protested vigorously. Their jingoes even urged that the United States be taught the same sort of lesson Russia had learned.

Roosevelt, who did not want to irritate the Japanese unduly over what was to him a petty domestic issue, was constrained by the fact that the states controlled their own educational systems. He did let Tokyo know how he felt about "the infernal fools in California, and especially in San Francisco, [who] insult the Japanese recklessly, and in the event of war, it will be the Nation as a whole which will pay the consequences." Here the president was rightly concerned about the larger impact of the "foolish offensiveness of idiots" in San Francisco who segregated the ninety-three students. He worried as well about a series of rhetorical and even physical attacks against Japanese in the city.

Roosevelt ultimately worked out a compromise, the Gentleman's Agreement of 1907, in which in exchange for San Francisco's rescinding the segregation policy, the Japanese promised informally to keep their citizens from emigrating to the United States. Even though this affair turned out to be a tempest in a teapot, when Roosevelt sent the United States' new Great White Fleet around the world in 1907 Japanese-American relations were so tense that observers feared that a "goodwill" visit to Tokyo could spark an incident that would result in full-scale war. In order to avoid that incident, almost all American sailors were kept on board at Tokyo harbor for fear the inevitable bar-room brawl would lead to a diplomatic confrontation. This potentially dangerous situation stemmed from an obscure action by an independent local school board that the president could not control.

The Democratic party in California, which did not win a gubernatorial election between 1894 and 1938, made substantial gains in 1908 when it adopted the anti-Japanese issue as its own. Hoping to take the state house in

1912, California Democrats helped convince Woodrow Wilson to affirm the policy of Chinese and Japanese exclusion. Wilson, whose views on racial issues were not especially progressive, did not need much convincing.

Nevertheless, in 1913 Wilson was not at all pleased when the California legislature drew him into another crisis with Japan when it barred aliens, almost exclusively Japanese, from owning land. As in 1907, jingoes in Tokyo called for war and again a president tried to intervene in California state politics. On this occasion, Wilson was unsuccessful in convincing Californians to revoke their legislation. Despite heated words on both sides of the Pacific, with the American General Board of the Navy even beginning to look over contingency plans for war, the crisis subsided. From the Japanese perspective, the racist statute enacted by the sovereign state of California constituted a general American insult against their proud nation.

This issue became an irritant again in 1924 when Tokyo, primarily as a face-saving gesture, tried to obtain a small symbolic quota under a new immigration bill that assigned quotas to Europeans but denied them to Asians. They were refused that courtesy. Secretary of State Charles Evans Hughes's plea to Congress not to exclude the Japanese "in the interest of our international relations" fell on deaf ears. So angered were the Japanese by the American slight that they proclaimed a "National Humiliation" day and one citizen even committed suicide in front of the American embassy. Needless to say, these immigration restrictions contributed to the hostility with which some Japanese viewed the United States right up to Pearl Harbor. Japan finally received a quota in 1952, during a period when Washington was trying to keep its new Asian ally in its Cold War camp.

In still another example of a president's inability to conduct his own Japanese policy, in 1912 the influential chairman of the Senate Committee on Foreign Relations, Henry Cabot Lodge, introduced a resolution that became known as the Lodge Corollary to the Monroe Doctrine, which again needlessly slapped Japan in the face. When Lodge heard that private Japanese businessmen were trying to buy land from Mexico around Magdalena Bay in Baja California, he proclaimed, supported by the Senate in a 51-to-4 vote, that such property could not be transferred to a private company with connections to a government in the other hemisphere. Lodge and his colleagues who voted for the resolution were influenced and encouraged by the sensational and wildly exaggerated treatment of the issue in William Randolph Hearst's West Coast newspapers. The Lodge Corollary had no legal standing. Nevertheless, the Japanese government urged their businesspeople to steer clear of Baja California—and, of course, added another incident to its catalogue of American insults to which it would respond in the future. Despite the Lodge Corollary's extralegal nature, the State Department referred to it on at least four other occasions to warn foreign governments about similar perceived violations of the Monroe Doctrine.

There were ways to resolve Japanese-American territorial conflicts. As he analyzed the prospects for a Japanese-American war that might begin over rivalry in China, Theodore Roosevelt began to back away from a vigorous defense of the Open Door. Between the lines of two carefully prepared executive agreements, the Taft-Katsura memorandum of 1905 and the Root-Takahira agreement of 1908, Roosevelt indicated that he was ready to accept Japanese predominance in China. He realized the United States could not project its power so many miles from its shores, especially considering the fact that the Philippines colony was a "heel of Achilles" in the military sense. As Roosevelt said in 1910, the Open Door Policy "completely disappears as soon as a powerful nation determines to disregard it, and is willing to run the risk of war rather than forego its intentions."

The public, as well as the business community, however, would never have accepted the jettisoning of the Open Door Policy. Roosevelt's realistic approach to the limits of American power might have headed off the almost inevitable clash between the United States and Japan in 1941. Yet he was reluctant to use his "bully pulpit" to denounce the popular policy. Thus, his little-understood executive agreements of 1905 and 1908 with Japan were forgotten when William Howard Taft and Woodrow Wilson expressed support for the Open Door and ignored the drift of their predecessor's policy. Roosevelt's fear of the political implications of appearing to truckle to Tokyo kept him from trying harder to keep the United States from meddling in what some on both sides of the Pacific had begun to consider the Japanese Caribbean.

Roosevelt preferred to use executive agreements, which bound only his administration, for his delicate diplomacy with Japan, because like John Hay and others before him, he worried about what might happen to treaties after they were submitted to the Senate. In 1905, for example, Senate Democrats blocked consideration of a treaty Roosevelt had concluded with the Dominican Republic in which the United States assumed control over that bankrupt nation's customs houses. Not to be outdone, an angry Roosevelt circumvented the Senate by drawing up an executive agreement that accomplished his original purpose. As for the Senate, he felt that its power to weaken or kill a treaty "should be rarely used," as was the case with his veto power. The Senate did finally approve a new Dominican Republic treaty in

1907. In 1911 and 1912, the Senate again rejected customs receivership treaties for Honduras and Nicaragua, respectively, with President Taft, in the latter case, employing Roosevelt's precedent to establish an informal protectorate over that Central American nation.

Roosevelt, who believed strongly that the United States had to play an increasingly more active role in the world, understood the implications of his position for the presidency and for the balance between the legislative and executive branches of government. "The President," he pointed out, "can never again be the merely domestic figure he has been throughout so large a part of our history." The problem for him, however, was that few Americans were then prepared to accept an end to their traditional isolationist policies when it came to the Europeans' internecine squabbles. Thus, he found it necessary to shield the public and Congress from his secret diplomacy at the Algeciras Conference in 1906, when his agents played a role in settling the Moroccan problem in a way that protected the interests of the Anglo-French Entente. This crisis originated with a vigorous German challenge to French hegemony in Morocco. When Congress approved the superficially innocuous Act of Algeciras, it declared that nothing in it could be interpreted as departing "from traditional American foreign policy which forbids participation by the United States in the settlement of political questions which are entirely European in their scope." Had Americans discovered the sort of wheeling and dealing in European politics in which their president was engaged, they would have been horrified. Roosevelt's deception made a mockery of the way the American democracy was supposed to conduct its foreign policy.

Roosevelt also made a mockery of the Constitution's delegation of shared responsibility for military policy—the president commands the armed forces but Congress pays for them—when he dispatched the Great White Fleet on its celebrated 'round-the-world trip in 1907. He knew that many in Congress opposed such a voyage because of the cost and because of the danger of igniting a war with Japan. Thus, he did not announce his intentions to send the fleet around the world when it began its voyage, even though he did not have the appropriations to pay for the venture. By the time Congress discovered the truth, it was too late—it had to pay for the return trip or leave the Great White Fleet marooned in an ocean halfway around the world.

In 1908, an incident involving Roosevelt and the publisher of the *New York Times,* Adolph Ochs, made a mockery of the free press in a democratic society as well. During that year, a reporter for the *Times,* William Bayard Hale, obtained an exclusive two-hour interview with Kaiser Wilhelm II of

Germany. The kaiser made so many intemperate and undiplomatic remarks to Hale that Ochs felt compelled to send the article to the president before publishing it. When Roosevelt told Ochs's agent that the article could cause a European crisis, the publisher killed the story. This was not the only time that the most important newspaper in the United States asked a president's advice about printing a controversial story.

Despite his interest in involving the United States in a rational way in foreign politics, Roosevelt was not above using a diplomatic incident for domestic political gain. When alleged American citizen Ion Perdicaris was seized by Raisuli, a Moroccan warlord in 1904, Roosevelt threatened to send the Marines to North Africa. As he told a cheering Republican national convention in Chicago in 1904, he wanted "either Perdicaris alive or Raisuli dead." A bemused John Hay, the original author of the demand, observed, "It is curious how a concise impropriety hits the public." Privately, Roosevelt admitted he had no intention of using force to extract Perdicaris—whose claims to American citizenship were dubious—from Raisuli's clutches.

Although the term "military–industrial complex" did not come into vogue until the 1960s, such a complex existed during the Progressive Era, centered around naval development. Roosevelt was one of the chief popularizers of the idea that the United States needed a first-class navy to protect its interests around the world. Others in the United States, including members of the influential lobby, the Navy League, promoted naval building for their own pecuniary interests. Most Americans, however, saw little need to incur the costs of building a large navy since their country not only was impregnable but was little involved in international politics. Why build a navy, they asked, if there was no danger from enemies abroad?

To respond to this rational query, legislators and administration aides often warned about the dramatic growth of the navies of Germany and Japan, two aggressive *commercial* rivals in Europe and Asia, during the annual debates over naval appropriations. As a Tennessee representative who opposed increased naval expenditures commented in 1908,

> We all remember a year or two the racket was worked on Germany, and every fall at the meeting of Congress we were told of the appalling danger of destruction and conflict with Germany. It was worked and reworked and worked over and over again until it became as frazzled as a last year's whip crack and then that was abandoned and they substituted in lieu of it poor old Japan in the Orient.

The emphasis upon those two countries as nations against whom the United States should be arming contributed to growing feelings of mutual hostility. The same sort of thing happened during the Cold War when the Soviet threat was depicted in the darkest possible terms whenever Congress considered defense appropriations.

Not as powerful as the armaments lobby, a peace lobby, which involved many Americans, also flourished during the Progressive Era. Its spirited activities on behalf of the disarmament and arbitration movements helped promote those causes in the United States. In fact, pressures from influential Americans such as industrialist Andrew Carnegie, the most prominent financial angel of the peace movement, helped compel Theodore Roosevelt to become a sponsor of the Second Hague Conference in 1907, much against his better judgment. Railing privately against the "peace-at-any-price, universal-arbitration" types, Roosevelt did achieve a measure of revenge when he refused to appoint any "peace men" to the American delegation.

The American president was not alone in his concern about the effectiveness of a peace lobby that did not seem to understand *Realpolitik*. Leaders in democratic European nations, especially England and France, also were compelled against their will to make gestures in the direction of disarmament and international cooperation. Indeed, peace groups in several countries joined together in a transnational lobby that increased their potency.

Bolstered by their international colleagues, American peace lobbyists were nonetheless not strong enough to overcome fierce nationalist opposition in Congress to the idea of the arbitration of disputes. Beginning in 1897, when confronted by stiff opposition from Irish-Americans, among others, the Senate voted down a relatively innocuous Anglo-American arbitration treaty. In 1908, Secretary of State Elihu Root concluded equally innocuous treaties with twenty-four countries. The Senate effectively killed them when it withheld its consent unless it was given the right to decide by two-thirds' vote the terms of each specific arbitration case that arose under the treaties. Similarly, in 1911, after Pres. William Howard Taft submitted arbitration treaties with England and France to the upper house, senators amended the treaties in ways that permitted them to decide when they would become operative. That was too much for Taft, who let his pet projects drop, complaining that the Senate "had truncated them and amended them in such a way that their own father could not recognize them." He knew, as Root learned three years earlier, that the terms presented by the Senate would be rejected by America's treaty partners.

The Taft administration made another gesture toward international amity in 1911 when the United States and Canada concluded a reciprocity agreement. In the debates in both countries, business and agricultural leaders from different geographic regions naturally took positions for or against the agreement depending upon its impact on their interests. Yet the most important factor in the debate may have been the support for the agreement expressed in many American newspapers. They rarely pointed out their own self-interest in editorials awash with arguments about how the agreement would improve the economy. The newspaper industry itself stood to gain dramatically if Canadian lumber for newsprint entered the United States duty-free. Although Canadians ultimately rejected the agreement, American newspapers influenced the more positive outcome of the debate in the United States.

Domestic Canadian politics were responsible in part for the defeat of the agreement in Ottawa when Conservatives attacked Liberals for selling out to the United States. When the issue of free trade comes up for debate in Canada, the opposition party, regardless of its economic views, invariably attacks the party in power for caving in to Washington. American diplomats are not alone in having to contend with such demagoguery.

Taft was more successful restructuring economic relations with nations in the developing world where the slogan "Dollar Diplomacy" characterized his policies. At first glance, the slogan seems to refer to the role financial and industrial interests played in pushing the government into new entanglements, particularly in Central America and China. The truth is more complicated. No doubt corporate leaders were committed to economic expansion abroad during the period. But they preferred stable European markets to those in the more volatile Third World. In many cases, the Taft administration urged American bankers to enter areas vital to American security but not very promising in terms of financial return. When bankers complained about the risk of investing in Nicaragua, for example, the administration promised them that if worse came to worst, the American military would protect their investments. Thus, American business leaders reluctantly accepted the offer, involved themselves financially and politically in the domestic affairs of the host nations and, when revolutions or defaults occurred, demanded that their government support their local favorites. Taft's policy of substituting "dollars for bullets" still could result in military intervention—as Latin Americans contended, "After [J.P.] Morgan comes the Marines."

AMERICA'S INTERNATIONAL PROBLEMS during the Progressive Era paled before those posed by World War I. From the start of the war in 1914 to the failure of the Senate to approve the Versailles Peace Treaty in votes in 1919 and 1920, domestic, partisan, ethnic, and economic considerations affected virtually every international issue.

Even during the interregnum between his election in November 1912 and his assumption of the presidency in March 1913, partisan politics complicated Woodrow Wilson's diplomatic strategies. The academic specialist in domestic politics, who said "it would be the irony of fate" if he had to concentrate on foreign policy, first was compelled to select William Jennings Bryan as his secretary of state. A three-time loser for the presidency, completely inexperienced in foreign relations, Bryan was still Mr. Democrat. Tradition demanded that he be offered the most prestigious position in the new administration. Bryan knew even less about foreign affairs than his chief and was a much less sophisticated thinker in general. The man who in 1906 had to ask what the Balkans were presided over a State Department that soon confronted the greatest world crisis in a century.

In addition, Wilson initially opposed rewarding party loyalists with major diplomatic appointments. For example, he did not want to appoint Tammany Hall judge James W. Gerard—"a pompous ass" according to the president-elect—to the important post of ambassador to Germany. Yet, he bowed to party pressures and posted very amateur diplomats such as Gerard to several key European capitals. No doubt he thought he had not sacrificed his principles too much since he did not expect to become involved in continental problems during his tenure. To be sure, the alliance systems and arms races had increased tensions in Europe in recent years, but the powers had made it safely through a series of crises beginning in 1905 without going to war with one another. Most observers were confident they would also be able to finesse the crisis created by the assassination of Austrian Archduke Franz Ferdinand in Sarajevo on June 28, 1914.

When the big war finally came six weeks later, Wilson, like the rest of the world, was shocked. Even more shocking, it did not end in a month or two but continued on for four years, affecting the United States even more dramatically than it had been affected during the last world war from 1793 to 1815.

At the onset of the Great War, most Americans were mildly Anglophilic, with the establishment, including Wilson, strongly Anglophilic. But as much as 20 percent of the population, coming mostly from ethnic communities, was strongly pro-German because of links to mother countries. The German-Americans, the second largest nationality group in America, generally supported Berlin. Their most important organization, the National German-American Alliance, boasted two million members. German policy-makers overestimated the power of the alliance in their calculations about the likely posture the American government would adopt during the war. Germany also could count on the support of Irish-Americans who opposed the English, adhering to the principle that the enemy of my enemy is my friend, and Jewish- and Scandinavian-Americans who disliked Russia, another German foe.

The intensity of these groups' feelings toward the combatants in 1914, compared to that of the somewhat more lukewarm pro-British sentiment in the rest of the population, posed problems for Wilson. As he said in 1914, "We definitely have to be neutral since otherwise our mixed populations would wage war on each other."

Economic factors also weighed heavily on the president. The United States was sliding toward a depression in early 1914. Its industrial plant was operating at only 60 percent capacity, and during 1914 the nation experienced the largest number of business failures in its history. The economy began to turn around when the most prominent neutral in the world became the prime supplier of the belligerents, in this case mostly the Allies since the British navy controlled the Atlantic. For example, during the first six months of the war, American exports of explosives increased 1,500 percent and exports of iron and steel increased tenfold. The agricultural export trade experienced comparable gains. As Thomas Jefferson, the originator of the idealist tradition in American foreign policy, boasted about an earlier European conflict, "The new world will fatten on the follies of the old."

When the British began to violate American neutrality, as they had done in previous wars, Wilson naturally protested. As the violations increased, the intensity of his formal written protests increased to a point where wags suggested that the State Department was running out of stationery. But he could never threaten to sever economic links to the British. Had they called his bluff, the United States would have been catapulted back into recession. Such an outcome would have ruined the economy and, more important, the Democrats' electoral prospects. After all, the only reason that the minority party won in 1912 was because Wilson ran against two Republicans, Taft and Roosevelt.

Wilson's approach to the loan issue illustrates the crucial relationship between his neutral strategies and the economy. When the war began, he adopted a new and highly moral policy of prohibiting American bankers from loaning money to belligerents. "Money is the worst of contrabands— it commands all other things," declared an even more moral Secretary of State Bryan. In late 1914, when the British began to run out of cash to buy American products, Wilson reversed himself on credits and then, in early 1915, on loans. He had concluded that the traditional legal practice of permitting belligerents to make loans in neutral countries, which he had earlier opposed in a burst of idealistic fervor, had suddenly become a practical necessity, considering the positive effect the war trade was having on the American economy—and on his political future.

Most of those credits and loans went to one side, the Allies. Trade with the Allies increased fourfold between 1914 and 1918 while declining precipitously with the Central Powers. Of course, the Germans could have contracted loans as well if they could have found bankers to deal with them; in much the same way they would have purchased munitions in the United States, if they could have found a way to get them across the British-controlled Atlantic. With money and war supplies flowing primarily to the British, the Germans claimed, not without reason, that Wilson's holier-than-thou neutrality was skewed.

Further, when the Germans introduced limited submarine warfare in early 1915 in order to challenge British control of the seas, Wilson declared that he was going to hold them to a greater degree of responsibility for submarine infractions than for the less lethal infractions committed by the British navy. Although by the end of 1916, Wilson became exasperated with British infractions, which increased in quantity and quality throughout the war, he—and London—realized that while he could threaten the Germans with a severance of relations or worse if they did not halt the illegal aspects of their submarine warfare, he could not threaten the British in the same manner because their trade was essential to American prosperity.

To be fair to Wilson, the issue of British violations of American neutrality, which did not cost lives directly, was far less volatile than the issue of German violations, which began with their declaration of limited submarine warfare in the winter of 1915. When, in late March, one American went down with the *Falaba,* a torpedoed British passenger vessel, few of his fellow citizens expressed concern. But after 128 American lives were lost when the *Lusitania,* another British passenger vessel, was sunk six weeks later, many of those same citizens were horrified and demanded immediate satisfaction from the Germans. In terms of the U.S. interpretation of neutral rights to travel on belligerent passenger vessels, the sinkings of the *Falaba* and the *Lusitania* were identical cases. The magnitude of the losses in the latter case was the key for an emotional populace.

The Germans recognized their public-relations problem and the intense popular pressures on Wilson to respond strongly against them. Writing from Berlin, Ambassador Gerard explained the Germans' delaying strategy. They were trying to "keep the *Lusitania* matter 'jollied along' until the American people get excited about baseball or a new scandal and forget" about the sinking.

Unfortunately for the Germans, the public and Wilson would not be "jollied," especially after one of their submarines sunk the *Arabic* in August. They were compelled to make the first of two conditional pledges limiting submarine activity. When the Germans apparently broke the pledges on January 31, 1917, Wilson found it difficult to keep the United States out of the war.

Three months earlier, few observers would have predicted such an outcome. In the election of 1916, Wilson ran on the slogan "He Kept Us Out of War" against Republican Charles Evans Hughes, who appeared somewhat more interventionist. Hughes's candidacy was not helped by the unpopular hawkish approach Theodore Roosevelt took in his campaigning for the Republican ticket.

In 1915 and 1916, although Americans saw no reason to involve themselves in the Great War, many agreed with Republicans that the nation should devote more resources to building its defenses. Originally reluctant to push for a preparedness program, Wilson changed his tune as the election approached. His belated conversion to preparedness was clearly a response to Republican attacks against his defense policy.

Wilson had incorporated in the Democratic party platform a strong statement against the role of ethnic groups in the political debate about neutrality policies—"by arousing prejudice of a racial, religious or other nature [hyphenism] creates discord and strife among our people," and affects American foreign affairs. He directed his attention to German-Americans primarily but he was also concerned about Irish-Americans. In July 1916, under pressure from Irish-Americans, the Senate passed a resolution calling for clemency for Irish rebel Roger Casement, who was about to be executed by the British. Wilson refused to intervene in the case, which cost him some traditionally Democratic Irish-American votes. On the other hand, Theodore Roosevelt, who even more than Wilson directly attacked German-Americans for their "moral treason to the Republic," hurt Hughes with that traditionally Republican voting bloc. Ironically, after expressing concern about hyphenism, Wilson appealed to Polish-Americans and other Eastern Europeans for their votes when he promised support for self-determination at war's end.

Jewish-Americans constituted another such group that tried to exercise its influence during the war and in this case, unlike the others, was quite successful. Led by the American Jewish Committee, which was founded in 1906, Jewish-Americans had earlier lobbied for several years for the termination of the 1832 commercial treaty with Russia because of violent Czarist anti-Semitism. In 1912, President Taft terminated the treaty, in good measure because of the effective lobbying activities of the committee. During the war, some American Jews, particularly in the new American Zionist Federation, were instrumental in helping to convince Wilson to support the British Balfour Declaration that promised Jews a "homeland" in Palestine.

In another foreign policy issue that had a bearing on the campaign of 1916, Wilson's approach to problems relating to the Mexican Revolution was affected in good measure by the need to appear to be a strong president who could defend the nation against cross-border incursions. The revolution had posed problems for Wilson since his earliest days in the White House. The first major crisis occurred in 1914, after he sent the Marines ashore to seize Vera Cruz in an attempt to destabilize a counterrevolutionary Mexican dictator. Congressional and public opposition led him to terminate the occupation without accomplishing his goals.

Americans were not as pacific about the most serious Mexican-American crisis during Wilson's presidency. Capitalizing on Pancho Villa's raid into New Mexico in early 1916, Republicans demanded a strong response from the president. When he sent Gen. John J. Pershing into Mexico to find and punish Villa for his rampages, he ran the risk of war with the government of Mexico, which was not at all pleased with the violation of its sovereignty. Yet Wilson felt he had to do something since the Republicans had called for even more vigorous measures against the despised "greasers" to the south. He therefore risked full-scale war with Mexico at a time when he was deeply involved in more important crises relating to World War I. He pulled back from the abyss before the election, despite the fact that war with Mexico might have been popular with the voters.

Wilson successfully countered Republican criticism of his foreign policies through his preparedness program and limited Mexican operations. His neutrality policies, however, could not keep the United States out of World War I. When the Germans declared unlimited submarine warfare on January 31, 1917, and then began intentionally sinking American ships, Wilson was forced to take action. In 1916, Congress had tried to head off the crisis with its Gore-McLemore resolution, which would have barred Americans from traveling on armed belligerent vessels. Wilson's operatives on Capitol Hill defeated the resolution after a difficult fight, contending that it represented a shameful surrender to illegal and immoral submarine activities. The president was not so successful in 1917 when, in the wake of the German proclamation of unlimited submarine warfare, he tried to obtain congressional approval to arm American merchant vessels for protection against the submarines. He was forced to arm the vessels without that approval when a group of senators, whom he labeled "a little group of willful men, representing no opinion but their own," filibustered his proposal to death.

The arming of the merchant vessels was only a stopgap measure. Wilson finally asked Congress for a declaration of war on April 2. In an eloquent and stirring address to a nation that harbored a sizable minority opposed to war entry, the president stressed issues broader than just submarine warfare, the presumed *casus belli*. Above all, he promised that American belligerency would lead to a more progressive international system. Instead of telling his constituents that the war had been caused by such evils as nationalism, arms races, and alliance systems, and that all parties were to some degree to blame, Wilson painted the Germans in the darkest of terms. On the other hand, the Allies, including the new czarless-but-not-yet-Leninist Russia ("a fit partner for a league of honor"), appeared as virtually blameless progressive democracies. Americans were thus set up for disillusionment when they found out about their imperialist allies and, especially, when a new world order did not replace the old one as Wilson had promised. Yet the president felt he had to "sell" the war in idealistic, black-and-white terms in order to rally as much of the population as possible around the idea of accepting that "fearful thing," and perhaps to convince himself of the wisdom and morality of his action.

The perceived need to sell the war also led Wilson to create the Committee on Public Information, or the Creel Committee, named after its chair, journalist George Creel. Critics judged this committee, which produced government propaganda directed to American citizens, to be too partisan. With its War Cooperating Committee in Hollywood, thousands of speakers, and even committees to change textbooks to present a more favorable image of the British, the committee, according to one official, became the "greatest adventure in advertising" in history. During World War II, officials in Franklin D. Roosevelt's comparable Office of War Information exercised more discretion when it came to activities that could be interpreted as partisan propaganda on the homefront.

In addition, Franklin Roosevelt did not go as far as Wilson in curbing free speech and civil liberties during war time. Wilson's Espionage Act of 1917 and sabotage and sedition acts of the following year made it difficult for op-

ponents of the war to make their cases in public. People who spread defeatism or uttered or printed disloyal statements about the United States
could suffer fines and imprisonment. Under those laws, over 1,500 people
were arrested for disloyal utterances, among them Eugene V. Debs, the
Socialist party leader who consequently had to run for president in 1920
from his jail cell.

Finally, in terms of the homefront, the world crisis permitted Wilson to
manage the economic life of the nation in a way that even Debs did not
imagine. Through his War Industries Board and other such agencies, the
president directed business and labor to concert their energies for the war
effort.

Franklin Roosevelt's agencies were even more intrusive during World War
II. In both cases, although the economy returned to the laissez-faire system
after the wars, the pendulum never swung all the way back to the prewar situation. The experiences in both wars influenced the development of America's contemporary welfare state in a variety of ways.

EVEN MORE THAN the entry into the war, the conflict over entry into the
League of Nations became mired in domestic politics. Wilson contributed
to his own difficulties, beginning with his call for a vote of confidence for
his foreign policies in the congressional elections of 1918. As is usual in by-
elections, the party in power lost, although not because of foreign-policy
issues. Nevertheless, Republicans argued that Wilson no longer represented
American opinion on foreign policy since his politically unwise call for a
mandate had been rejected. As Wilson's *bête noire* Theodore Roosevelt commented, "Mr. Wilson has no authority to speak for the American people at
this time. His leadership has just been emphatically repudiated by them." In
addition, the president's failure to take a truly bipartisan delegation with him
to Paris made the resulting Treaty of Versailles "Wilson's treaty" and thus a
major issue of partisan contention as the 1920 election neared.

Aside from party politics, senators and representatives of both parties were
genuinely concerned about the way the president had enhanced his powers
at their expense during the extraordinary period of crisis since 1914 and also
about how the League of Nations might further weaken their prerogatives.
For example, in cooperation with the Allies, Wilson sent thousands of American troops into the Russian Civil War without congressional approval or
meaningful consultation and relied increasingly on a personal advisor, Col.
Edward M. House, to undertake secret missions about which he could not
be compelled to report to Congress. In many ways, House operated as na-

tional security advisors and their National Security Council staffs operated from the 1960s through the 1980s, far from congressional oversight or scrutiny. Given such activities by the president and his minions, no wonder Congress rankled at being told to approve the epochal—and controversial—peace treaty that had been negotiated without its advice.

When the Republicans won the Senate by one seat in 1918, they organized the committees, including the key Committee on Foreign Relations. The Republicans owed their victory to a disputed election in Michigan in which a seat was probably stolen from Democrat Henry Ford. From his powerful position as chairman of the Committee on Foreign Relations, Henry Cabot Lodge developed a clever strategy of parliamentary delay until he was able to rally opposition nationwide and muster enough votes to defeat Wilson's treaty. Had the Democrats been in control of the Senate, Wilson might have been able to ram the treaty through quickly and the United States would have joined the League of Nations. Certainly, the vast majority of Americans approved of his diplomatic handiwork when he returned from Paris in July 1919.

From the start, however, there were dissenters. In early March, thirty-nine senators had joined a Lodge-led "round robin" to denounce the treaty as it then stood. Wilson hoped he had met most of their concerns when he renegotiated several articles. But the senators were supported by many ethnic groups, who were among those most vocal in denouncing the peace treaty and the League of Nations. Irish-Americans disliked the fact that England had not only its vote but the votes of five commonwealth nations in the proposed international organization. German-Americans were angry with the harsh peace treaty that blamed the Fatherland for the entire war. In addition, liberals and progressives, upset about the end of domestic reform in 1917 and the reactionary Red Scare of 1919, saw the peace as a vindictive one that supported the imperialist policies of America's allies. The Red Scare itself contributed to increased nationalism and xenophobia, which encouraged isolationist attitudes and was intimately related to American anti-Bolshevik activities in the Soviet Union. The symbiotic relationship between domestic and foreign anti-Bolshevism appeared again in the United States during the early Cold War.

The Red Scare influenced and was influenced by the very unstable economic and social conditions in 1919. Four million Americans went on strike, several cities experienced race riots or anarchist bombings, and the rapid demobilization of the armed forces created intense competition for jobs. Radicals were not the only ones to be blamed for the instability. Agitators also targeted immigrants from southern and eastern Europe, their numbers threatening to increase because of dislocations caused by World War I, for contributing to America's problems. Thus, 1919, marked by its heightened nationalism, was not a propitious time to try to convince the most isolationist of peoples to join an international organization.

Interestingly, few influential leaders raised their voices to challenge the absence of a racial equality clause in the League Covenant. Wilson, who might have gone along with one despite his better judgment in order to win concessions from the Japanese, knew that many southern opinion leaders would have used that issue to justify their distaste for the treaty.

Despite the widespread opposition to various aspects of the treaty, Wilson might still have been able to win the day had he been able to reach more American citizens on his successful speaking tour in 1919. His task certainly would have been easier with electronic media. From the thirties onward, American presidents increased their natural advantages over Congress and the media with their ability to command the airwaves for speeches concerning national security issues. But such technological innovations came too late to help Wilson. (They were a mixed blessing, however, as the tail began wagging the dog. Ultimately, as we will see, the electronic media often determined the way presidents handled their foreign policies.)

When the treaty finally reached the floor of the Senate in November 1919, and then again in March 1920, more than two-thirds of the senators voted for American entry into some sort of League of Nations. But the issue had become so politicized that a stubborn and seriously ill Wilson in effect said no League unless you accept my unadorned document, and the Republicans said no League unless you accept our treaty laden down with reservations. The president and the Senate were in political gridlock, much to the disappointment of most Americans who approved of the League of Nations concept.

Critics have assailed Wilson for committing the "supreme infanticide" by refusing to permit Democrats to desert his ship when it appeared that the only way the United States was going to enter the League was with the Republican-amended document. At the time, however, he felt that the vote in March 1920 would not be the last vote on the issue—the American public would have a chance to opt for his League in "a great and solemn Referendum" in the election of 1920. Here, former professor Wilson, one of the nation's foremost experts on the American political system, made another tactical blunder. Rarely had foreign policy figured prominently in presidential elections. The election of 1920 was no exception, with domestic issues deciding the outcome as they had in the 1918 by-elections. Moreover, although the Democrats and their standard bearer James M. Cox were clearly pro-League and would even accept clarifying reservations, the Republican position was more ambiguous. Many pro-League Republicans and independents who preferred Warren G. Harding's domestic program were able to cast their ballots for him in good conscience since they expected that he would work for League entry, albeit with reservations. They were sadly mistaken, of course.

THREE

From War to War,
1920–1944

THE UNITED STATES did not join the League of Nations and was relatively inactive in international—albeit not economic—politics during the 1920s. Returning to "normalcy," disillusioned by their experience in World War I, Americans hoped once again to steer clear of foreign entanglements, particularly those dealing with the major powers in Europe and Asia. Even had they wanted to participate in international affairs more fully, presidents were hamstrung in developing internationalist policies because of the prevailing isolationist sentiments to which most Americans clung. For example, before Wilson left office, such sentiments directly affected his Asian policies. He had dispatched a military force to war-ravaged Siberia, primarily to keep an eye on the Japanese who had moved in earlier. The public and its representatives in Congress demanded the return of their boys, thus weakening Wilson's leverage against what he perceived to be the predatory Japanese. In this case of congressional meddling, things worked out for the best as the Japanese eventually withdrew their occupation forces.

A near-universal disdain for the Byzantine diplomatic practices that had allegedly produced World War I and the wrangling over the peace treaty reinforced traditional American isolationism. If there was to be any contact with the outside world, it had to reflect a new, more open, diplomatic style that took into account the public's opinion. Although American—and democratic European—diplomats could still ply their traditional trade on occasion, they were forced to practice a more public form of diplomacy, as seen in the era's many conferences that were thrown open to the media.

Despite the American preference for isolationism in the twenties, major foreign policy issues did arise, including disarmament, recognition of the Soviet Union, immigration restriction, and entry into the World Court. Domestic political considerations colored the United States' posture on all four issues.

After flexing its muscles over the Treaty of Versailles, the allegedly isolationist-dominated Senate shifted course almost at once to demand that the president convene a major international conference. Sen. William E. Borah, one of the "irreconcilables" who led the fight against the League of Nations, introduced a resolution in December 1920 calling for an international conference to limit arms. Congress supported the resolution overwhelmingly, 74–0 in the Senate and 332–4 in the House. This hearty endorsement of Borah's proposal was difficult to ignore.

President-elect Harding was not pleased with the resolution that most Americans greeted enthusiastically. Disarmament advocates devoted a week to the cause in June 1921, during which they collected petitions signed by 6 million citizens, an effort comparable to the Nuclear Freeze movement of 1983. To be sure, Harding and his secretary of state ultimately agreed that a disarmament conference would be a good idea; they preferred, however, to work on the complicated issue without being pressured by the public and Congress and without Borah and his crowd assuming credit for the popular initiative. In a 1923 Senate resolution, the independent Borah also called for the international community to make war a public crime. Not initially attractive to American foreign policy professionals, that resolution became one of the foundations for the Kellogg-Briand Pact of 1928, which made illegal the resort to arms for offensive purposes.

Disarmament in the abstract was popular with penny-pinching Americans, but not if the United States had to obtain it through entanglements with the outside world. For example, at the 1932 Disarmament Conference, Pres. Herbert Hoover had an opportunity to strike a deal with the French on a relatively serious disarmament proposal. But in exchange for accepting the American position, the French wanted either an American treaty of territorial guarantee or a reduction in their World War I debt. Hoover, who genuinely believed in disarmament as the way to international amity, dared not accept the controversial French quid-pro-quos in an election year and the conference fell apart.

Another case of usurpation of foreign policy initiatives from the executive involved recognition of the Soviet Union. So many groups had come out for nonrecognition that it would have been political suicide for either the Democrats or Republicans to suggest it. Wilson could have recognized the new Russian government at its inception or soon after. The longer he delayed, the more opposition developed to the revolutionary regime.

Fearful of enhancing the status of radicalism and communism in the United States through recognition of the Soviet Union, the American Federation of Labor, the American Legion, and the Catholic church, among others, opposed opening the door to communist diplomats. No influential organizations or leaders suggested otherwise and the issue was put on hold until the onset of the Depression, when the prospect of increased Russian trade, as well as their possible support against Japanese aggression in Manchuria, won converts to the cause of recognition.

Thus, from 1917 to 1933, the United States refused to recognize the Soviet Union. This entirely unique American record for nonrecognition of odious regimes was broken in the years from 1949 through 1978, over which time five presidents refused to establish formal relations with the People's Republic of China while treating the Nationalist Chinese on the island of Formosa as the "real" China. As in the case of the Soviet Union, influential pressure groups, led by the legendary China Lobby, tied the presidents' hands on this matter, which for other major powers had always been a simple legalistic issue—if the government controls its own territory for a reasonable period of time it deserves recognition. This situation was somewhat different than that in civil war–torn Mexico in 1913, when Woodrow Wilson decided not to recognize a "regime of butchers." Then a case could have been made that the Huerta government in Mexico City had not yet established control over a major portion of the country.

The Soviets were not the only ones to be slighted by American policymakers because of domestic politics. In a far more important action against foreigners, for the first time in American history (with the exception of Chinese exclusion) Congress enacted legislation in 1921 and 1924 to restrict immigration on the basis of national origin. At issue was the perceived watering down of America's Anglo-Saxon and northern European stock by the peoples of southern and eastern Europe who had flocked to the country during the three decades prior to World War I. Characteristic in his racist views was John Hay, who had earlier spoken out against Russian pogroms.

Democracy and Diplomacy

At the same time, he also argued against Jewish immigration to the United States, which would be the "mere transportation of an artificially produced disease growth to a new place."

The new laws established quotas that discriminated against those who wanted to emigrate from such nations as Greece, Italy, Russia, Rumania, and Poland. Although none of those discriminated against reacted the way China and Japan did during Theodore Roosevelt's administration, immigration restriction on the basis of national origin affected America's relations with those countries and its image abroad. The quota system was renewed in 1952 over a presidential veto. When it was finally jettisoned in 1965 during the Johnson administration, one of the main arguments used by proponents of reform involved the impact of quotas on U.S. foreign relations.

This race-based approach to immigration compelled Americans to refuse to accept many Jews from Hitler-dominated Europe in the late 1930s, the war years, and even the postwar years. During the Depression, the issue was not just the need to maintain a northern European–based culture in the United States—there was a real fear that increased immigration from southern and eastern Europe would produce hundreds of thousands, even millions of new workers who would take jobs away from Americans. Later, the three-cornered conflict among Arabs, Jews, and the British over Palestine was exacerbated from 1945 through 1947 when the United States, among others, refused to accept the remnant of European Jewry languishing in displaced-persons camps. Some DPs, who preferred to emigrate to the United States, had no choice but to try to slip into Palestine, despite a British blockade and Arab hostility provoked by the fear that they would soon be outnumbered by Jews in the Holy Land. Even after Americans learned about the Holocaust, they refused to alter the 1924 quotas.

The xenophobia that contributed to immigration restriction in the twenties also made itself felt in the several battles over American entry to the World Court. Although after 1920 the United States never seriously considered entry into the League of Nations, all members of the international system, whether in the League or not, could join the associated World Court. Throughout the twenties and thirties, a majority of Americans, including all the presidents, supported World Court membership. But the needed approval of at least sixty-six senators proved difficult, except when the accession treaty was encumbered with reservations unacceptable to the Court. Thus, even though both parties endorsed Court membership in the 1924 campaign, when the Senate added a major reservation to an accession treaty that it finally approved in 1926, the Court found the reservation unreasonable.

One of the main arguments used by opponents of American membership in the Court revolved around the rhetorical question posed by the *Chicago Tribune* in 1925—"Do you want your fate settled by judges with names like Didrik Galtrup, Gjedde Nayholm and Wang Ch'ung-hui?" "How many friends can Uncle Sam count on if he submits his affairs to the World Court?" Chicago, of course, was the heartland of American nationalism—a place where Mayor William H. "Big Bill" Thompson promised to "punch the snout" of the king of England if he ever came to his town and where the state constitution was amended so that "American" and not English would be the official language of Illinois. As late as 1935, fear of such emotional nationalist opposition led twenty-six senators initially favorable to American membership in the World Court to join ten hardliners to kill another accession treaty. They were prodded by a vigorous anti-Court campaign led by right-wing priest Father Charles E. Coughlin and publisher William Randolph Hearst, whose efforts produced over 200,000 telegrams to Washington. In the end, enough senators joined their colleagues, one of whom proclaimed "to hell with Europe and the rest of the nations," to keep the United States out of the Court.

The debate over the Court demonstrates how in a democracy a minority can flout the will of a majority, including the president, when it feels strongly about the issue. In the United States, most of the time, a minority shouting loudly, as in the case of the National Rifle Association on gun-control issues, is more powerful than the less-impassioned majority, especially when the president does not want to risk political capital on a relatively minor matter. Some theorists not only accept the situation but suggest that this is the way a democracy should work. If every person in the United States felt strongly about many issues and worked hard for them, the government could not operate. Perhaps, but in the case of the World Court, and the League for that matter, the president's ability to conduct an effective foreign policy in the best interests of the nation was weakened by a strong minority of short-sighted isolationists and nationalists armed with specious and often racist arguments against responsible internationalism. Comparable arguments were made in recent times by opponents of an alleged Third World–dominated United Nations and its "blue-helmeted" "New World Order" police force or the alleged power of the World Trade Organization of the General Agreement on Tariffs and Trade (GATT).

During the twenties, the United States practiced isolationism when it came to *political* relationships with the powers and their new institutions. Nevertheless, the sorrowful experiences of World War I spurred the development of internationalist and dovish groups that exerted pressure on the Harding and Coolidge administrations. In 1918, both the Council on Foreign Relations and the Foreign Policy Association were founded as citizens' lobbies to produce greater awareness about the world and the United States' role in it. Older peace groups such as the World Peace Foundation and the Carnegie Endowment for International Peace were even more important. Their leaders and members wrote letters and signed petitions to buttress American support for the Washington Naval Disarmament Conference and the Kellogg-Briand Pact. During the twenties and thirties, at least fifty different peace groups flourished in the United States; their activities reached as many as 50 million Americans. In one year, one group sent out 2.6 million pieces of mail itself.

A director of the Carnegie Endowment, Columbia University professor James T. Shotwell was in Paris when Foreign Minister Aristide Briand first suggested a politically significant nonaggression treaty between the United States and France, which Washington was later able to convert into the harmless multilateral Kellogg-Briand Pact to outlaw war. But officials in the State Department were initially furious with the clever French attempt to bind the United States to its elaborate security system through the use of a pseudo-alliance, a neutrality or nonaggression pact. Shotwell's well-meaning but naive participation in that unwelcome démarche caused some in the department to consider employing the Logan Act of 1798, which prohibits private citizens from engaging in diplomatic activities, against the busybody professor.

Shotwell's superior at the Carnegie Endowment, Columbia University's Pres. Nicholas Murray Butler, contributed to popular pressures for a positive response to Briand's démarche. The State Department was prepared to ignore France's informal proposal until the *New York Times* published a letter from Butler in its influential letters-to-the-editor page. Periodically, a letter to the editor in the *Times* (or any of several other elite publications) or, as in recent years, a column on an "op-ed" page can make diplomatic waves, as was the case, for example, in early 1993 when former president Richard Nixon publicly presented proposals for dealing with Russia, which received enough favorable attention that Pres. Bill Clinton had to consider them. Leaders of most other major powers have never had to worry about such a prestigious—and independent—institution as the *New York Times* while trying to win elite and popular support for their foreign policies.

The peace groups were not alone in their attempts to influence foreign policy in the twenties. In general, they fought an uphill battle against those who wanted to continue doing business in traditional ways in the international arena. For example, the armaments lobby worked diligently to see that the disarmament movement did not cut too deeply into its profits. At the Geneva Naval Conference of 1927, William Baldwin Shearer, a master lobbyist for American shipbuilders masquerading as a journalist, helped scuttle proposals that affected his industry's balance sheets.

When it came to American military intervention, peace groups were more successful. A new Progressive party nominated dovish Sen. Robert LaFollette (R-Wis.) as its presidential candidate in 1924. One of the key planks in his platform concerned opposition to American military involvement and protectorate relationships in Latin America. Although the Progressives did not win in 1924, LaFollette polled more than 16 percent of the popular vote. Furthermore, antiwar pressures in Congress, the media, and the public in general influenced Pres. Calvin Coolidge's policy in the most important American military activity of the twenties. Coolidge's dispatch of American Marines to Nicaragua during a revolution in 1927 produced an outpouring of anti-interventionist sentiment that limited his options. The president hoped to assist the pro-American government in Managua in its battle with liberal rebels. But most Americans wanted the Marines out of the country as soon as possible, which forced Coolidge to arrange an election to provide the cover for withdrawal.

Throughout this period, and most other periods in American history for that matter, the public has generally acted as a restraining force on presidents bent on intervening in places that do not appear to be vital to national security. Indeed, popular opposition to intervention in Nicaragua in the 1920s parallels the position taken on the same issue by the public sixty years later. Coolidge's Nicaraguan crisis may also have been the first time that an American leader talked about a communist takeover in the hemisphere when Secretary of State Frank B. Kellogg warned about the dangers of "Mexican-fostered Bolshevik hegemony in Central America."

The Marines did not pull out of Nicaragua in 1928 because of the revolt led by guerrilla chief Gen. Augusto Sandino. America's ultimately unsuccessful counterrevolutionary war against Sandino was unpopular in the United States. In the 1928 election, the Democrats challenged not only the substance of the action but also the legality of Coolidge's undeclared little war. Fortunately for Coolidge and for his Republican successor, Herbert Hoover, their party was still far too dominant to be affected seriously by the attack on their Nicaraguan foreign policy, just as Ronald Reagan and George Bush were able to win elections in 1984 and 1988 despite their unpopular Nicaraguan initiatives.

Hemispheric neighbors and near neighbors were affected as well by Prohibition. It was not difficult to smuggle alcoholic beverages through or over America's long and porous land and sea borders. On occasion, smuggling from foreign sources led to international incidents, the most famous of which embroiled the United States in a minidispute with Canada. In 1929, an American Coast Guard vessel sank a Canadian rum-runner, *I'm Alone,* in international waters. The Canadians lost one crewman in the encounter, a tragedy for which the United States was ultimately forced to apologize and pay damages.

These problems paled before those posed by the illegal importation of drugs into the United States a half-century later. The related issues of American drug use and crime led several administrations to fight the drug war at the source, with major economic and military programs in producer countries. For a score of Latin American and Asian nations in the 1980s, diplomatic interactions with the United States were determined by the widespread use of drugs in American society. That is, the U.S. government intervened in places such as Bolivia because it was unable to control some of its citizens' apparently insatiable demand for drugs, in much the same way that it was unable to control the demand for alcohol in the 1920s.

DESPITE RELATIVE American political isolation in the twenties, American businesses expanded exponentially worldwide with implications for foreign policies well into the future. During the decade, exports doubled while foreign investments grew fivefold. Characteristic of this growth were the strong market positions achieved by U.S. Rubber in Malaya, Anaconda Copper in Chile, General Electric in Germany, RCA in Poland, Borden in England, and several oil companies in the Middle East.

Private investors did not expand their operations abroad completely unfettered. The administrations of the twenties established an informal procedure in which corporations were expected to float loan proposals past State Department bureaucrats who had economic *and* political expertise. Those bureaucrats advised against making loans to countries that the United States had not recognized or that owed money to the United States, to foreign monopolies in competition with American businesses, or to socially unacceptable enterprises. In the latter category, the State Department advised one group not to invest in the Pilsner Brewing Company in Czechoslovakia, but not because of the political or economic impropriety of the loan. To the contrary, the company and Czechoslovakia were good risks. The problem was Prohibition and the unseemly prospect of Americans becoming involved with "demon rum" abroad. To be sure, no "law" mandated State Department approval of foreign investments. But since Americans often called upon their government for support or protection abroad, most businesspeople, including those who wanted to invest in Czech beer, accepted State Department advice. Not surprisingly, the State Department worked hard to frustrate American investment in the Soviet Union during the twenties. In that case, however, the Ford Motor Company and International Harvester, among other large corporations, rejected department warnings and collaborated with Josef Stalin on his vaunted Five-Year plans.

Of all the places into which American businesses and capital moved aggressively, Latin America was the most important in terms of future political implications. Over 1,000 American companies exercised considerable economic influence in three-quarters of the nations of Latin America. Economic influence led to considerable political influence, especially in Central America. American businesspeople, sometimes acting independently of American diplomats, bought politicians and even armed their cadres in innumerable attempts to maintain a favorable economic climate for their companies. At the time, the U.S. government approved of the manner in which its security and economic interests were being protected in Latin America. The chickens came home to roost in the form of passionate anti-imperialism and anti-Americanism during the thirties and the years after World War II.

With war clouds on the horizon and with European Fascists establishing pockets of support in several Latin American nations, the United States, under Franklin Roosevelt's Good Neighbor Policy, began to separate itself from some American business interests in the hemisphere. More and more during the thirties, the State Department urged corporations to become less overbearing with their Latin American clients before it was too late. The department adopted this position not necessarily because it had given up the idea that it should support American enterprises abroad. Policymakers were concerned that the arrogant behavior of those enterprises could result in the expulsion of all American economic influence from some countries and even lead to German spheres of influence in areas of strategic importance. The State Department backed up its new approach in the late thirties by failing to support the more aggressive claims of American oil companies in Venezuela and Mexico. Such behavior suggests that the relationship between Washington and specific business interests operating abroad is more complicated than crude economic determinists have posited.

THE GREAT DEPRESSION created immense pressures on American politicians to alleviate unemployment and economic stagnation. The policies they adopted impacted other countries struggling to improve the lot of their own citizens, and ultimately affected international politics in general. For example, the United States tried to protect sectors of its economy against lower-cost foreign competition in order to save American jobs. The Smoot-Hawley Tariff of 1930, primarily aimed at improving the domestic economy, had an impact abroad. Economic nationalism made it much harder for other nations to sell their goods in the United States and, for that reason, to buy American goods as well. The high tariff, which did little to boost the domestic economy, may have increased the severity of the depression around the world. Not surprisingly, the tariff paralleled comparable economic nationalist policies from the major powers that led to a shutdown of two-thirds of all world trade. By 1932, twenty-five of America's trading partners had enacted retaliatory trade legislation that contributed to a 50 percent decline in U.S. exports. No wonder Vice-President Al Gore used the example of Smoot-Hawley to skewer Ross Perot in their important televised debate over the North American Free Trade Treaty (NAFTA) in 1993.

Like many historians, Gore may have exaggerated the impact of the tariff on the trajectory of the depression. Other factors contributed to the decline in U.S. exports as well. Indeed, it is possible that contemporary observers were taken in by the way the Democrats used the issue to pillory the Republicans. According to the British ambassador, Democrats "carried on a species of guerrilla warfare, asking the electorate to censure the Republicans . . . for having . . . unnecessarily and wantonly exposed the country to a wave of foreign resentment."

Whatever the true significance of the Smoot-Hawley Tariff, for politicians concerned about getting elected, it was—and is—generally easier to enact trade barriers against foreign competition than to argue that in the long run most consumers would benefit from being able to buy goods at the lowest prices. Moreover, in a world operating with few economic barriers, the more a nation imports, presumably the more that nation is able to export. That is easy to say, but in the short run, as seen in the United States in the late 1980s and early 1990s in terms of competition with Japan, politicians score heavily by talking about unlevel playing fields controlled by foreigners who are throwing autoworkers off the assembly line.

Similarly, there is no doubt that at the London Economic Conference of 1933 Roosevelt was constrained from approving measures to boost the international economy, which in the long run could have boosted the U.S. economy. He refused to cooperate with the European powers' currency stabilization proposals because he thought they would be harmful to the *immediate* prospects for American recovery. Politicians who must be reelected periodically find it difficult arguing that short-term losses might bring long-term gains. Further, Roosevelt did not worry very much about the impact on Europe when he took the United States off the gold standard. In that case, he apparently was influenced by the positive reaction from the public—and from the stock market—when Walter Lippmann suggested in one of his columns that such a move was imminent. Later in the thirties, American diplomats, especially Secretary of State Cordell Hull, linked the deleterious impact of economic nationalism not just to the world's economy but also to the rise of Fascism and Nazism in Europe. Allied planning for the postwar world envisaged the erection of a series of multilateral institutions, such as the International Monetary Fund (IMF) and GATT, which would foster cooperation and lower tariffs.

The weakness of the virtually unregulated American banking system during the go-go years of the twenties also contributed substantially to the worldwide economic downturn. The World War I reparations and loan-redemption system during that decade began with loans from American banks to the Germans to repay the British and French who repaid the Americans. When the American banking system self-destructed after the crash in 1929, the international repayment system collapsed.

The United States could have ameliorated the situation by canceling most or all of the Allied debts. Some Republican leaders approved of the idea in principle but realized that it was politically unpalatable since the war loans had been financed through the sale of bonds whose redemption would have to have been supported by higher taxes. In fact, in 1932 both Hoover and his Democratic opponent, Franklin D. Roosevelt, might have considered canceling Allied debts in exchange for a cancellation of German reparations had they not had to run for election.

The worldwide repercussions of a failure of the American banking system were not unique to the Depression. When American savings and loans institutions began to default in record numbers in the late 1980s, government measures to bail out investors impacted on the national deficit, the value of the dollar, and interest rates, all of which had some effect on other nations' economic, political, and external relations. When the gargantuan American economy sneezes, other governments may catch a cold, with implications for their political survival as well as for their relations with the United States.

However one evaluates the relationship between economic nationalism and rising international tensions, after 1931 the United States confronted an unprecedented series of crises that led ultimately to its entry into World War

II. Throughout the period, as might be expected, domestic considerations played a major role in determining the American government's responses to those crises. Moderate interventionists, from Hoover's Secretary of State Henry L. Stimson during the Manchurian Crisis of 1931–33 through Roosevelt as late as the fall of 1941, were severely constrained by what they perceived to be pervasive isolationist sentiments. Although many leaders in both parties felt that the United States had to assume some responsibilities in a system sliding again toward world war, the issues were so controversial and the efforts needed to educate the public so herculean that politicians feared electoral defeat if they proclaimed that U.S. interests extended to the Rhine.

Congress, dominated by isolationists, made things difficult for Roosevelt. In 1935, the Senate's Munitions (or Nye) Committee investigated American entry into World War I in an effort to keep the country out of the next war. The committee had been prodded by the publication of sensational journalistic exposés and books in 1934 about munitions profiteers, materials used successfully by the indefatigable Dorothy Detzer of the Women's International League for Peace and Freedom to lobby for a congressional investigation. The Nye group's seemingly authoritative report contained no smoking guns but suggested that American entry into the Great War had something to do with the machinations of bankers and munitions makers, linked to the British, who did not have their country's national security interests at heart. The Nye Committee's report, as well as the Senate's rejection of entry into the World Court, brought together an uneasy coalition of pacifists and internationalists in the Emergency Peace Campaign in 1936–37, the largest peace organization in American history to that point. With branches in over 1,200 American cities, the group pressured Congress to adopt measures to keep the United States out of war. While their pleas for a reconsideration of the World Court decision fell on deaf ears, many politicians endorsed their more isolationist proposals. Roosevelt and other moderate internationalists were powerless to challenge the growing notion that American participation in World War I had been a mistake and that Congress had to remain on guard against another attempt by a president, allegedly influenced by irresponsible lobbies, to construct unneutral policies that would lead the nation into a war it did not have to wage.

The passage of neutrality acts during 1935–37, prohibiting loans and the sale of munitions to belligerents and keeping American vessels out of war zones, was one way Congress tried to keep America out of World War I [sic]. Roosevelt failed in several attempts to moderate the acts by obtaining presidential discretion to distinguish between aggressors and their targets. Only after World War II began, in November 1939, was he able to obtain modifications that permitted Americans to sell arms on a cash-and-carry basis to belligerents.

Underscoring the power of the isolationists as late as 1938, a proposed amendment to the Constitution known as the Ludlow Amendment, which would have taken the war-declaring power away from Congress and given it to the people through a direct popular vote, was introduced in the House. According to one senator who opposed the amendment, it "would be as sensible to require a town meeting before permitting the fire department to put out the blaze." The fact that it failed to emerge from committee to the floor by a margin of only twenty-one votes reflected the powerful forces in opposition to Roosevelt's attempts to develop a more interventionist foreign policy.

Historians have criticized Roosevelt for moving too slowly in leading the United States toward accepting its international responsibilities. Perhaps, but his prime concern until 1938 was his massive and controversial New Deal reform program. He feared losing support for his domestic legislation in conflicts over foreign policy issues. Owing to the seniority system, the most conservative members of his coalition, the southern Democrats, generally controlled the key congressional committees. Already uneasy about the more radical New Deal propositions, most of them were even more uneasy about moving too quickly into the international arena. Some liberal Democrats were also poised to oppose Roosevelt if he entered the European and Asian maelstroms. They remembered what had happened to Progressive reform when the United States entered World War I.

In the critical period from 1939 through 1941, Roosevelt handled this problem more adroitly than did reform president Lyndon Johnson when he led the United States into the Vietnam War through stealth because of his need to protect his own massive reform program, the Great Society. In the end, Johnson lost his credibility because of his unwise political tactics. At all times, presidents contemplating controversial foreign activities have to take into consideration the impact of those activities on their domestic programs. Indeed, when seeking to shepherd his major economic reform package through Congress in the spring of 1993, Pres. Bill Clinton walked very carefully around the minefield of the Bosnian civil war for fear of weakening his domestic coalition. As a State Department official allegedly said, the administration understood the moral issue at stake in Bosnia but "the survival of the fragile liberal coalition represented by this presidency" was also at stake and it represented an even higher moral issue. Interestingly, during that same period, both the United States and the United Nations pulled their punches on increasing pressure on Serbia because they did not want to hurt Russian president Boris Yeltsin, who was hoping to keep that contentious issue quiet until his nation's historically pro-Serbian electorate had an opportunity to vote on *his* domestic program.

Although it did not help Roosevelt in his battles with the isolationists in the late thirties, his powers as chief diplomat were secured, and to some degree enhanced, by the landmark Supreme Court ruling in *United States v. Curtiss-Wright Export Corporation* in 1936. In that case, the Curtiss-Wright corporation challenged Roosevelt and Congress's right to place an arms embargo on Bolivia and Paraguay during the Chaco War. According to Justice Sutherland's opinion,

> In this vast external realm . . . the President alone has the power to speak or listen as a representative of the nation. . . . [Congress] must often accord to the President a degree of discretion and freedom from statutory restriction which would not be admissible were domestic affairs alone involved. . . . Moreover, he, not Congress, has the better opportunity of knowing conditions which prevail in foreign countries.

During the Vietnam era, Congress took issue with Sutherland's constitutional interpretation, particularly the notion that the president knows what is going on in the world better than anyone else.

In the fall of 1937, Roosevelt made his boldest move toward intervention prior to the outbreak of world war with his Quarantine Speech directed against the Japanese who had just begun their war in China. He talked about taking strong, if undelineated, actions to stop them. When the president evaluated the press response to his speech the next day, he became convinced that isolationism was so powerful in the United States that he would be unable to lead his nation toward greater involvement in the Asian war. He may have been mistaken in his analysis of the reaction to his talk about "quarantining the aggressors." Historians claim that he misread the evidence and that the public supported a more assertive policy in Asia. Whatever the evidence, Roosevelt backtracked soon after the speech and took a more cautious approach toward interventionism over the next few years.

Public opinion that matters is not always what people think but what presidents think they think. Although successful professional politicians are generally adept at evaluating public opinion—how else could they get elected and reelected?—they have sometimes blundered, as was the case with Roosevelt at a crucial point in 1937 when he may have overestimated the pervasiveness of American isolationism.

The United States was not alone in its isolationism in the thirties. Politicians in England and France also confronted publics unenthusiastic about collective security. Only one power consistently called for joint action against German and Japanese aggression—the Soviet Union. Although the United States finally recognized the Russians in 1933, the lukewarm American response to Soviet pleas for collective security against Fascism after 1935 was affected by domestic anticommunism. For many Americans, Communism was the ultimate enemy. Whereas Japanese militarism and German Fascism posed only military threats to their neighbors and no immediate threat to the United States, Communism, directed by conspirators in Moscow, could come to the United States through its ideology, not just with the Red army and navy.

Indeed, many American isolationists echoed European pro-Fascists who argued "Better Hitler than Blum." Leon Blum was the socialist-leaning leader of the French government. Whether confronting Japanese aggression in Asia or German aggression in Central Europe, the message was the same. Whatever those aggressors were up to, at least they were sworn enemies of the chief enemy of Western civilization, the worldwide communist conspiracy. As late as 1937, Americans still placed Stalin above Hitler on their least-favored leader list. When the Soviet Union invaded Finland in late 1939, many isolationist but anticommunist leaders urged the president to do more to aid the brave Finns battling Communism and at the same time opposed increased support for the British and French who were only fighting Germans.

In addition, some prominent American businesses enjoyed cordial economic relations with Hitler's Germany. Twenty of the nation's top 100 corporations maintained special agreements with their German counterparts, which could have affected American national security. For example, Standard Oil's agreement with I.G. Farben denied the American company the right to make aviation fuel for the United States.

Domestic anti-Semitism also colored American policies during the thirties. Anti-Semitism, then widely shared, made many Americans easy prey for those who contended that interventionist sentiment was influenced, as isolationist spokesperson Charles A. Lindbergh charged in 1941, by the Jews whose "greatest danger to this country lies in their large ownership and influence in our motion pictures, our press, our radio, and our government." Lindbergh's wildly exaggerated charges had some basis in fact. As Hitler's persecution of the Jews increased dramatically after the enactment of the Nuremberg Laws of 1935, the small but disproportionately influential American Jewish community was among the most fervent opponents of his regime. Throughout the thirties, that community led a vigorous, and to some degree successful, boycott of German goods. They were not as successful in reforming the immigration laws to permit more Jewish refugees to enter the United States. The quota for all Germans, Jew and gentile alike, was 27,000 per year, and since the Nazi government prohibited German Jews from emigrating with their money and valuable possessions, they ran afoul of the immigration laws' antipauper provisions. Nor were Jews and their supporters in the United States (and England) successful in convincing the British, who held the mandate for Palestine, to permit appreciably more refugees to enter the Holy Land.

According to public opinion polls, 80 percent of American citizens approved of their immigration laws in the 1930s, which, according to one congressman, were supposed to keep out "bolsheviks, wops, dagoes, kikes, and hunkies." In February 1939, two-thirds of Americans polled opposed a congressional bill that would have raised the quota to permit 20,000 German-Jewish children to enter their country. In a later era, in 1956, when spokespersons for 20,000 anticommunist Christians from Hungary who fled Soviet oppression petitioned Congress to set aside the meager quota assigned to "hunkies," their request was accepted.

Aside from these general influences, specific domestic considerations figured prominently in Roosevelt's responses to the series of crises that shook Europe from 1935 to 1939. When the Italians invaded Ethiopia in 1935, a year before the 1936 election, the president weighed his options with an eye to the Italian-American vote. Italian-Americans, who generally supported Democrats, were split in their approval of Benito Mussolini. The dictator even sent agents to the United States to work with their former countrymen to influence American policy toward Rome. Fear of reprisals from Italian-Americans was not the only reason Roosevelt was satisfied merely with the condemnation of Italy and a moral embargo, but they troubled a candidate who was surprisingly pessimistic about his chances of winning the 1936 election.

Roosevelt was far less concerned about a small and uninfluential group of African-Americans who lobbied for greater support for Ethiopia in the war. That support took many forms: poet Langston Hughes wrote a "Ballad of Ethiopia," several American blacks volunteered to fight in the Ethiopian army, and their entire community cheered the victory of Joe Louis, the "Brown Bomber," over Italian heavyweight Primo Carnera in 1935. The emperor of Ethiopia, Haile Selassie, was not enthused about such support since he did not consider his people to be related to black Africans. In 1937, after the war was over, African-Americans founded the Council of African

Affairs but it was not until the 1970s that their attempts to influence American policy on the continent, particularly South Africa, began to have some effect.

The Spanish Civil War (1936–39) was a more important prelude to World War II than the Italo-Ethiopian War. Like Italian-Americans in the earlier war, the American Catholic community, generally supportive of the fascist counterrevolution in Spain, influenced Roosevelt's cautious policy toward the social democratic republic, the legitimate government in Madrid. Catholics, who were more often found in the Democratic than Republican columns, had been told by their hierarchy that the war in Spain, which some saw as a conflict between democracy and Fascism, was a war between Communism and Christianity. Throughout the twenties and thirties, the American Catholic church, among the most conservative in the world, was a leading opponent of atheistic Bolshevism, and indeed, any force that threatened the traditional position of the church. Spain became a secular state when the republic was established in 1931. Fascist leader Generalissimo Francisco Franco promised the church that it would return to its old economic, social, and political prominence in a fascist regime.

Whatever domestic pressures he felt, Roosevelt coordinated his policies with the British and French, who, in their attempt to localize the conflict, instituted an arms embargo against the Spanish Republicans and turned a blind eye toward Italian and German violations of nonintervention pledges. These two policies, acceded to by the Roosevelt administration, spelled doom for the elected government in Madrid, which though supported by the Soviet Union was not its puppet until perhaps the last months of the war.

At least 3,000 American citizens traveled to Spain to join 30,000 other International Brigadeers fighting for the republic. The Americans had to be smuggled into the country because the United States and the European democracies had forbidden such private intervention. Their heroic and romantic volunteer participation in the war, celebrated in the media of the day, helped popularize the cause of the republic in the United States. By 1938, a clear majority of Americans expressed support for Madrid and, had the war gone on, perhaps would have forced Roosevelt's hand on the arms embargo or emboldened him to somehow aid the republic that he himself favored.

The International Brigades were organized by the Soviet Union. Because Moscow was the only major power to call for and even to take action against Fascism, the American Communist party enjoyed its greatest legitimacy in its controversial history. To be sure, the vast majority of Americans still opposed Communism. But many intellectuals, writers, performers, and college students were attracted to that cause because of what they perceived to be the democracies' feckless appeasement policies.

As the president and his aides contemplated responses to fascist aggression in Europe and Africa and Japanese militarism in Asia, they were able to evaluate their constituents' attitudes with a new tool, the modern public opinion poll. Polls are blunt tools that provide unsubtle snapshots of opinion at a discrete point in time. Yet their availability increased the confidence of leaders in their abilities to determine more accurately the peoples' policy preferences.

During the late thirties, pioneer pollster George Gallup served this need for solid information about the public's opinions. Unbeknownst to Americans, his polls were not entirely private or independent. For one thing, Gallup pollsters sometimes asked Roosevelt and his aides to suggest questions for a poll. Moreover, Gallup often gave the administration advance peeks at poll results so that it could prepare a response following their publication. Since polls not only report opinion but also make it by reporting it, Roosevelt gained quite an advantage over his adversaries. As other respected pollsters entered the field, some became known primarily as Republican pollsters while others maintained loyalties to Democrats. As president, Richard Nixon so distrusted the alleged biases exhibited by pollsters that he established his own polling operation.

Polls relating to complicated and remote foreign policy issues are less useful to decisionmakers than those relating to more familiar domestic issues. They certainly are not much help in a fast-moving crisis. If anything, because of the president's presumed expertise in this area, the public has generally been willing to follow him when he announces that a national security–threatening event has occurred. In the absence of such an event, presidents since the thirties could be certain that Americans would invariably tell pollsters that they did not want to intervene militarily abroad.

Such was the case from 1935 through 1941 when Americans clearly expressed their policy preferences to the pollsters—they wanted to stay out of war. Roosevelt had other indications that isolationism was a powerful force in the United States. During the mid-thirties, Father Charles E. Coughlin's weekly radio commentaries, which reflected isolationist, even profascist views, was one of the most listened-to programs.

When World War II broke out in September 1939, Roosevelt initiated a cautious policy of moral, political, and economic support for the British and French that began with Cash and Carry neutrality and moved through the Destroyer Base Deal in September 1940 and Lend-Lease in February 1941.

He wanted to do more to aid the democracies but was hamstrung by strong isolationist sentiment that he felt might affect the outcome of the 1940 presidential election in which he ran for an unprecedented third term. Isolationism also came to be a partisan issue, with Republicans much more than Democrats finding themselves in that camp. Thus, when Roosevelt pushed the Fourth Neutrality Act through Congress in the fall of 1939, a majority of those opposing the revisions favorable to the Allies were Republicans.

Isolationism was challenged not only by the president but by interventionist groups, particularly the Committee to Defend America by Aiding the Allies. Members of that bipartisan committee, led by Republican newspaper editor William Allen White, held meetings, wrote newspaper and magazine articles, and petitioned representatives to support increased aid to Britain and France to keep the Germans from reaching the Atlantic. The White House had earlier enlisted the widely respected White to head up the Non-Partisan Committee for Peace through Revision of the Neutrality Act. His group was successful in the fall of 1939. Again, by the spring of 1940, the fact that more and more Americans told pollsters that they were prepared to do more to aid the Allies suggested that White's interventionist lobby was having some effect. The close relationship between his presumably independent and spontaneously developed committees and the White House was not known at the time. During the Vietnam War, both the Johnson and Nixon administrations enjoyed support from comparable "independent" committees of public-minded citizens and, as was the case with the White committees, they too received under-the-table direction from the White House. In both cases, even though presidents used the cloak of national security to defend this practice, they certainly raised questions about the nature of the American democratic system and the ability of citizens to mount a challenge to an administration engaged in such deceitful activities.

Another influential citizens' lobby led by Grenville Clark did not have FDR's official blessing. Clark's informal group played a major behind-the-scenes role mobilizing support for passage of America's first peacetime draft law, which was enacted in September 1940. FDR approved of the controversial idea but did not want to raise it during the election campaign.

Not all groups involved in the debate over adopting a more interventionist posture were favorable to the president. In September 1940, the day after Roosevelt announced the Destroyer Deal, in which he traded overage American vessels to the British for bases in their empire, isolationists formed their own potent lobbying group, the America First Committee. Less bipartisan than the Committee to Defend America by Aiding the Allies, America First fought unsuccessfully against the Destroyer Deal as well as Lend-Lease the following winter. But after the United States had gone so far as to loan goods to the British in their war effort, a relatively popular proposal, America First's message became simpler and more acceptable to many Americans—the United States does not belong in the war.

Roosevelt secretly ordered the FBI to keep tabs on the committee, claiming that it was working with German agents. The agency used many of the same sorts of illegal means to monitor the activities of America First as those ordered by presidents Johnson and Nixon to keep tabs on another antiwar movement. In the latter case, both presidents also defended their actions in terms of the relationship of foreign governments to the movement. In the year before Pearl Harbor and during the Vietnam War, neither antiwar movement maintained significant ties to the "enemy." They were "all-American" dissenters. Even less defensible was Roosevelt's request to the FBI in September 1941 to investigate a handful of congressmen, who were outspoken opponents of his interventionist foreign policies, for alleged subversive activities.

At first, Roosevelt's interventionism was not an issue in the 1940 election. The president and Republican nominee Wendell Willkie maintained an informal and tacit gentleman's agreement to leave foreign policy out of the campaign. Willkie, a moderate and something of an internationalist, generally approved of Roosevelt's policies of aid to the Allies, including the controversial Destroyer Deal, and did not object to the institution of selective service in September. Had the president suspected that Willkie would not support the unprecedented deal, he might have waited until after the election to announce it. However, the Republican standard bearer did disapprove of the way his opponent arranged the deal in "the most dictatorial action ever taken by any President" because it was an executive agreement and not a formal treaty.

In October, when it appeared that he was going to lose, Willkie broke the gentleman's agreement on foreign policy and began to charge that a vote for Roosevelt was a vote for war and that "if you elect me president, I will never send American boys to fight in any European War." At the time, the president thought it possible that the United States would be in the war in the near future because of the threat to American national security posed by expansionist Germany and Japan. Yet he understood that realistic talk about the possibility—not even probability—of future American intervention might result in the loss of the election. Thus, he promised "again, and again, and again" the "mothers and fathers of America" that "your boys are not going to be sent into any foreign wars." This was pure demagoguery since Roosevelt expected that American boys might soon have to fight in World War II. However, as one prominent historian argued in the president's defense, FDR was like the doctor forced to tell the patient the little white lie that a life-saving medicine really does not taste bad. Perhaps, but is such lying permissible in a campaign for president? Roosevelt's position was understandable, if not acceptable, given Willkie's cheap shot. Nevertheless, many of the same people who accepted his white lie in 1941 were angered in 1965 by Lyndon Johnson's apparent white lie during the 1964 campaign when he told prospective voters that the war in Southeast Asia would be fought by Asian, not American, boys. Or as Sen. J. William Fulbright (D-Ark.) noted in 1971, "FDR's deviousness in a good cause made it easier for LBJ to practice the same kind of deviousness in a bad cause."

Furthermore, although Roosevelt won the election in part by assuring Americans that he was not going to get them into war, the fact that he lulled them into a false sense of security made it all the more difficult to sell them on the need for intervention during the following year. Right up to Pearl Harbor, only a very small minority of Americans told pollsters that they thought their country belonged in the war in the absence of a direct attack on its territory, although increasingly larger numbers of people were willing to support measures to stop an Axis victory. But that support did not necessarily mean that a majority of Americans wanted to go to war. Indeed, when selective service came up for renewal in August 1941, the bill made it through the House by a 203–202 margin.

Roosevelt's white lies continued on through 1941. On September 4, 1941, the USS *Greer* was fired upon by a Nazi submarine in an act that Roosevelt labeled "piracy, legally and morally." He used the event to issue a "shoot-at-sight" order—American naval officers could shoot at any submarine they saw in their vicinity even though the subs took no hostile action against them. Most Americans applauded the strong—and illegal—action against German submarines. Of course, Roosevelt had neglected to inform the nation that the *Greer* had been tailing the sub for several hours, relaying its position to British planes overhead. One wonders what the response would have been had the president informed them completely about the nature of the attack on the *Greer*. In a comparable situation in 1964, Lyndon Johnson withheld crucial information from the public about the Gulf of Tonkin attack. Both presidents, no doubt, would have used the defense of "national security" to explain their deviousness.

Although it was not a matter of presidential deceit, most Americans did not understand why the United States found itself in mortal combat with Japan, aside from the obvious attack on Pearl Harbor. The war that finally came to the United States on December 7, 1941, was intimately related to America's Open Door Policy. The Japanese felt compelled to knock out the fleet in Hawaii because the United States refused to accept their military and political gains in China. During the long negotiations between the two countries, the China issue emerged as the most difficult to resolve. The Japanese contended that their Greater East Asia Co-Prosperity Sphere was akin to the Monroe Doctrine. They did not meddle in the American baili-wick; Americans should not meddle in theirs. But most American policy-makers had accepted the Open Door Policy, a policy that revolved around the myth of the China Market, as vital to their national security interests. Ever since the turn of the century, if not earlier, the penetration of that untapped market of hundreds of millions of consumers appeared to be one sure way to guarantee perpetual economic stability and growth. Had Amer-icans known that the Japanese attacked Pearl Harbor because of a squabble about a phantom China Market, they might not have been as supportive of the war resolution.

THE ROOSEVELT-WILLKIE election marked a turning point in the influ-ence of foreign relations on presidential elections and, of course, vice versa. Reflecting the United States' leadership in the international system, issues relating to foreign affairs were important factors in every campaign from 1940 through 1988. If no specific issue arose to split the candidates, they argued that, at the least, they were more experienced diplomats or tougher than their opponents and thus the electorate would be safer from external attack during their presidencies. Aware of this development, other nations began paying special attention to the "domestic" content of American for-eign policy as early as a president's third year in office.

This could be seen, for example, in Roosevelt's diplomacy in 1943 and 1944. Critics have objected to the way he deferred political decisions con-cerning the postwar world until final military victory. Thus, he may have lost the opportunity to limit the Soviet spheres of influence while they still bat-tled the Nazis inside their own country. Roosevelt preferred to keep the issue of postwar Eastern Europe out of the headlines because of the votes of some ethnic groups, especially Polish-Americans, who would take umbrage if some of their motherland was "given away" to the Soviet Union in a hard-nosed bargain. Indeed, when the Republicans raised that issue in the 1944 election, the president announced that he was supportive of Polish territorial claims. His support weakened substantially at the Yalta Conference three months after he had been elected to a fourth term. Had he made the territorial concessions he made at Yalta before the election, the Republicans would have had a potent campaign issue. In addition, he at first kept the details of the Yalta compromises secret. When they began to leak out, the realistic arrangements the Big Three had made over the disposition of Eastern Europe and other territories looked all the more nefarious because they had been kept secret. Over the next decade, the "sellout" or "conspiracy" at Yalta became a prominent theme in Republican politics.

As with the failure to level with the American people in the 1940 and 1944 elections, Roosevelt's unwillingness to explain the hard geopolitical issues to his constituents made things much more difficult for his successors when the idealistic postwar world he talked about during the war did not materialize. Here he was repeating the mistakes Woodrow Wilson made when he brought the United States into World War I under rhetorical false pretenses.

The controversial Polish and East European issues, could, however, work two ways for the president. On occasion, American diplomats exaggerated the power of the ethnic groups, especially the Polish-American bloc, during negotiations with the Russians in order to obtain concessions. For example, at the 1943 Teheran conference, Roosevelt told Stalin that "as a practical man" he had to consider the views of 6 million Polish-Americans in signing off on proposals for Poland's postwar boundary.

However, groups such as the Polish-Americans were more of a problem than an asset for American presidents in their negotiations. After the 1944 election, Roosevelt and then his successor, Harry S Truman, claimed that they could not accept publicly a spheres-of-influence settlement as proposed by Josef Stalin and Winston Churchill, even had they wanted to, for fear of alienating European-Americans whose homelands were about to disappear behind the fast-lowering Iron Curtain. Churchill could much more easily accept such an amoral deal not only because his public was more realistic but also because he did not fear the political power of such groups in Britain.

Undersecretary of State Sumner Welles, who headed up the Interdepartmental Committee on Foreign Nationality Problems, warned as early as 1942 that nationality groups in the United States, numbering as many as 40 million members, "might try to influence foreign policy." The following year, the Office of Strategic Services (OSS) reported that 215 major organizations representing those groups produced at least 250 regular publications.

Not all groups that hoped to influence American policy toward the bel-

Democracy and Diplomacy

ligerents posed problems for the president. Many Americans who were An-glophilic because of blood or cultural ties warmly greeted Clarence Streit's popular book, *Union Now with Britain*. In addition, a very effective lobby, made up exclusively of European-Americans, the Citizens' Committee to Repeal Chinese Exclusion, contributed to the climate in 1943 that enabled Roosevelt to terminate a policy that was a standing insult to China, the Allies' major partner in Asia. The president would not have pushed very hard on this potentially controversial issue had not the committee prepared the way for him. And finally, all through the war, the Council on Foreign Rela-tions worked closely with the State Department, albeit under the table, on a successful propaganda campaign for the United Nations.

As Roosevelt considered his options for postwar Europe, he was severely constrained in posing any sort of postwar counterweight to the Red army by the Americans' historic unwillingness to maintain a peacetime military establishment. He led his allies to believe that the United States would retreat to its shores once the war was over, confronted by demands to balance the budget and return to "normalcy." Here he was mistaken, with anticommu-nism ultimately defeating isolationism and budget-balancing during the late 1940s.

Roosevelt, unlike Wilson, did not use his Office of War Information (OWI) during World War II for partisan domestic advantage. Nevertheless, the OWI forged a cooperative relationship with American media to guaran-tee that they followed the government line. For example, Hollywood agreed to submit scripts to the OWI to make certain that its films did not offend an ally or suggest themes harmful to the war effort. This practice resulted, among other things, in American films about the Soviet Union being submitted by the Film Bureau of the OWI to the Soviet Embassy in Washington for tech-nical advice and in producers eliminating stock "Negro" characters so as not to upset the African-American community being wooed by another people of color, the Japanese.

The relationship between the OWI and the film industry led to a situa-tion where, for the first time, a major American medium became almost an official medium—and few citizens were aware of it. Studio executives ac-cepted the relationship not just because they were patriotic. The govern-ment controlled the lucrative foreign film market, contracts for thousands of training films, and scarce resources—including movie stars in uniform—needed in film production. Elmer Davis, the head of OWI, was pleased with Hollywood's cooperative attitude. "The easiest way to inject a propaganda idea into most people's minds," he contended, "is to let it go through the

medium of an entertainment picture when they do not realize they are being propagandized."

Several of the themes developed by the OWI to rally maximum support
for the war effort came home to haunt postwar administrations. For example, the constant attempt to make China an equal member of the Big Four
and to sell its struggle against Japan as part of the fight of democracies against
dictatorships affected domestic politics during the early 1950s. If the Chinese
were so democratic, so strong, even so American-like, how could it be that
they fell to Communism only four years after the end of World War II? In
One World, Wendell Willkie's 1943 best-selling memoir about his global diplomatic mission for Roosevelt, the Republican leader contended that "China
was not an alien country, full of strange customs, but a warm-hearted, hos-
pitable land filled with friends of America."

The Soviet Union was another place Willkie found friends of America.
The wartime depiction of Russia once again as a fit partner for a league of
honor, a depiction reinforced by Moscow's heroic military effort and rhetorical liberalization during the conflict, led to recriminations later about naive
or fellow-traveling American diplomats being too soft on the Reds at such
places as Yalta. Roosevelt offered periodic exaggerated praise for the brave
Russians because of his need to counteract widespread public opposition to
this important alliance of necessity. Such vocal anticommunism reinforced
Stalin's paranoia about the capitalists delaying a second front and led to his
veiled threats of a separate peace with Berlin. Roosevelt had good reasons to
paint an overly pleasant view of the Soviet Union. Nonetheless, his strategy
backfired spectacularly during the Cold War era when it was brought up
against presidential candidate Adlai Stevenson, among other Democrats, in
the 1952 election.

From time to time, the Left also caused Roosevelt problems in the media
and elsewhere. For one thing, despite the president's public encouragement
of the Soviet Union, some decried the failure of the United States to launch
a second front in Europe in 1942. More important, liberals disagreed vigorously with Roosevelt's accommodationist policies toward fascist Spain and
Vichy France. The president had maintained diplomatic relations with those
two nonbelligerent allies of Hitler because he believed that such a distaste-
ful and amoral posture made sense in terms of the nation's global strategic
interests.

The war did produce a good measure of bipartisanship beginning with
Roosevelt's appointments of Republicans Henry L. Stimson as secretary of
war and Frank Knox as secretary of the Navy in 1940. He was also success-

ful in convincing Republicans to support the United Nations in the postwar world. Unlike Wilson's League, the new world organization did not become a partisan football at the end of World War II. The Republicans' Mackinac Declaration of 1943 helped to assure that when the time came, Democrats and Republicans would accept entry into the United Nations. From 1943 through the early years of the Cold War, the two Democratic presidents enjoyed support from former isolationist Sen. Arthur Vandenberg (R-Mich.) who beat the drums among his skeptical colleagues for bipartisan internationalism.

All was not exactly sweetness and light between the parties during the global conflict, however. As the 1944 election approached, Republicans attacked Roosevelt's conduct of foreign and military affairs. When late in the campaign, à la Willkie four years earlier, Republican candidate Thomas E. Dewey began criticizing Roosevelt's wartime policies, the president lashed back, calling his opponent and supporters isolationists, a label that had come to be associated with defeatism and appeasement in the thirties. One bit of Democratic doggerel created for the 1944 campaign poked fun at "Dewey, Tom on matters foreign, sounds a lot like Harding, Warren."

The Republicans, moreover, sought to red-bait the president during the campaign, raising an issue used with far greater success in succeeding campaigns. After they criticized Roosevelt for being too conciliatory toward the Soviet Union, he asked former ambassador Joseph E. Davies to warn his friends in the Kremlin not to respond. Had Josef Stalin publicly defended Roosevelt's conduct of Soviet-American relations, the president might have lost the election.

In addition to raising questions about Roosevelt's competence, some Republicans accused the Democratic leadership of having been unprepared for Japan's surprise attack on Pearl Harbor. Chief of Staff Gen. George C. Marshall had briefed the Republican nominee about the ability of the United States to decode Japanese messages in 1941, an ability that was still contributing to the success of the naval war in the Pacific. Dewey took the high road and did not reveal this information during the campaign. Other Republicans would certainly have been even more aggressive on the Pearl Harbor issue had they known about the codebreaking.

The future of the British mandate in Palestine surfaced as another contentious issue during the war. Both parties were concerned about the Jewish vote, which was sizable in several large states, especially New York. Politicians who felt that the idea of a Jewish state in Palestine might not have been in America's national interest found they had to deal carefully with this matter. With New York Republican Dewey running for president in 1944 and 1948, Palestine became embroiled in electoral politics as each party vied for the Jewish vote by adopting platforms attractive to Zionists.

The disposition of Palestine was not just a Jewish issue. Prominent leaders in both parties and in the country in general supported the idea of a Jewish homeland on moral grounds. The Christian Council on Palestine, founded in 1942, consisted of 600 clergymen devoted to the Zionist ideal. A large lay committee, the American Palestine Committee, chaired by Sen. Robert Wagner (D-N.Y.), and including 68 other senators, 200 representatives, the heads of the CIO and A. F. of L., and many other national leaders who were not politicians, joined to advance the cause of a Jewish state. Despite the existence of gentile political action committees, at bottom many politicians adopted specific positions on immigration to Palestine and other regional political plans because of the Jewish vote in the United States. As one Israeli diplomat later commented, "The Almighty placed massive oil deposits under Arab soil. It is our good fortune that God placed five million Jews in America."

Jewish-Americans were certainly not passive observers on the issue of a Jewish state. They developed a powerful Zionist lobby, as first represented by the American Zionist Emergency Council, with which American presidents and legislators had to deal from the election of 1944 to the present. And although some in the Jewish community still opposed a Jewish state as World War II came to a close, once Israel was established in 1948, almost all Jewish-Americans supported its continued existence.

The Jewish community had not been very successful in influencing the administration's policy toward the Holocaust. When word about Hitler's death camps first leaked out late in 1942, the United States might have taken a variety of actions to save hundreds of thousands of lives, including helping more Jews in occupied countries to escape and bombing the concentration camps. Jews split among themselves about the wisdom of pressuring Roosevelt on the issue for fear of reinforcing the notion of anti-Semitic Americans that the war was being fought on behalf of the Jews. Indeed, the president more than likely worried about that issue when he relegated the rescue of the Jews to a matter of low priority.

Another ethnic minority group, the Japanese-Americans, did not fare well during World War II. In the weeks after Pearl Harbor, 110,000 Japanese-Americans, primarily on the West Coast, citizens as well as aliens, were rounded up and put in concentration camps for the duration of the war, allegedly to keep them from aiding the enemy and also to protect them from the ire of other Americans who fumed over the sneak attack in Hawaii. We now know that national security had little to do with the incarceration of the Japanese-Americans. If Americans were concerned about sabotage and espionage from that community, why were not the Japanese-Americans on Hawaii or the German- and Italian-Americans treated in a similar fashion? The reasons behind the internment of the West Coast Japanese-Americans had more to do with American racism in the region and jealousy over that community's economic success than with national security. Pearl Harbor offered American racists the opportunity finally to accomplish their self-perceived historic task of destroying the prosperous Japanese-American community.

Little did Americans suspect then that in less than a decade Japan would become a vital American ally in a new crusade. Of course, few imagined that even before the last American soldier returned from World War II combat theaters, their country would become involved in the most dangerous international conflict in its history, a conflict that lasted almost fifty years and ultimately affected—even determined—virtually every diplomatic, political, economic, social, and cultural activity.

FOUR

The Cold War's Darkest Days, 1944–1960

WHEN FRANKLIN ROOSEVELT told Josef Stalin in 1943 that Americans would not accept the stationing of troops abroad in peacetime, he, like most of his fellow citizens, assumed that the United States would return to the sort of normalcy that marked the twenties, albeit this time with some participation in an international organization. He could not have imagined that within a few years hundreds of thousands of American soldiers, integral parts of a huge peacetime military-industrial complex, would be on permanent guard in Europe and Asia; or could he have imagined that his country would become the leader of a peacetime military alliance and give away billions of dollars in foreign aid. Of course, in 1943 he could not foresee the Cold War with the Soviet Union, which produced the state of extreme tension necessitating those unprecedented actions from the most insular of major powers.

Those who study the relationship between opinion and policy in the American democracy often talk about the way the public establishes the boundaries within which presidents are constrained to act. In 1943, those boundaries were clear to Roosevelt. But the fact that they were expanded so quickly and dramatically demonstrates the power of the president to influence the public to permit him to do things that only a short time earlier would have been considered unimaginable.

The transformation of American attitudes from isolationism to interventionism in all areas of the globe is one of the most important developments in modern history. American policymakers accomplished that transformation through constant—and sometimes hysterical—appeals to their constituents to convince them that the United States had to assume leadership of the democracies and their empires in the postwar world.

The general suspicion and hostility that Americans felt toward domestic Communists and fellow travelers made the interventionists' job somewhat easier. As tensions with the Soviet Union increased, so too did repression of Communists at home: the more closely they were linked to Moscow, the easier it became for politicians to persecute them and for conservative isolationists to accept interventionism. Earlier, isolationist Americans reflected such attitudes when they embraced the cause of aid to Finland in its Winter War with the Soviet Union in 1939–40.

The government's propaganda assault against Communists—and their ideas—at home and abroad colored all aspects of American life and culture from the end of the war to the seventies and even later. Some of that propaganda reflected sincere attempts by presidents and others to awaken the United States to its international responsibilities and expanded security interests. But they sold their message in more apocalyptic terms than were necessary or desirable.

In the private sector, without much prodding, journalists and film, radio, and television producers struck patriotic and anticommunist themes. Clever communist agents looking like average Americans lurked behind every lamppost, engaged in a conspiracy to take over the country. In a situation comparable to but more pervasive and long-lasting than the postwar Red Scare of 1919, Americans were willing to surrender civil liberties to protect themselves against this new mortal danger. On the radio and in motion-picture theaters, patriots revealed the nature of that danger as they explained how "I Was a Communist for the FBI" or how "I Led Three Lives." In the schools, frightening atomic bomb–raid drills reinforced the Red Menace for a generation of young Americans. And it worked. An insular, antimilitarist, penny-pinching people became an interventionist, internationalist, generous nation almost overnight. But that remarkable conversion, based upon a caricature of world politics, came with some costs.

One cost was paid by the State Department. Although there were not many former members of the Communist party in the department, or other branches of government for that matter, the Cold War at home led to the dismissal of experts who were allegedly soft on Communism and the resignation of others who were demoralized by the U.S. party line to which they had to adhere or risk being branded a subversive. Further, the firing of some foreign service officers produced timidity on the part of those who remained who might have challenged hard-line policies in the Third World in particular. More important, the government lost the services of experts who understood the history and culture of other countries—China and Vietnam, for example—who might have suggested alternate policies in the fifties and sixties. Finally, one wonders what their presence in the State Department or other parts of the Washington foreign policy establishment could have meant for the apparent attempts by the Soviet Union, as early as 1952, to move from Cold War to peaceful coexistence.

The State Department and several other agencies were gutted by Loyalty Review boards established by Truman. He tolerated the boards, which often dismissed government employees on flimsy evidence without due process, because his party was under attack for being too friendly with Communists and fellow travelers. In the private sector, after being pilloried by the House Un-American Activities Committee for its harboring of Communists and for making subversive films, Hollywood established a blacklist and even began making fiercely anticommunist films to curry favor with the government. From labor unions to the universities, liberals attempted to prove their patriotism during the dark days of the Cold War by discharging those with then- or former communist leanings. The Red Scare, which ruined the lives of hundreds of thousands of Americans and which affected all aspects of the national culture from 1947 through the early 1960s, was a direct product of the diplomatic conflict between the Soviet Union and the United States.

One did not have to be a Communist to become a victim of the Red Scare. In September of 1946, Secretary of Commerce Henry A. Wallace spoke out against the developing Cold War and called for diplomatic compromises with the Soviet Union. The president fired the former vice-president, who appeared to be challenging the official line. Truman privately described him as "a pacifist 100 per cent" linked to "parlor pinks" who "are a sabotage front for Uncle Joe Stalin." The dropping of the progressive Wallace also symbolized a shift in domestic priorities away from radical New Deal programs that might smack of socialism. Many progressive causes fell by the wayside during the early days of the Cold War because of their presumed communist taint. For example, because the Communist party had long made civil rights one of its more prominent causes, FBI chief J. Edgar Hoover, among others, contended that subversives lurked behind the struggle against segregation.

The Red Scare was not manufactured out of whole cloth. Through its actions abroad and even in the United States, the Soviet Union made it easy for Americans to fear and hate Communism. From 1946 through 1950, the West was rocked by a series of spy scandals in North America and Great Britain involving domestic Communists who allegedly stole the "secret" of the atomic bomb, among other classified materials.

Yet even such sensational events would not have aroused the American public sufficiently had it not been for the Truman administration's efforts to demonize the Soviet Union. Americans were shocked by Winston Churchill's Iron Curtain speech at Fulton, Missouri, in March 1946. President Truman, who had seen the speech in advance, privately endorsed the popular British leader's clarion call for vigilance and unity to meet the threat to world peace posed by the Russians. In early 1946, however, many influential observers, who expressed dismay about the breakup of the wartime coalition, thought that the former prime minister had overstated his case. Thus, the president treaded cautiously that year in bringing the United States into a full-scale cold war.

Churchill may have had a greater impact on Russians than on Americans. Stalin reacted angrily to his warnings, which were, after all, directed to the United States, not the USSR. But one of the problems with crude public diplomacy, as reflected in the Iron Curtain address, is that it often exacerbates international tensions. Indeed, Churchill could have been perceived as responding to a comparably bellicose public speech, primarily intended for Stalin's own constituents, which the Russian leader had delivered the previous month to herald a new party line.

Despite major East-West conflicts throughout 1946 and early 1947, many Americans were still not prepared to return to the interventionist mode of the World War II years. As Truman wrote about the period immediately following the war, "The tide of public opinion was impossible to stem. Every momma and poppa . . . had to have her boy home right immediately, and every Congressman, of course, wanted to be reelected." The president faced pressure from scores of "I Wanna Go Home" and "Bring Daddy Back Home" clubs that formed as the war came to a close.

In the spring of 1945, the United States had 12.3 million people under arms. One year later, force levels plummeted to 1.5 million, a figure the brass claimed was 1 million less than required to handle its assignments. Many in Truman's cabinet worried about the "frenzied demobilization" as Secretary of the Navy James M. Forrestal labeled it. But what else could he expect in a democracy that had always viewed a large peacetime military establishment as unnecessary, expensive, and even dangerous?

The American public's subsequent willingness to accept a large peacetime military establishment was influenced in part by Truman's dramatic and impassioned request to Congress in March 1947 for $400 million to aid Greece and Turkey in their struggles against the Soviet Union and their surrogates. Senator Vandenberg advised the president to "make a personal appearance before Congress and scare hell out of the country" so that Americans would finally realize how seriously the Soviet Union threatened national security. Or as Undersecretary of State Will Clayton put it, "The United States will not take world leadership effectively unless the people of the United States are shocked into doing so." Only then would they and their provincial representatives on Capitol Hill be willing to commit so many resources in peacetime to defend nations thousands of miles away.

Privately exasperated with the undemocratic faction he proposed to support in the Greek Civil War, Truman nonetheless publicly described the conflict as one between freedom and communist dictatorship—"It must be the policy of the United States to support free people who are resisting subjugation by armed minorities or by outside pressures." Defending such exaggeration during the early Cold War, Thomas A. Bailey, a leading diplomatic historian wrote, "Deception of the people may in fact become necessary. . . . The yielding of some of our democratic control of foreign affairs is the price we have to pay for greater physical security." Perhaps, but even hardline Secretary of Defense James Forrestal worried about exaggerations such as those that appeared in the Truman Doctrine. He was "a little fearful that [public opinion] may swing too strongly the other way now" because Americans "see things precisely in black and white terms."

The black-and-white vision of the nation's friends and foes was Truman's creation. He felt, rightly so, that Americans might not have been enthusiastic about his doctrine if he described the situation in Greece as a civil war between an autocratic king and left-wing heroes of the World II antifascist resistance dominated by Communists or had he noted that the Soviet Union had some legitimate historic claims on territory controlled by the autocratic Turkish regime that had cravenly opted for neutrality during World War II.

The selling of the Containment program embodied in the Truman Doctrine became a major activity for the foreign policy establishment. In March 1948, in the wake of the Soviet takeover of Czechoslovakia, the administration, aided by those industries in the private sector that would profit through an arms buildup, exaggerated the crisis in order to convince Congress to accept its massive funding proposals for the Marshall Plan and the armed services. One aide remarked during the period, "Almost 80 percent of your time . . . is management of your domestic ability to have policy, and only 20 percent, maybe, dealing with the foreign." Three years later, another major, albeit secret, blueprint for fighting the Cold War, NSC 68, stressed the absolute necessity of persuading people about the dangers they confronted. The authors of that document pointed out that the Soviet Union "does not have to be responsive in any important sense to public opinion."

There is nothing wrong with a democratic government trying to educate and lead its citizens to support a policy in the national interest. The problem was the way the presidents and their agents went about that task. Like Wilson in 1917 and Roosevelt during World War II, to explain the Soviet-American conflict in less than apocalyptic terms ran the risk of losing considerable support for the huge financial and personal sacrifices being demanded. This has been and continues to be one of the major problems of a democratic foreign policy, whether one considers the shrill Federalist attacks against crazed mobocrats in Paris in 1793 or George Bush's comparisons of Saddam Hussein to Adolf Hitler in 1990.

The early strident propaganda campaigns of 1947–49 may have been necessary to secure passage of the Truman Doctrine, the Marshall Plan, and the Point Four programs, and to assure American entry into the North Atlantic Treaty Organization. But the selling of the Red Menace in the late forties made it harder to unsell that image after Stalin's death in 1953. In addition, the notion that most anticolonial activity in the world was the product of the puppet masters in the Kremlin made it more difficult for Americans to accept later that there were places in the Third World where the locals had legitimate grievances against Western overlords. George F. Kennan himself, the reputed father of the Containment policy, complained early on about the unwise globalization and militarization of his doctrine. It is also likely that the constant repetition of exaggerated anti–Soviet themes had an impact on the presidents and their advisors, who came to believe their own propaganda in a subconscious feedback process. Finally, by depicting the enemy in such terms, Truman increased Russian fears of an aggressive America and justified their legendary paranoia.

All democratic societies confront the problem of how to explain complicated foreign policy problems, which do not pose an immediate national security threat, to their populations. Unless the message is simple and exaggerated, allegedly short-sighted citizens might reject the costs and sacrifices demanded of them to achieve some obscure long-term goal.

Parts of the Containment program were sold in terms of their benefits to the economy. During the war, economists—and politicians—worried about a return to depression-like conditions once war-related spending and employment programs closed down. In November 1944, even before the Cold War was on, one of its architects, Assistant Secretary of State for Economic Affairs Dean Acheson, warned that "we cannot have full employment and prosperity in the United States without foreign markets." Most of those markets were in Western European countries or their colonial possessions.

In July 1946, Acheson, now undersecretary of state, appealed to Congress to approve the unprecedented $3.8-billion reconstruction loan to England for an "investment in the future." When the time came during the following year to sell Congress and the public on the much more ambitious Marshall Plan, the administration made comparable arguments about the relationship between the American economy and a recovering European economy. Despite the fact that exports were less than 10 percent of total American GNP, key sectors of the American economy, such as the automobile and steel industries, and especially wheat growers who shipped half of their product abroad, depended upon the export trade. In addition, Americans imported certain crucial raw materials from the Europeans' imperial possessions for their own military-industrial plant. Thus, the needs of the American economy demanded the rebuilding and protection of Western European states, and their well-being depended in part upon retention of their empires. As a byproduct of this policy, the United States supported Paris's attempt to restore its colonies in Indochina both to maintain that market for France and for an emerging Japanese ally who had lost its major trading partner when China went Communist in 1949. The globalization of the Containment program, which saw the United States becoming intimately involved in Third World revolutions, had a good deal to do with the perceived weaknesses in the American economy.

Although such economic rationales made sense to some in the American political and corporate establishments, most politicians—and certainly the public—needed less complicated reasons to provide foreign aid on such a massive scale in peacetime. Thus, the argument that hungry people are likely to become Communists proved to be the clincher for those concerned about the costs of the Marshall Plan. That argument was among the most prominent employed by the Committee for the Marshall Plan to Aid European Recovery, another of those allegedly private and independent citizens' committees organized to support a government initiative.

The massive aid plan was originally offered to all European countries, including those in the Soviet bloc. There is no doubt that Congress would have rejected any bill that included foreign aid to Communists. But a cynical Truman felt reasonably certain that the Russians would never accept an economic program with the capitalistic strings and oversight that the United States attached to it.

All of the original Containment programs, save NATO, represented unilateral American initiatives. Even had the United Nations been more viable, it is highly unlikely that Congress and the public would have accepted international control over aid packages contributed by the United States. To the present day, a significant portion of the population fears the alleged drift toward one-world government that greater reliance on the United Nations might bring in its wake.

If the many exaggerated alerts to the Soviet danger were not bad enough in terms of contributing to fear of the Kremlin in the United States, the election of 1948 certainly reinforced it. As early as November 1947, presidential aides James T. Rowe and Clark Clifford told Truman that as the next election approached he should stress foreign affairs—"There is considerable political advantage to the Administration in its battle with the Kremlin. . . . The worse matters get . . . the more is there a sense of crisis. In times of crisis, the American citizen tends to back up his president." Here Rowe and Clifford echoed Tocqueville, who wrote that "it is chiefly in its foreign affairs that the executive power of a nation finds occasion to exert its skill and strength. If the existence of the Union were perpetually threatened . . . the executive government would assume an increased importance." What was more perpetually threatening than the long Cold War?

Clifford was also instrumental in convincing the president, against the firm opposition of Secretary of State George C. Marshall and others, to take the lead in recognizing Israel in May 1948. Whatever foreign policy rationale he advanced, Clifford was concerned about the Jewish vote in the fall election. That vote had already figured prominently in the by-election of 1946 when on October 4, 1946, Truman called for the British, who still held the League of Nations' mandate for Palestine, to admit 100,000 Jewish refugees into the Holy Land. Two days later, Republican leader Thomas E. Dewey countered with a demand that they let in several hundreds of thousands more. The British, who saw these public challenges to their policies as crassly related to American domestic politics, were furious with Truman. Their intemperate foreign minister contended that the United States had adopted its position on the refugees because there were "too many Jews in New York." That remark almost cost his government a favorable hearing on Capitol Hill for the vital reconstruction loan.

Since 1876, every winner of a presidential election had taken New York.

At the time, Jews constituted 14 percent of the state's population and 20 percent of the population of New York City. Further, the American Zionist Council's Emergency Committee on Zionist Affairs was an effective lobby that evolved in 1956 into the American-Israeli Political Action Committee (AIPAC), which represented the views of thirty-eight Zionist organizations and had an annual budget of over $12 million by 1991.

The New York vote was not the only factor that affected Truman's pro-Israeli policies prior to the 1948 election. The Democratic party, which was in difficult financial shape in that campaign, relied on the fundraising of Abraham Feinberg, a strong supporter of Israel, who, with Truman aide David Niles and the president's former Jewish business partner, Eddie Jacobson, exercised influence in the Oval Office. Truman claimed that he was never lobbied so much on any issue as the recognition of the state of Israel. To be fair, the Zionists needed to lobby hard to balance almost monolithic pro-Arab sentiments in the State Department, which revolved around Western Europe's need for Middle East oil as well as the long-term interests of American oil companies. The department's officials, who were not running for office, had no reason to take the Jewish vote into account as they recommended policy options. Additionally, many of the so-called Arabists suffered from "localitis," a common affliction in the diplomatic corps in which foreign service officers associate themselves 100 percent with the interests of their host countries. It was not just foreign service officers who weighed in against Israel and the Jewish lobby. Western intelligence agencies were riddled with anti-Israeli, pro-Arab operatives. And much of this was known to Israeli intelligence and Zionist leaders.

American Zionists also led Zionists around the world in helping to finance the impoverished Jewish state. No laws prohibit citizens from buying bonds or from otherwise making contributions to a nation with whom the United States is at peace. On other occasions, particularly in Nicaragua in the 1980s when American liberals and leftists sent aid to the Sandinista government, such activities could work at cross purposes to official policy.

As in most elections, the political debate in 1948 focused on domestic issues, but one of those issues, the Democratic party's alleged dalliances with Communists and fellow travelers, had foreign policy overtones. The Democrats had used that same issue to assail their competitors on the Left in the Progressive party. Neither the Democrats nor the Progressives were helped in late July and early August when former Communists Elizabeth Bentley's and Whittaker Chambers's charges about Communists in government hit the front pages. Republican candidate Dewey also criticized Truman's apparent appeasement of Communism in such places as Greece and China, although he did not exploit the Berlin crisis, which had begun in June. Other Republican leaders lambasted Roosevelt's wartime diplomacy, especially his actions at the Yalta Conference. Not a major issue in 1948, the conference became a potent one for Republicans in the years to come. In fact, more than twenty years later, when Soviet premier Leonid Brezhnev suggested that President Nixon meet him for one of their periodic summit conferences at the Black Sea resort of Yalta, the president refused to meet at a city that symbolized for him, and the rest of his party, the first major Soviet victory in the Cold War.

Despite the attack on Truman's softness on Communism, the Democratic party was able to retain the votes of Greek-, Polish-, and Italian-Americans who saw the president as supportive of their homelands. The Nationalities Division of the Democratic party made special appeals to those groups. Since the late nineteenth century, both parties had maintained active nationalities divisions, which to some degree helped to keep ethnic politicians viable by pandering to their demands for an American policy favorable to their homelands.

Even though other Republican leaders criticized Truman's foreign policies, they were not a major issue for Dewey. Confident of winning, the challenger did not veer too far from bipartisanship on foreign policy aside from raising the issue of Israel's borders in late October as the Jewish state and its Arab enemies wrangled over terms to end the Israeli War for Independence (1948–49). Truman responded by calling for an even larger part of the Negev Desert for Israel than demanded by Dewey, as each candidate jockeyed for advantage with Jewish voters. It was true, of course, that most American Jews traditionally supported Democratic candidates. As many as 90 percent had voted for Roosevelt in 1944. Running scared as a likely loser, Truman could not take one Jewish vote for granted and thus curried favor with them. His defenders could say, as Roosevelt's defenders had said in 1940 and 1944, that Republicans shamelessly introduced apolitical national security questions into the election for partisan purposes.

In 1948, the major critique of Truman's foreign policies came from the Left. Progressive party candidate Henry Wallace charged that the Containment policy was leading the United States toward a dangerous confrontation with the Soviet Union. By the time Wallace aired those arguments, they fell on mostly deaf ears—Americans had already been firmly converted to the Cold War perspective shared by both major parties. Indeed, if anything, Wallace's attack on Truman's foreign policy helped the president by making it more difficult for the Republicans to accuse him of being soft on Communism.

In election campaigns during the first two decades of the Cold War,

attacks from the Left against either Democratic or Republican foreign policies were singularly unsuccessful. Most Americans accepted the notion that
those who supported accommodation with the Soviet Union or who were
outspoken advocates of disarmament or who accused the United States of
practicing imperialist policies in the Third World were unpatriotic or dupes
of the Communists. And people who defended the right of those to make
such critiques were themselves found guilty of un-American activities by association. During the Vietnam War, critics of American policy were most
successful when they concentrated on the practical mistakes made in that
particular war and not when they assailed the alleged immorality of the
entire American diplomatic record.

Truman was embarrassed during the 1948 campaign by the plans of the
National Association for the Advancement of Colored People (NAACP) to
bring the issue of race relations in the United States to the United Nations.
According to the NAACP, the country was in violation of the UN Charter
because of segregation. The Soviet Union tried to convince the world body
to consider the issue in October 1948 but was voted down. Throughout
much of the Cold War, particularly during the 1950s and 1960s, the Russians
challenged American influence in emerging Third World countries in part
by stressing its enemy's abysmal record in race relations. On occasion, African
diplomats traveling by car between Washington and New York confronted
segregated facilities. The situation was so unpleasant that the State Department's protocol office maintained a special section to help Africans find
housing and schooling in the nation's capital.

Racism in New York City was one of the reasons offered by Russian premier Nikita S. Khrushchev in 1960 for moving the United Nations to
another location. In its ideological battle with the Soviet Union, the United
States was handicapped by its record in race relations when it contended that
its "democracy" was the system to be emulated. Many in the government
recognized this issue, as when the attorney general argued in 1952 in support
of ending segregation, "It is in the context of the present world struggle
between freedom and tyranny that the problems of racial discrimination
must be viewed." Looking at that issue from another perspective, President
Kennedy asked several years later, "Why can a Communist eat at a lunch
counter in Selma, Ala., while a black American veteran cannot?" In a related
vein, Kennedy might have taken J. William Fulbright's candidacy for secretary of state more seriously had it not been for the Arkansas senator's dismal
civil rights record.

Democracy and Diplomacy

WHITE HOUSE AIDE Clark Clifford correctly recognized that foreign affairs was one area in which a president could generally rally the population. Truman and his successors were aided immeasurably in that area by the development of new institutions such as the Central Intelligence Agency and the National Security Council in 1947, which increased their control over foreign policy making. In addition, the availability of radio, and then television, made it easier for the president to go directly to the public to explain matters of national security. The electronic media willingly surrendered airtime to presidents when they wanted to tell their constituents, in presumably nonpartisan speeches, about dangers that loomed abroad. Ironically, since the country did not have an official government newspaper or television station, as is the case in more authoritarian states, the public accepted such messages over "free" airwaves more readily than overt propaganda that might have come through government channels. Some began to question those messages during and after the Vietnam War when they perceived the presidents as dissembling and when alternate information sources demonstrated that policymakers were not omniscient.

Senator Fulbright labeled the years from 1940 through the Vietnam War an "era of perpetual crisis." Because of a long series of extraordinary events in the international system, Congress frequently relinquished some of its prerogatives to the president, who presumably could act with more dispatch and consistency than the more cumbersome and unpredictable bodies on Capitol Hill. Sometimes, as in the case of Truman's unilateral decision to involve the United States in the Korean War, Congress approved of presidential actions after the fact. On other occasions, as in the cases of Formosa, the Middle East, and Vietnam, it offered a virtual blank check to the president, in the form of open-ended resolutions, to take whatever measures he deemed necessary to defend the nation's security.

Not everyone in Congress was pleased with these developments. The period from the end of World War II through the seventies long has been considered as one dominated by healthy congressional bipartisanship, except for election years, with both parties accepting presidential leadership in the vitally important international sphere. A careful analysis of this common assumption suggests otherwise, with Republicans and Democrats often splitting along partisan lines on foreign affairs. Indeed, Truman enjoyed less support from Congress during the Korean War than did Johnson during the Vietnam War. In general, when it came to matters relating to the defense budget there was more bipartisanship than when the issue revolved around foreign trade and aid.

Surprisingly, Truman had little trouble bringing the United States into NATO in 1949. Here he was aided once again by Senator Vandenberg, whose resolution supporting such an alliance breezed through the Senate with only four dissenting votes in the summer of 1948. Further, in early 1951, in a "Great Debate," the president beat back a congressional attempt to limit his ability to dispatch troops to Europe without its consent. He was aided immeasurably by a private nonpartisan group, the Committee on the Present Danger, which, among other things, ran twelve national radio programs in prime time in the spring of 1951 to influence the debate. The prestigious committee included leaders from the Council on Foreign Relations, college and corporate presidents, and former government officials. Appearing at the time as a progressive organization struggling against neanderthal isolationists in Congress, the committee was reborn in 1976 as a conservative anticommunist organization, ironically using many of the same arguments that its members presented in 1951.

Truman confronted more Republican opposition when it came to foreign aid appropriations called for in his Point Four and other aid programs. Attacking such aid as "globaloney," critics in Congress severely limited the amount of funds allocated to the programs. Sen. Robert A. Taft (R-Ohio), a potential Republican presidential candidate, denounced an important foreign aid bill for India and threatened to make it, and comparable bills, an issue in the 1952 election campaign.

Although the United States has given away billions in foreign aid since that point—and much of it in military and not economic or humanitarian aid—many in Congress assailed such allegedly wasteful expenditures. Despite Americans' self-image as a generous donor to Third World countries, they have devoted a smaller percentage of national wealth to such aid than many of their Western allies, except for the early years of the Cold War. When that "war" ended in the early 1990s, and with it the fear of Third World nations falling to Communism, foreign aid became an even harder sell for presidents on Capitol Hill.

Aside from cutting back Truman's foreign aid requests, Congress took the lead in promoting policies for Spain and China that were originally unacceptable to the president. Beginning in 1948, supporters of a Spanish lobby in Congress began to pressure him to normalize relations with fascist Spain, which was accomplished late in 1950. In the discussions about aid to and recognition of Franco's regime, one congressman referred to the dictator as a "very, very lovely and lovable character." An even more powerful lobby, the China Lobby, urged its many supporters in Congress to compel the president in 1948 to send more aid to the fast-failing Chinese Nationalists, even though there was little the United States could do to save that government from falling to the Communists in their civil war (1945–49).

Pressure from Republicans was also responsible for Truman's dispatch of conservative Gen. Albert C. Wedemeyer to China in 1947 to investigate the prospects for the Nationalists in the ongoing civil war. His report, which called for more aid to Nationalist leader Chiang Kai-shek, but which also denounced him for his corruption and ineptitude, was kept secret so as not to embarrass America's ally. It was also kept secret because the public might have inquired why tax dollars should be sent to such a corrupt and inept leader. The alleged "suppression" of Wedemeyer's report later resulted in more grist for the Republicans' mill in their criticism of Truman's China policy.

Truman's swift decision to support South Korea following North Korea's invasion of June 25, 1950, across the 38th parallel, despite the fact that Secretary of State Acheson had publicly declared in January that the peninsula was not within the country's primary security perimeter, and after the Joint Chiefs had privately decided that it was of no strategic value, was partially in response to domestic political considerations. Truman and the Democrats were already feeling the heat from the increasingly more effective Republican charge that they had "lost" China the previous fall when the Communists raised their flag over Beijing. Then, in February 1950, a relatively obscure junior senator, Joseph McCarthy (R-Wis.), became a sensation with his charges that Communists in the State Department had abetted Mao Tse-tung in his destruction of "freedom" in China. Walter Lippmann wrote of McCarthy's attacks on Acheson, "No American official who has represented his government abroad in great affairs, not even Wilson in 1918, has ever been so gravely injured at home."

Truman never gave Congress the chance to declare war in Korea. In the past, presidents had sent armed forces into many a skirmish without a declaration of war. But never had a president exercised his power as commander-in-chief to involve the United States in a major war. The Korean "War," which Truman labeled a "police action," cost more American lives than the declared wars of 1812, 1846, and 1898 combined. Had Congress suspected that the war would last three years and require a massive investment in lives and treasure, it might not have accepted so easily the usurpation of its power. The Korean War marked a major turning point in presidential-congressional relations over the war-declaring power, paving the way for presidential wars in Southeast Asia and elsewhere.

A limited war, the conflict in Korea was tailor-made for partisan wrangling. When the war started, one of Senator Taft's aides suggested that the powerful Republican leader withhold support for Truman's decision to help South Korea so that if the policy failed, which appeared likely, he would be positioned to use the war for political advantage. When Taft rejected that cynical advice and approved of the police action in Korea, Truman's press secretary commented, "My God! Bob Taft has joined the U.N. and the U.S."

But the administration could not expect Taft and his colleagues to remain on board for long. Thus, when Truman considered the expansion of the war into North Korea in the summer of 1950, he feared that the prudent but not-anticommunist-enough decision to halt at the 38th parallel could affect the prospects of his party in the by-elections in November. Truman announced the decision to permit UN Commander-in-Chief Gen. Douglas MacArthur to cross the 38th parallel at a cabinet meeting where the major item on the agenda was the election. Still ringing in the Democrats' ears was the attack from a Republican congressman against the "Hiss [Alger] Survivors Association down at the State Department who wear upon their breasts the Cross of Yalta." (Hiss, a State Department official accused of spying for the Soviet Union, was ultimately convicted of perjury.) It was also during this period that Congress passed the McCarran Internal Security Act over Truman's veto. Supporting the throwback to the alien and sedition laws, Sen. Karl Mundt (R-S.D.) proclaimed, "If we are going to ask our boys to die fighting in Korea and other areas, we certainly should protect them from sabotage behind their backs at home." One wonders how the world would have changed had Truman not been influenced by political concerns to try to liberate North Korea. His allies in Europe certainly thought it was an unwise move.

When the battle lines became fixed around the 38th parallel in the late winter of 1951, after a successful Chinese counterattack had repelled MacArthur's advance, the partisan wars heated up. With the conflict stalemated, it no longer seemed as serious a threat to national security and thus became fair game for the Republicans. MacArthur exacerbated the situation when, on several occasions, he appealed over the head of the president to Republicans and citizens generally to support more aggressive strategies to defeat the Communists, saying, among other things, "there is no substitute for victory."

Whether or not MacArthur's demands to bomb and maybe even invade China were sound, when he appealed publicly to the opposition Truman finally had to relieve him of his duty—"MacArthur left me no choice—I could no longer tolerate his insubordination." Aside from the general's clear insubordination, his call for escalation, eagerly accepted by many Republicans, frightened America's allies and enemies alike. At home, however, the vast majority of Americans supported the general over the president, with some on Capitol Hill and in state legislatures calling for Truman's impeachment. In a most unusual situation, Congress invited the cashiered general to address a joint session where he was greeted as a conquering hero and where one congressman who had listened in awe commented, "We saw the hand of God in the flesh, and we heard the voice of God." By the time the 1952 presidential election came around, the MacArthur affair had blown over. Yet the Democrats' conduct in the Korean War was a powerful issue for Republicans. Americans had been reluctant to switch leaders in the middle of previous wars. This stalemated war was another matter. As the conflict continued through 1951 and 1952, more and more Republican politicians expressed dissatisfaction with the administration's military and diplomatic strategies.

Even without the unprecedented no-win or limited war, the odds were stacked against the Democrats in 1952. They had been in power for twenty years, it appeared to be time for a change, and their candidate, Adlai E. Stevenson, was no match for the popular World War II hero Dwight David Eisenhower. The allegedly sorry diplomatic record of the Democrats, which included the "loss" of China, the Russian "theft" of the atomic bomb, and the no-win war, contributed to Republican confidence. Two of the three main themes in their election equation—KC2 or Korea, Communism, and Corruption—involved foreign policy issues. (Sometimes they referred to the "three Cs," using the alternate spelling, Corea.) And, to the Republicans, behind the alleged foreign policy failures lay the Communists in the State Department who had been responsible for the sellout at Yalta and the loss of China. In fact, the Republican vice-presidential candidate, Sen. Richard M. Nixon (R-Calif.), had made his name through his investigation and "prosecution" of Alger Hiss.

In addition, Republican spokespersons, although not Eisenhower, attacked the defensive policy of containment and called for the offensive policy of rollback. Nixon called Stevenson "a graduate of Dean Acheson's cowardly College of Communist Containment," while Sen. Alexander Wiley (R-Wis.) referred to containment as "pantywaist" diplomacy. The Republicans promised to be more aggressive, as reflected in the 1951 Kersten Amendment to the Mutual Security Act, setting aside funds for the development of a 100,000-person émigré army to liberate Eastern Europe.

The rollback policy, which became an important part of Republican rhetoric, created false hopes among East Europeans that the United States would come to their aid when they rebelled against Soviet-installed regimes, as was the tragic case with Hungary in 1956. The policy also made America's Western European allies nervous because of fears that the battlefields for roll-back would be in their own backyards. Although the Republicans never did institute rollback, as demonstrated by the policy's abject failure in 1956, they continued their rhetorical assault on the Soviet Union and the namby-pamby Democrats. In July 1959, Congress unanimously approved the Captive Nations Resolution, which set aside the third week in July every year as Captive Nations Week. Eisenhower disapproved of the resolution at the least because of its timing, which coincided with Vice-President Nixon's visit to Moscow. Soviet leader Nikita S. Khrushchev, who was not amused by Congress's action, complained that "this resolution stinks."

Ultimately, of course, the Soviet Union did roll back. Supporters of the assertive Republican rhetorical policy, which was used more to capture votes and attack Democrats than to liberate Eastern Europeans, now claim that it was not a failure. Their periodic embarrassment of the Soviet Union scored propaganda points and, despite the lack of American support in 1956 for Hungary (and in 1968 for Czechoslovakia), supposedly encouraged several generations of Eastern Europeans to believe that the world did not consider their plight as acceptable or normal.

The general assault on the Democrats as being too soft on Communism became a common theme in all elections from 1952 to 1988. The Democrats came to be associated with people for whom peace was more precious than defending national security, people who were interested in disarmament and shied away from military confrontation, even though, ironically, they were also the "party of war" with their war entries in 1917, 1941, 1950, and in Vietnam.

In the 1952 campaign, Eisenhower also promised to go to Korea if elected. This meant very little in practice but held out the hope that if he went there, the war might end sooner. Interestingly, in discussing the war during the campaign, the Republican candidate effectively used a phrase similar to one used by Lyndon Johnson in the 1964 campaign. Promising to bring American boys home, Eisenhower said of the war in Korea, "Let it be Asians against Asians." The war turned out to be the second most important issue for all voters and the most important issue for independents. Unlike his party's promise of rollback, Eisenhower redeemed his campaign pledge to go to Korea, although the trip he took in late November 1952 did not accomplish as much in ending the war as did both his later veiled threat to use nuclear weapons against the North Koreans and Chinese if the war dragged on much longer and Stalin's death in March 1953, which produced a new and less aggressive Soviet leadership.

The Korean War ended in July 1953. The fact that the Chinese "volunteers" had fought alongside the North Koreans made it impossible for the United States to normalize relations with Beijing for the foreseeable future. With the cries of "Who lost China?" from the campaign of 1952 still ringing in American ears, and the powerful China Lobby committed to restoring the Chinese Nationalists to the mainland, the question of recognition was put off not just during the Eisenhower administration but through the Kennedy and Johnson administrations as well. As with the opposition that developed in the United States to the Soviet revolution, once the Chinese Communists had been demonized, it was difficult to undemonize them without paying a heavy political price.

DURING THE Eisenhower administration, the Central Intelligence Agency, headed by Secretary of State John Foster Dulles's brother, Allen, expanded its covert activities dramatically. It enjoyed "victories" in Iran and Guatemala and suffered "losses" in Egypt, Tibet, Indonesia, Ukraine, and Eastern Europe, among other places. The CIA kept knowledge of U.S. involvement in these victories and losses, and the means used to pursue them, from the American people. During World War II, Americans accepted the idea that their intelligence services should be engaged in covert activities, including murder and sabotage, which seemed justified to protect national security. Such activities in peacetime, like the overthrow of a freely elected government in Guatemala, were another matter. In 1954, World War II hero Gen. James Doolittle, who prepared a report on the American intelligence community, told the president, but not the public, that "we must learn to subvert, sabotage, and destroy our enemies by more clear, more sophisticated and more effective methods than those used against us. It may become necessary that the American people will be made acquainted with, understand and support this fundamentally repugnant philosophy." Presidents from Eisenhower to the present chose not to discuss this issue with the public, or with most members of Congress for that matter. They determined that not only would national security be endangered by revealing such activities but that the public might not understand why "repugnant" and undemocratic actions were vital to national survival.

The CIA-engineered coup in Iran, which in 1953 restored the shah of Iran to power over his nationalist prime minister, has often been interpreted as another example of "dollar diplomacy." The Iranians threatened the interests of British oil companies, which in turn pushed their government to intervene on their behalf. As with much of dollar diplomacy, the story is far more complicated. In the wake of the successful coup, President Eisenhower appointed Herbert Hoover Jr. to negotiate a restructuring of the Iranian oil industry. Hoover's biggest problems revolved around convincing American oil firms, which were quite satisfied with their operations in Saudi Arabia and other areas of the Persian Gulf, to join an Iranian oil consortium in order to protect perceived U.S. national interests in that strategically important country. The oil firms did so only after Hoover obtained the Justice Department's promise to waive antitrust laws prohibiting American companies from cooperative activities that might restrain trade.

The CIA also exercised its influence over the media. During the days before the 1954 coup in Guatemala, Allen Dulles misinformed a relative of the publisher of the *New York Times* that the paper's man in Central America, Sidney Gruson, was possibly subversive. The CIA chief asked his friend to speak to the publisher about getting Gruson out of the area. Gruson's superiors in New York did order the correspondent, a very experienced observer of the Guatemalan scene who might have blown the whistle on the U.S.-backed coup, to stay away from the country. More important, it was during this period that the agency began to recruit journalists to work as stringers and informants, thereby compromising the free press.

The Eisenhower administration concurrently introduced a "New Look" military policy to maintain national security while trimming the defense budget. The Republicans, after all, prided themselves on being small-government budget-balancers. Although never as extreme as it was caricatured, the new policy did place more reliance on a nuclear arsenal than had Truman's in order to get "more bang for the buck" by "substituting machines for men." This approach, which involved economic considerations as much as military doctrine, had major implications for Eisenhower's diplomacy as well as for the diplomacy of his counterparts in Moscow and Beijing. Without concomitant spending in the conventional arms area, the Eisenhower administration was constrained from considering possible military adventures it might have entertained. Its enemies, furthermore, feared that in the absence of an ability to offer a graduated response to their thrusts and parries, the White House might push the nuclear button over a relatively marginal issue. U.S. allies were equally concerned that war would lead to the incineration of Europe, the presumed site of the major battles, since the United States had evidently turned away from developing a conventional response to a Soviet conventional first thrust.

Budget-balancing also led to strong American interest in rearming Germany, a prospect that added to East-West tensions by making a solution of the two Germanies problem less likely. This economy-driven attempt to induce Germany to pay a fair share of the Western defense burden even concerned some of its former enemies in NATO. Throughout history, domestic economic considerations have often led democratic states to adopt military decisions that had profound strategic and political implications. The British decided at the turn of the century that they could no longer afford to maintain a serious naval presence in the Western Hemisphere, given their more pressing interests in Europe and Asia. That decision led to British acceptance of American hegemony in the hemisphere.

WHEREAS THE Republicans had assumed the offensive in the election of 1952, the Democrats, again led by Stevenson, played that role in 1956. Stevenson called for a ban on the testing of hydrogen bombs and also attacked the Eisenhower-Dulles strategy of brinkmanship. Eisenhower, who objected strongly to the injection of the nuclear issue into the election, considered the Democratic candidate a "small politician." When the Soviet leader foolishly wrote to the president during the campaign and called for an H-bomb test ban, he inadvertently hurt Stevenson, much to the Republicans' pleasure.

Stevenson also shamelessly attacked Eisenhower from the Right. As in the earlier Republican charge of "Who lost China?" he now asked who had allowed North Vietnam to fall to Communism in 1954 and repeatedly questioned the effectiveness of American policy for failing to take advantage of weaknesses in the Soviet bloc.

The election also influenced the calculations in October 1956 of both Anglo-French and Russian leaders about crises in the Middle East and Hungary, respectively. The British and French, and their Israeli ally, hoped that they could get away with an invasion of Egypt to overthrow Gamal Abdul Nasser during the campaign. Eisenhower, they reasoned, could not afford to oppose them, given the unpopularity of the anti-Western Egyptian leader and the importance of the Jewish vote. They were wrong. Eisenhower claimed that he "gave strict orders to the State Department that they should inform Israel that we'd handle our affairs exactly as though we didn't have a Jew in America." Similarly, the Russians thought they could smash the Hungarian rebellion both because of the attention given to the Suez Crisis and because Eisenhower would be reluctant to take risky actions in the international sphere during the height of the campaign. Eisenhower was furious at his allies and the Russians, albeit for different reasons. Yet both crises may have contributed to his victory margin, since voters usually rally around experienced presidents during crises.

At the end of the campaign, on October 29, a desperate Stevenson attacked Republican policies in the Middle East, a ploy that may have attracted some of the minority of Jewish-Americans who were planning to vote for the GOP. But again, as in 1952, the Democrats held a losing hand against the popular Eisenhower.

Although Eisenhower was able to oppose Israeli gains during the Suez War and to take positions that alienated Jewish voters, the Jewish lobby remained a formidable group. A bitter John Foster Dulles complained hyperbolically about "how almost impossible it is in this country to carry out a foreign policy not approved by the Jews. Marshall and Forrestal learned that. I am going to try and have one." Early in his tenure at the State Department, Dulles asked the Israeli government to inform its allies in the United States to ease their pressure on Washington. Even before the 1956 war, when the United States and Great Britain were involved in Project Alpha, a promising peace plan for the Middle East, Dulles worried about the Jewish vote. He informed the British prime minister that the plan had to be completed quickly before the election because "the Zionist voters would make it impossible for the United States to continue with a policy of strict neutrality." Of course, given the ease with which Eisenhower won the 1956 election without the Jewish vote, Dulles was exaggerating. The Jewish lobby did, however, exercise enough influence with Congress after the Suez War to make it impossible for the president to threaten sanctions in order to force an unconditional Israeli withdrawal from the Sinai Peninsula in early 1957.

Typical of other administration problems posed by the lobby was the embarrassment suffered when the touring King Saud of Saudi Arabia was not given an official welcome by New York Mayor Robert Wagner in 1957 because of his country's anti-Jewish—and anti-Catholic—policies. Two years later, Nasser sparked a comparable incident when he barred American ships carrying Israeli goods from using the Suez Canal and instituted a blacklist against firms trading with Israel. In retaliation, in April 1960, the Seafarers' Union in New York City, prodded by friends of Israel, refused to unload goods from Egyptian vessels. (In 1969, the International Longshoreman's Association led a comparable boycott when its members refused to unload goods on Swedish vessels because of that country's opposition to America's policies in the Vietnam War.) In addition, the Senate passed an amendment to a foreign aid bill authorizing the president to cut off aid to Egypt until Nasser opened the canal to American vessels carrying Israeli goods. These actions angered both Eisenhower and the Egyptians. Supporters of Israel could argue at this juncture, and at many other junctures during the Cold War, that their lobbying activities were in the national interest, not just the interest of Israel. Israel was a democratic ally of the United States defending Western principles against Arab nationalism and communist expansion into the region. American presidents and diplomats, worried about oil and the gains the Soviet Union had made by adopting an anti-Israel policy, did not always see things that way.

THROUGHOUT MOST of Eisenhower's two terms, the Democrats controlled both houses of Congress. Because of this reality, the president had to work closely with the opposition to push through his foreign programs. Indeed, as an internationalist who subscribed to the general bipartisan consensus that had obtained since the late forties, Eisenhower discovered that the Democrats were his most supportive allies against isolationists and unilateralists on Capitol Hill. Some Democrats even saw in their much-trumpeted loyal bipartisanship a way to use Republican disunity on national security matters as a political issue.

Eisenhower was keenly aware of the criticism Truman earned for entering the Korean War without congressional consultation. Consequently, he asked for advance approval for possible intervention in his Formosa Resolution of 1955, which authorized the president to take whatever action necessary to defend Nationalist China, and his Middle East Resolution of 1957, known as the Eisenhower Doctrine. The latter authorized the president to send economic and military assistance and even troops to the region if a Middle Eastern government requested them. During congressional consideration of the resolution, Senate Majority Leader Lyndon B. Johnson (D-Tex.) demonstrated his and Congress's power when he informed Eisenhower that he could not gather enough votes for the Middle East Resolution unless the president killed a pending UN sanctions resolution against Israel.

Eisenhower accepted such horsetrading from Johnson. His problems with the Republicans were more difficult. A typical example was the proposed Bricker Amendment to the Constitution, which was defeated in the Senate in February 1954 by one vote. The amendment, supported by the Daughters of the American Revolution and the American Medical Association, among other influential groups, would have severely crippled the power of the president to make executive agreements without congressional approval and would have made it virtually impossible to conduct diplomacy with the necessary "secrecy and dispatch" for which John Jay argued in the 63rd *Fed-*

eralist. Eisenhower opposed the amendment because "the President must not be deprived of his historic position as spokesman for the nation in its relations with other countries."

Like Truman, Eisenhower continued the practice of negotiating executive agreements with countries for bases and financial support when the consummation of a treaty of alliance was problematic. For example, executive agreements that permitted the United States to establish air bases in Spain enabled the president to bind that fascist dictatorship to the NATO alliance without having to confront liberals in the Senate who would have objected strenuously to a formal treaty.

Eisenhower did not always have his way with Congress. He was unable to muster support in 1956 to defeat Public Law 726, in which Congress halted aid to Yugoslavia until it was satisfied with a presidential report that the maverick communist state was really on the American side in the Cold War. Several years later, the distinguished diplomat George F. Kennan complained that he never would have accepted the post of ambassador to Yugoslavia had he known about all the difficulties he would have with a meddling and uninformed Congress. Looking at congressional meddling during the same period, Senator Fulbright worried that "for the existing requirements of American foreign policy, we have hobbled the President by too niggardly a grant of power." Of course, in a few years, Fulbright changed his tune in dramatic fashion and sought ways to rein in the president.

The National System of Interstate and *Defense* (italics mine) Highways Act of 1956 was one program both parties in Congress and the president could agree upon. Those concerned about the expense were brought on board somewhat disingenuously by the argument that the act was a defense measure that would enable the military and the citizenry to move about more efficiently if they were at war with the Soviet Union. The original federal commitment to highway building originated as well as a defense measure. In 1919, when a military caravan took sixty-two days to cross the United States, government officials were convinced that they needed to develop a highway network. The officer in command on that transcontinental trek was Lt. Col. Dwight David Eisenhower.

Highways were more popular than seaways. Backed by American railroad and shipping interests and coal producers, among others, critics in Congress had long made it impossible for presidents to construct the much-needed St. Lawrence Seaway with Canada. With opponents railing about a "socialist ditch," the Senate defeated a promising seaway treaty in 1934. In 1954, in part because of increased need for Canadian ore, much of the domestic opposition vanished as Congress approved the Wiley-Dondero bill to build the seaway. Congress moved with some dispatch in this case because Canada, preparing to go it alone, had already initiated negotiations between Ontario and the state of New York, acting independently of Washington, to clear the way for the first stages of a seaway.

All Americans, regardless of foreign policy orientation, were shocked in 1957 when the Russians launched into orbit *Sputnik,* the first space satellite. Two months earlier, they had successfully tested the first intercontinental ballistic missile. Americans had long felt secure that their country was the clear number one in scientific innovation. When the Russians beat them into space, observers blamed the American educational system. The result was massive new spending for higher education, including the $1-billion National *Defense* (italics mine) Education Act. *Sputnik,* a product of Soviet-American Cold War rivalry, helped to change the face of American higher education. Moreover, the increased government funding that was focused on defense-related science and technology dramatically affected research strategies and even the curricula in many colleges and universities, and not always in directions that those interested in the traditional liberal arts preferred.

Eisenhower, however, was serious about balancing the budget and thus resisted demands from Congress for an unlimited commitment to the space race. He supported the development of the National Aeronautics and Space Agency (NASA) in 1958 and wanted "to know what's on [the] other side of the moon, but I won't pay to find out this year." Part of his problem was the costly rivalry between the services that led to each building its own missile system, supported by Army, Navy, and Air Force lobbies in Congress and in the defense community. In an attempt to gain more control over the process and to lower defense costs, Eisenhower tried to reorganize the Defense Department. When Congress balked, he enlisted the support of 100 top business executives to lobby their representatives to accept his cost-cutting and streamlining initiatives. They were only partially successful, however.

Sputnik became a partisan political issue as well. Democrats assailed Republicans for permitting the Soviet Union to surpass the United States in rocketry and missiles, a development that was, according to Sen. Henry Jackson (D-Wash.), "a devastating blow to the prestige of the United States." Democratic Senate Majority Leader Lyndon Johnson held hearings on the affair before his Intelligence Subcommittee of the Armed Services Committee. Eisenhower could have improved his political position by announcing that the then-secret U-2 flights not only were a major scientific breakthrough but also revealed that Russian missile advances did not yet threaten national security. Several of the president's advisors urged him to take the heat off the administration through such a revelation. Tempting as this option appeared in the political sense, Eisenhower felt it was not in the nation's best interest to boast about the U-2. The issue of the alleged failures of the Republican space and missile programs figured prominently in the 1960 election campaign.

The Russians again demonstrated their advances in military technology when they shot down a U-2 on May 1, 1960. Eisenhower's spokesperson first denied that the plane was a spy plane and then, when confronted by the evidence that the Russians had been holding back, not only admitted it but maintained that the United States was correct in pursuing its U-2 program. Both Eisenhower and Russian premier Khrushchev had high hopes for the Paris summit meeting, which was to take place just after the shootdown. Khrushchev apparently expected that Eisenhower would not take responsibility for the program and blame his aides, an option he held open to him. Not realizing how Eisenhower's admission of lack of control over his underlings might disturb the American electorate, the Russian leader miscalculated and then made things worse by demanding an apology before the summit could formally begin. He failed to understand how impossible it would have been for the president of the United States, in an election year, or any year for that matter, to issue such a humiliating apology. Or perhaps he did understand. There is some evidence to suggest that Khrushchev was under intense pressure from his military not to conclude any disarmament treaties at the once-promising meeting and thus he may have purposefully set out to scuttle the summit.

Because of the way Khrushchev appeared to disrupt the conference, its failure and the administration's blundering did not become issues in the election of 1960. If anything, the Republican candidate Vice-President Richard Nixon was helped as the Cold War suddenly became chillier. After all, he had enhanced his legendary anticommunist credentials when he challenged Khrushchev rhetorically in a highly publicized informal debate in Moscow the previous year.

Other Cold War issues were important, however, especially the Democratic charge that Republican defense policy had produced not only a *Sputnik* gap but a much more serious missile gap. Despite the Democrats' intricate charts and missile counts, there was no missile gap and they suspected it, thanks in part to intelligence gathered by those infamous U-2 flights. It was true, however, that the Democrats may have been deceived by Pentagon informants who painted an inaccurate, bleak picture of the missile race simply because they wanted the United States to build more missiles.

Paradoxically, had Kennedy maintained the missile gap fiction through his administration, the United States might have been better off. The Russians knew there was a missile gap but they were the ones who were far behind. American expression of fear about Soviet rockets comforted Moscow in 1960. Fidel Castro later claimed that he also believed the Democratic line as well as Khrushchev's numerous boasts about Soviet capacity. That was one of the reasons why he felt that the United States would not risk war if Moscow brought nuclear weapons to Cuba.

After less than one month in office, Secretary of Defense Robert S. McNamara told journalists that there was no missile gap and that the United States was well ahead of the Russians. This declaration may have induced the Russians to speed up their defense programs to try to catch up to the United States and perhaps even motivated them to place missiles in Cuba to close the gap. McNamara later admitted he made a mistake in blurting out the true nature of the missile gap. Part of his problem was inexperience in handling on-the-record press conferences that had come to play an ever more important role in diplomatic affairs.

Taking the offensive in the campaign, the Democrats also criticized the Republicans' liberation or rollback policies. What had Eastern Europe to show from eight years of Republican policies, they asked? The Democrats did not promise rollback themselves; they did imply that if they were returned to office, Eastern Europeans could look forward to a more promising future.

The 1960 election was the first in which the inexperience in foreign relations of one of the candidates, the youthful senator from Massachusetts, became an issue. As vice-president, Richard Nixon had traveled around the world. John F. Kennedy had to demonstrate that he could manage American foreign policy in the dangerous nuclear age. He succeeded in allaying American fears about his inexperience in the first televised presidential debate in which he appeared to be as mature and knowledgeable as Nixon. In a comparable situation in 1976, Americans became more confident about former Georgia governor and peanut farmer Jimmy Carter's foreign policy expertise when Pres. Gerald R. Ford apparently became confused during a televised debate and claimed that Poland was not part of the Soviet empire.

The issue of Cuba also arose during the Kennedy-Nixon debates, when the Democrat attacked the Republicans for not doing more to remove Fidel Castro from power. Although they had not been briefed specifically about the matter, Kennedy and his advisors knew in general that plans were afoot to assist anti-Castroites to overthrow the Cuban leader. When Kennedy made the charge, Nixon was at a disadvantage because he could not explain all that he knew about Eisenhower's secret anti-Cuban policy, including the training of a rebel army to invade the island. Kennedy endangered national security by cynically using the issue for partisan purposes during the campaign. Of course, as we have seen, that was not unprecedented.

Kennedy, who also accused the Republicans of having "lost" Cuba, understood the rules of the game. On one occasion during the campaign, he playfully asked his aides, "How would we have saved Cuba if we had the power?" He answered his own question sardonically, "What the hell, they never told us how they would have saved China."

Professional diplomats do not like the idea of presidential campaign debates or even presidential press conferences, which the democratization of society and the development of electronic media have fostered. On those occasions, either because of a mistake, an inadvertent leak, or for partisan advantage, presidents sometimes say things that seriously complicate specific foreign policies.

Although the televised debates hurt Nixon in 1960, that same medium gave him a boost when it broadcast the sensational events at the fall UN general meeting. Khrushchev's truculent speech in September, as well as the astounding oft-repeated telegenic images of his famous shoe-banging temper-tantrum, helped Nixon on the grounds that he had already established his ability to deal with the fiery Soviet leader. For his part, Khrushchev later claimed that because he wanted Kennedy to beat the hard-line Nixon, he delayed until after the election the planned release of two American RB-47 pilots who had been shot down over his country. He feared that such welcome news during the campaign might contribute to Nixon's chances for victory. Twenty years later, the Iranians helped defeat their self-proclaimed arch-enemy, Jimmy Carter, when they delayed releasing American hostages until well after the election.

Before Kennedy took office, President Eisenhower offered a valedictory to his constituents. His farewell address ranks second only to Washington's in terms of importance. Eisenhower warned about the "grave implications" of the growing influence of the military-industrial complex in "every city, every State house, every office of the Federal government." He had fought for eight years, not always successfully, to balance the budget, and, especially, to curtail the military's spending and economic and political power. Billions of dollars each year went to fighting the Cold War, billions that meant jobs in congressional districts and corporate profits. No doubt there was waste, duplication, and competition between the services, and even deceitful public relations campaigns to sell the American people on the need for those expenditures. (During the Reagan administration, a Defense Department official asserted that up to 30 percent of the Pentagon budget of $150 billion was wasted.)

Congress, the Department of Defense, and the military industries constituted the triumvirate of the military-industrial complex that engaged in a weapons-procurement program often driven by domestic political considerations, not foreign or defense policy needs. The complex looked even more disreputable when retired military and congressional leaders took up key positions in defense industries, taking advantage of their expertise and old contacts to win contracts for their firms. Millions of workers throughout the country became dependent on the weapons-procurement system for their livelihood, with those in the huge aerospace industry in California and Washington state two notable examples. It was not surprising that the district with the most extensive military installations was that represented by L. Mendel Rivers (D-S.C.), the long-time chair of the House Armed Services Committee. Key legislators such as Rivers were not the only ones so favored. During the Reagan administration, Secretary of the Navy John Lehman adopted a "home porting" system that brought coastal installations to many new districts and thus increased the constituency on Capitol Hill that would support his plans for increasing naval expenditures. Further, some Pentagon appropriations were part of a "black budget" not revealed to Congress.

The system had its supporters. One of the main arguments used for the arms buildup required by NSC 68 in 1950 had been the positive impact of defense spending on the economy, a sort of military Keynesianism. Of course, NSC 68 suggested that the nation could not afford guns and butter and thus recommended drastic cuts in social welfare and most other domestic programs except those related to military and internal security issues.

On the other hand, critics have suggested that by devoting so many resources to research and development in the military area, the government lured many of the country's brightest scientists into defense work. Their absence in the private sector helps to explain why the United States fell behind its industrial rivals in key sectors of the economy in which it once led the world. By 1961, 65 percent of all high-tech research and development funds came from Washington, 85 percent of which was militarily oriented. Germany, and particularly Japan, two nations with much smaller defense establishments, were free to devote a larger proportion of their resources to nonmilitary research and development than the United States. Their success supports historian Paul Kennedy's argument that all of the number one powers declined since the sixteenth century because they devoted an increasing proportion of gross national product to defending their far-flung empires while their rivals devoted their energies to modernizing domestic infrastructures.

The American arms industry not only produced weapons of war for the U.S. armed forces. It also became one of the leading producers of weapons for U.S. allies and other nations. American (as well as other major powers') arms transfers, often more related to business than national security concerns, ultimately had an impact not only on the region in which the arms were sold but also on American foreign policy. For example, in the early nineties, one could see the unfortunate impact of profit-driven arms transfers on the internal stability of the former Yugoslavia and Somalia.

The arms race, particularly that dealing with atomic weapons, also led to an increased tolerance for governmental secrecy and lying. Concerned about Native Americans and others who were exposed to nuclear fallout during testing in the forties and fifties, former Secretary of the Interior Stewart L. Udall noted in 1993 that "the atomic weapons race and the secrecy surrounding it crushed American democracy. It induced us to conduct Government according to lies. It undermined American morality. Until the cold war, our country stood for something. Lincoln was the great exemplar. We stood for moral leadership in the world."

Eisenhower's call for restraining the behemoth of a military-industrial complex, while thrilling liberals and others who shared his concerns, fell on deaf ears. At least when the Democrats came into office in January 1961, American military procurement policies, aside from new budgeting systems, remained essentially in place. In 1961, Secretary of Defense McNamara requested congressional authorization to build 950 new missiles. The Joint Chiefs had asked for 3,000. McNamara felt he could meet security needs with only 450 missiles but had to ask for 950 because "that's the smallest number we can take up on the Hill without getting murdered." Moreover, after looking at the unfavorable trade balance, President Kennedy established a new Pentagon bureau in early 1961 to boost arms sales abroad.

The new president, however, introduced structural changes in his foreign policy–making machine, which impacted dramatically on the course of events over the next two decades. In order to maintain tighter executive control over foreign policy, Kennedy increased substantially the role of the president's advisor for national security affairs. Under Truman and Eisenhower, that post had been almost clerical, with the advisor serving as a coordinator and facilitator. Under Kennedy, National Security Advisor McGeorge Bundy began to develop an independent policymaking function, which slowly began to rival that of the secretary of state. Unlike the secretary, the national security advisor did not have to appear before Congress when summoned. With a relatively small staff insulated from the huge State Department bureaucracy, Bundy and, in particular, his successors Walt Whitman Rostow and Henry Kissinger, fashioned policies in relative secrecy. This development made it more difficult for Americans and their representatives to know just what the president was up to in the international sphere and culminated in the Iran-Contra scandal in the middle 1980s when NSC staffer Oliver North conducted a private covert foreign policy. Complicating matters as well was the enhancement of a little State Department in the Pentagon that blurred the distinctions between the two departments and increased their bureaucratic rivalries.

Such institutional changes did not interest most Americans, who thought the transition from Eisenhower to Kennedy would lead to a reorientation of their nation's Cold War and domestic policies. They assumed that the torch had been passed to a new generation with bold new ideas. No doubt, the Kennedy team was more youthful chronologically and stylistically than the Eisenhower team. Whether they would be able to—or even desired to— reorient American policy beyond campaign-year boiler plate, is another matter.

FIVE

The World Becomes More Complicated,
1960–1980

PRESIDENT KENNEDY did not talk directly about liberation or rollback in his stirring inaugural address. His message, however, "Let every nation know that we shall pay any price, bear any burden, meet any hardship, support any friend, oppose any foe to assure the survival and success of liberty," reinforced the main foreign policy theme of the campaign: the Republicans had not come close to victory in the Cold War. Kennedy's open-ended promise led Americans into many new ventures in the struggle against the alleged global communist conspiracy.

For one thing, stung by Soviet successes in space, Kennedy promised that within the decade the United States would win the space race by putting a man on the moon. He and his successor Lyndon Johnson gave the National Aeronautic and Space Agency (NASA) virtually a blank check to beat the Russians to the moon, diverting money that might have been used for other technological or medical breakthroughs. To be sure, there were valid reasons to accelerate the moon project, but the prime motivation was to gain a propaganda victory in the Cold War—to restore America's position as number one in applied science. In 1969, the United States did just what Kennedy had promised, albeit at great expense. By that time, the Russians had dropped out of the race, if there ever was one. And more important, American prestige in the world, at a nadir because of the Vietnam War, did not rise appreciably because of the impressive accomplishment.

From space to beneath the earth, Kennedy's vigorous challenge to the Russians affected the daily lives of Americans. For a while, he encouraged the building of atomic bomb shelters in the backyards of private homes. They soon became options, along with in-ground pools, screened porches, and attached garages, for suburban housebuyers. Aside from reinforcing the Russian suspicion that Kennedy might be preparing for a first strike and suggestions that Americans could survive a major nuclear exchange, the short-lived shelter program raised a host of philosophical issues about the measures that should be taken when the bombs began to fall and neighbors or relatives, who had not been prudent enough to build shelters, tried to get into one's cramped, nuclear family–sized shelter.

Kennedy's first major attempt to "bear any burden" to bring the contest to the Communists ended in fiasco in April 1961 at the Bay of Pigs in Cuba, where an American-sponsored invasion to overthrow Fidel Castro failed miserably. The president's defenders contend that he had inherited the program from the Eisenhower administration. But even had he had more qualms about the invasion's chances for success, it would have been difficult for him to call it off considering the vigor with which he had assailed the Republicans during the campaign for having done nothing to get rid of Castro.

The Bay of Pigs invasion called into question once again the independence of the free press in the American democracy. Beginning in the fall of 1960 and continuing on through the winter and early spring of 1961, newspapers and magazines ran a number of stories, some of which contained erroneous information planted by the CIA, that American-backed Cuban émigrés were training to invade their homeland. More important, a few days before D day, the authoritative *New York Times* received information about the invasion. After speaking to the president, the publisher decided to eliminate crucial details about the event to protect the lives of the émigré army and, more important, to protect national security.

By the time he leaned on the *Times,* Kennedy had become distressed about information that had already reached the press about the supposedly covert operation. "I can't believe what I'm reading," he told an aide. "Castro doesn't need agents over here. All he has to do is read our papers!" A few days after the failed invasion, he lectured the media:

If the press is awaiting a declaration of war before it imposes the self-discipline of combat conditions, then I can only say that no war ever posed a greater threat to our security. . . . Every newspaper now asks itself with respect to every story: "Is it news?" All I suggest is that you add the question: "Is it in the interest of national security?"

Kennedy was exaggerating his problems. Concerns about the difficulties of operating an effective diplomacy in a country with a free press proved unfounded. Thus, as in other crises, even during peacetime American newspapers practiced self-censorship. Of all people, Kennedy should have known better than to worry about an irresponsible press. Reporters and publishers refrained from printing anything about his astounding—and to some degree national security–threatening—philandering. Moreover, eighteen months later, during the Cuban missile crisis, James Reston of the *New York Times* decided not to run a story on troop movements in Florida after Kennedy told him it would not be in the national interest. Finally, when the president complained about negative press reports about American military and economic programs in 1962 in Vietnam, several publishers replaced their muckraking correspondents with less critical ones.

Since the 1960s, American conservatives have attacked the media for being too liberal. It is true that working journalists tend to be more liberal, on the average, than the rest of the population, but gatekeepers, editors, and especially publishers tend to be more conservative and more than willing to cooperate with an administration in the name of national security. As early as the Spanish Civil War, editors of the *New York Times* censored the dispatches of correspondent Herbert Matthews because they presented material that they felt could embarrass the United States.

The disaster at the Bay of Pigs did not damage Kennedy politically. When he appeared on television to accept personal responsibility, the public rallied around him. His approval ratings went up 5 percent, causing him to comment, "The worse I do, the more popular I get." Much the same thing happened after Jimmy Carter's botched rescue mission in Iran in April 1980. In general, Americans support a president in a crisis, even when things are going badly. Since 1945, presidential popularity has risen during international crises that social scientists label "rally events." Whether a foreign policy decision was popular or not, Kennedy realized what other postwar presidents had also realized—diplomatic activities were more important than domestic activities. As he told Richard Nixon a few days after the Bay of Pigs invasion, "It really is true that foreign affairs is the only important issue for a President to handle, isn't it? I mean who gives a shit if the minimum wage is $1.15 or $1.25 in comparison to something like this."

The fact that few citizens complained about the covert, unilateral character of the Bay of Pigs invasion, in which Kennedy was clearly involved in an illegal attempt to topple a sovereign government, demonstrated how well they had learned their Cold War catechism. They might have been less supportive had they known about the alliance the CIA had forged with the Mafia to assassinate Fidel Castro. This was not the first time the government used organized crime figures in a foreign policy venture. During World War II, Mafia kingpin Charles "Lucky" Luciano employed "family" connections in Sicily to help smooth the way for American invasion forces.

The government's ability to operate an effective covert diplomacy, shielded from both the media and Congress, was again demonstrated during the Cuban missile crisis. Few Americans knew what was going on in the White House during those thirteen days in October 1962 that constituted the most dangerous crisis of the Cold War. At the time, several American decisionmakers estimated the chances for a nuclear exchange at anywhere from 33 to 50 percent. In recent years, Russian scholars have revealed new and disturbing, but not necessarily conclusive, information about their country's strategies during the crisis. Considering that information, some decisionmakers now believe the odds for war to have been even shorter.

Domestic politics helped determine Kennedy's response to the Soviet introduction of offensive missiles into Cuba. As the 1962 congressional elections approached, he perceived himself a failure. Congress had enacted little of his New Frontier program, and in foreign affairs he had lost at the Bay of Pigs, been bullied by Khrushchev at the Vienna Summit in June 1961, accepted the neutralization of Laos, and stood by while the Russians built a wall between East and West Berlin. In addition, the first public claims that Russians had placed offensive missiles in Cuba came from a Republican senator, Kenneth Keating of New York. Keating, who was seen as a stalking horse for a potential Republican candidate for president, New York governor Nelson Rockefeller, may have received his information from contacts in the CIA who were distressed about Kennedy's threats to shake up the agency after the Bay of Pigs disaster.

Even the Russians understood the relationship between Kennedy's foreign policy and the elections. Khrushchev had earlier privately assured the president that he would take no action that might affect the outcome in November. Of course, he gave that assurance while he was implanting missiles in Cuba. The Russian leader told colleagues he hoped to keep the missiles a secret until November 6, the date of the congressional elections. After that point, when he planned to reveal to the world his great coup, he was certain it would cause Kennedy few political problems. The CIA discovered the missiles before the election.

Thus, when the time came to act, Kennedy was concerned about his political prospects, as well as national security interests. As in all crises, few leaders speak even in private about such selfish considerations. Nevertheless, they were a factor, for example, leading Kennedy to refuse to trade outmoded and soon-to-be-dismantled missile bases in Turkey in return for the bases in Cuba. Had he been willing to accept such an exchange at the onset of the crisis, the United States would not have had to risk nuclear war, either by invading or bombing Cuba, or even by enforcing the naval quarantine that was decided upon at the eleventh hour. In Kennedy's defense, he could not afford to "lose" the crisis because of national security concerns. That is, had the Russians won, they might have become emboldened to try even more dangerous actions that could have ignited a third world war for certain.

For whatever reason, although Kennedy initially refused to trade the missiles in Turkey for those in Cuba, that trade was part of the deal that resolved the crisis. But Kennedy kept that information from the public because it would have given the impression that Khrushchev's alleged aggression paid off—and that the president had lost the diplomatic duel. One wonders whether Kennedy would have moved so close to the brink had he suspected, as the head of the Soviet Institute of Military History asserted in 1989, that both strategic and tactical warheads had already arrived in Cuba and that Soviet commanders had been given the authority to use the tactical ones if necessary to repel an invasion.

In one interesting sidelight again involving the American media, when during the crisis the distinguished commentator Walter Lippmann suggested in his syndicated column that the United States make the swap of Turkish for Cuban missiles, the Soviets initially interpreted the column as an officially sanctioned trial balloon. From their perspective, the American media were closely related to ruling circles in Washington. During the crisis, a counselor from the Russian embassy sent several key messages to the White House through John Scali of ABC News.

The perceived American diplomatic tradition of operating according to moral principles and not mere *Realpolitik* had an impact on the peaceful resolution of the conflict when Robert Kennedy, among others in the inner decisionmaking group known as Ex-Com, opposed an air attack against the missiles or even an invasion of Cuba. He asserted that the United States was not the sort of country that perpetrated a Pearl Harbor–style sneak attack.

Most Americans applauded President Kennedy's skillful "crisis management." Indeed, his win over Khrushchev contributed to his party making a stronger than expected showing in the by-elections. As one Republican complained after he read the returns, "We were Cubanized."

After that most dangerous of Cold War crises, during which Kennedy and Khrushchev executed their last-minute retreat from the abyss, Soviet-American relations improved, symbolized by the signing of the Partial Test Ban Treaty in 1963. Since 1957, the National Committee for a Sane Nuclear Policy (SANE) had been lobbying effectively for disarmament. A small group with never more than 25,000 members, SANE, along with organizations such as Women Strike for Peace, popularized the argument that the testing of nuclear weapons was polluting the environment. SANE and its allies had demonstrated their political skills earlier. According to a 1955 Gallup poll, 17 percent of Americans considered nuclear fallout to be "a real danger." By late 1957, that number had risen to 52 percent, a product of an effective propaganda campaign led by SANE and Democratic politicians who had raised the issue during the 1956 campaign. When the Soviet Union announced a voluntary ban on testing in March 1958, the pressure on President Eisenhower became intense. Against his better judgment, he agreed in the fall of 1958 to a voluntary U.S. moratorium that lasted until 1961. Then it became Kennedy's turn to contend with the antitesting lobby.

Although SANE was interested in broader disarmament measures than just a test ban, its stress upon the amount of strontium 90 in the air and how that pollutant affected children's skeletal development created pressures on Kennedy to do something about the problem. Of course, Kennedy would not have agreed to the treaty had he not been assured that his scientists could monitor Soviet compliance from afar and that American weapons could be tested adequately underground. Khrushchev's public proposal of a partial test ban added to the pressure. Interestingly, the president encouraged SANE chair Norman Cousins to serve as an intermediary between himself and the Russian premier during the months prior to the conclusion of the treaty.

Kennedy did not at first face the same sort of public pressures over his Vietnam policies. By the fall of 1963, the United States maintained only 16,000 advisors in that country and most Americans remained unconcerned about this apparently limited commitment to defend the pro–Western Saigon regime against the National Liberation Front's (NLF or Viet Cong) insurrection. One reason for their seeming indifference was the administration's downplaying of the role those advisors played in the conflict. We now know that they were engaged in far more combat with the Communists than was reported in the media. For example, American pilots flew combat missions. Yet the administration described these as training missions, since one Vietnamese "student" always came along for the ride. Kennedy employed such subterfuges not to keep the information that the Americans had changed their role from advisors to "advisors" from the enemy. The Viet Cong and Hanoi knew that American forces were shooting at them. Kennedy wanted to keep that information from the American people.

The increase in advisors from 800 in 1960 to the 16,000 when Lyndon Johnson took office was intimately related to domestic politics. Although Vietnam was not a major political issue in 1961, Kennedy felt it could become one. After losing several duels with the Communists in 1961, he drew the line at South Vietnam. Indeed, he established his Vietnam Task Force immediately after the failure at the Bay of Pigs. He had decided that he could not afford the adverse domestic reaction, encouraged by Republicans, if he let the Saigon regime fall to the Viet Cong, a likely outcome without increased American military and economic support.

In the summer of 1963, Vietnam became a major public issue for the first time in Kennedy's presidency. The precipitant was not the war in the field, which was going badly, but the conflict in Saigon and Hue between the American-backed government of Ngo Dinh Diem and Buddhists. Self-immolation was the most sensational of the tactics employed by Buddhists to call attention to their struggle against an authoritarian regime. Shocking images in American newspapers and on television screens of burning bonzes centered attention on Vietnam and increased pressures on the Kennedy administration to "pacify" Saigon. Buddhist leaders, who understood the importance of the American media, informed journalists about self-immolations in advance in order to obtain maximum publicity for their ultimate sacrifices. American journalists knew that they were being used to create a groundswell of opinion against the Diem government but contended that the self-immolations were big, mediagenic news stories that had to be covered, irrespective of the impact on American foreign policy. Those stories played a role in Kennedy's decision to encourage an anti-Diem coup led by dissident military officers. This was not the only time that demonstrations, often planned for the convenience of American newspeople, had an impact on public opinion and policymaking.

Political instability in South Vietnam made Kennedy nervous about the prospect of a greater American commitment. Although the evidence is contradictory, he allegedly told at least three of his colleagues, aide Kenneth O'Donnell, Secretary of Defense Robert S. McNamara, and Sen. Mike Mansfield (D-Mont.), that he would deescalate—but only after the 1964 election. He did not want to run for reelection as the president who lost Vietnam. He privately admitted in 1963, "These people [the Vietnamese] hate us. They are going to throw our asses out of there at almost any point.

But I can't give up territory like that to the Communists and then get the American people to reelect me!"

In 1954, Eisenhower's press secretary had worried about how the Democrats might use the issue of Vietnam's fall to Communism had the Republicans allowed the agreements reached at Geneva to play themselves out. Later, both Lyndon Johnson and Richard Nixon made similar calculations as they considered the relationship between withdrawal from Vietnam and their electoral prospects in 1968 and 1972 respectively. The longer and larger the American commitment to Vietnam, the harder it became in domestic political terms to pull out of the war without, as Lyndon Johnson said, the "coonskin nailed to the wall." Had that happened, he contended, "there would follow in this country an endless national debate—a mean and destructive debate—that would shatter my Presidency, kill my administration, and damage our democracy."

Relatively free to escalate modestly in Vietnam, Kennedy was hobbled by Congress's Hickenlooper Amendment, which restrained a president's ability to conduct diplomacy in other parts of the Third World. Comparable to the Jackson-Vanik Amendment of 1974, which tied trade with the Soviet Union to its treatment of Soviet Jews, and the Clark Amendment of 1976, which prohibited aid to American friends in the Angolan civil war, the Hickenlooper Amendment of 1962 warned that foreign aid would be cut off to recipients who nationalized American properties without compensation or otherwise discriminated against American businesses. Presidents did not welcome such congressional assertiveness. Yet as the branch of government having the responsibility to approve trade and aid legislation, Congress had every right to attach such codicils to its bills, even if they did decrease executive flexibility in foreign policy making.

In contrast, Congress was far more cooperative with Kennedy when drafting the important Trade Expansion Act of 1962. With the Reciprocal Trade Act of 1934 due to expire in June of that year, the president obtained new powers from Congress to cut tariffs in specific cases, to compensate producers in the United States who might be hurt by increased foreign competition, and to provide training for workers displaced because of that competition. At the time, Americans were concerned about competition from the new Common Market. Ironically, their government had been encouraging the Europeans to integrate their economies since the early days of the Marshall Plan. Citizens of a strong and prosperous capitalist Western Europe would not find Communism attractive and thus would lessen U.S. Cold War burdens. But an integrated Common Market became a formidable competitor for many key American industries. This issue, marked by periodic threats of tariff wars that threatened the political unity of the Western alliance, continues to the present day as the United States schizophrenically applauds the development of the largest unified market in the world and opposes its exclusivity and subsidies.

At first glance, as in the case of the Common Market, Kennedy's proposal to establish the Peace Corps seemed to have little relationship to domestic politics. Once established, the Peace Corps earned mixed notices, depending upon the country to which the young people were sent and the sorts of activities in which they enlisted. But one thing was certain. The vast majority of volunteers came back to the United States sympathetic to those in the Third World who assailed Western imperialism and colonialism. Not surprisingly, a large number of former volunteers later participated prominently in the American anti–Vietnam War movement.

Kennedy did not live to see the formation of that movement, as he was gunned down in Dallas on November 22, 1963. According to the Warren Commission investigating the assassination, Lee Harvey Oswald was the lone deranged shooter who perpetrated the deed. To this day, many Americans do not believe that Oswald acted alone and, more important, find explanations for assassination plots in Kennedy's foreign policy initiatives. According to one popular conspiracy thesis, Kennedy was killed by forces in the American military or intelligence agencies who opposed his apparent readiness to pull out of Vietnam. The CIA itself was nervous about the president's alleged plans to gut the agency that he felt misled him at the Bay of Pigs and elsewhere.

DOMESTIC ISSUES were the paramount factors in Lyndon Johnson's successful presidential campaign in 1964. Johnson ran as a liberal Democratic reformer against Barry Goldwater, a conservative Republican candidate who allegedly threatened to dismantle the welfare state. The 1964 campaign, however, did involve one important foreign policy issue—the possible escalation of the U.S. role in the Vietnam War. Because of several comments he made, the loose-lipped Goldwater appeared as a mad bomber, willing to use nuclear weapons in that war. He had also voted against the popular Partial Test Ban Treaty of the previous year. One famous television ad for Johnson, which was so offensive that it was pulled after a few days, showed a little girl counting the petals she plucked from a daisy. Her innocent exercise ultimately turned into a countdown for a nuclear explosion. For his part, Senator Fulbright, who ramrodded the Gulf of Tonkin Resolution through the

Senate in August only to become a leading dove less than a year later, explained his enthusiastic support for Johnson ("the dumbest thing I've ever done") in terms of his fear that the dangerous Goldwater might make it to the White House and precipitate a world war. Goldwater charged accurately that Johnson was not telling the truth about American policies in Southeast Asia and had not developed a plan for victory.

To distance himself from the hawkish Arizona senator, Johnson maintained that while the United States was not going to shy away from its commitments, the war in Vietnam "ought to be fought by the boys in Asia to protect their own land," suggesting that a vote for him was a vote against further escalatory moves in Southeast Asia. At the time that he made those comments, several of his advisors were urging him to escalate in Vietnam. In fact, by approving OPLAN 34-A raids on North Vietnam, he had already secretly escalated. Supported by American air and naval units, South Vietnamese were slipping into North Vietnam on sabotage missions. There was such a mission, about which the American public did not know, just prior to the North Vietnamese attack on the *Maddox* in the Gulf of Tonkin on August 2. When Johnson appeared on television on August 4, after an alleged second attack on an American vessel in the gulf, he failed to inform Americans about the covert OPLAN 34-A raid. Had Americans known about the raid, they might have at least understood why the North Vietnamese attacked the *Maddox* and some might have even opposed the retaliatory air attack on North Vietnam. More would have joined the opposition had they known that the president himself was uncertain about whether the second attack ever occurred. As he said later, "For all I know our navy might have been shooting at whales out there."

The Gulf of Tonkin Resolution that Congress passed in the wake of the affair authorized Johnson to take any measure deemed necessary to defend the armed forces in Southeast Asia. This was the closest that Congress came to declaring war against North Vietnam. It was enough for Johnson. He referred frequently to the resolution to silence critics who accused him of conducting a war without congressional authorization. According to the president, "it was grandma's nightshirt—it covered everything." Privately he claimed that with his blank-check resolution, he did "not just screw Ho Chi Minh, I cut off his pecker."

When a president appears on television from the Oval Office to announce a national crisis, he is difficult to challenge. As the "Great Communicator" Ronald Reagan noted, "The biggest advantage a modern President has is the six o'clock news. Presidents can be on the news every night if they want to—and they usually want to." It is true, of course, that once Johnson's deceptions leaked out, and Americans discovered that Richard Nixon often lied to them as well, many became skeptical when other presidents or officials appeared on television to explain a crisis.

Safely reelected and armed with his Gulf of Tonkin Resolution, Johnson approved the bombing of North Vietnam in February 1965 and the assumption by American boys of the main ground combat role in Vietnam in July. As a sardonic commentator noted, "They told me that if I voted for Goldwater we would bomb North Vietnam. I voted for Goldwater and we bombed North Vietnam." President Johnson appeared to be as militaristic as Goldwater allegedly would have been. In April 1965, without consulting Congress, he sent Marines into a civil war in the Dominican Republic to contain phantom Communists. The president's aides elicited support for the intervention by exaggerating and even making up atrocity stories in which American citizens' lives appeared to be in imminent danger from bloodthirsty communist terrorists. The invasion of the Dominican Republic, even more than the bombing of North Vietnam, turned Senator Fulbright against the administration's foreign policies.

Johnson's escalation of the air and ground war in Vietnam in 1965 belied his campaign statements about his relatively dovish policy. As the conflict continued through 1966 and 1967, those statements contributed to a decline in his credibility, a key factor in the loss of public support for his Vietnam strategies.

Johnson decided to deflect attention from the crisis in Vietnam because he feared for his cherished Great Society programs. With huge majorities in Congress, he knew he had a brief and virtually unprecedented window of opportunity to introduce the most massive reform program in American history. Had Congress and the public been informed about the long-run costs of the war and the implications of the escalation, they might have demanded reductions in spending for the newly established domestic reform initiatives since it was not possible to afford both guns and butter. For that reason, Johnson rejected his advisors' proposals to raise taxes in 1966 to pay for increased military spending. Johnson did "not want to be the President who built empires or sought grandeur, or extended domain. I want to be the President who educated young children . . . who helped the poor . . . who protected the right of every citizen to vote."

The escalation in 1965, particularly the bombing, contributed to the formation and growth of the largest antiwar movement in American history. Through mass one-city demonstrations attracting as many as 500,000 participants, letter and petition writing, electoral politics, and draft resistance, the movement affected the Southeast Asian policies of both Johnson and Nixon. Indeed, two specific Vietnam foreign policy decisions were influenced by the movement, which, though it never captured the loyalties of a majority of citizens, had great strength among upper- and upper-middle-class citizens and their college-age children.

The first decision occurred during Johnson's administration. The spectacle of more than 35,000 young protesters besieging the Pentagon on October 21, 1967, compelled the president to launch a major public-relations campaign in November and early December, which emphasized that the ever-more-costly war was being won and that there was light at the end of the tunnel. When on the heels of this propaganda blitz, the Communists launched their country-wide Tet Offensive on January 31, 1968, many Americans found it difficult to understand how, if things were going so well, the enemy was able to put together such a large and initially successful operation. Although by the middle of February the offensive had failed, many were skeptical when Johnson proclaimed victory. This skepticism was a factor in declining public support for the president's policies in Vietnam and contributed to his monumental decisions of March 31, 1968, to limit the bombing, not to escalate, and not to seek reelection.

Johnson's decisions related clearly to the decline in approval ratings for his handling of foreign relations. Critics later claimed that he brought this upon himself because of his failure to rally support for the war in Southeast Asia. One of the main lessons drawn from America's failure in Vietnam was the folly of becoming involved in another limited war without first securing popular support for the long haul.

But Johnson faced a difficult problem. When he and his advisors made the war an American war in 1965, they viewed it as the prototype of the wars of the future in the Third World. The United States had to learn how to fight such wars with its nuclear arm tied behind its back and, as Secretary McNamara noted, "without the necessity of arousing the public ire." The danger was that hawkish Americans would demand swift and total victory using all available weaponry. Nuclear escalation could have led to a cataclysmic and final world war.

Walter Lippmann wrote earlier that democracies like the United States were generally reluctant to get into war, but once they started fighting, they fought ferociously to unconditional surrender. Similarly, George F. Kennan wrote that the American democracy was like a "prehistoric monster" who is "slow to wrath" but once in a fight "not only destroys his adversary but largely wrecks his native habitat." Or as a Union officer wrote of fighting Confederate guerrillas in Missouri, "There exists in the breasts of people of educated and Christian communities wild and ferocious passions . . . which be aroused and kindled by . . . war and injustice, and become more cruel and destructive than any that live in the breasts of savage and barbarous nations."

Had Johnson aroused passionate support for the war, perhaps by empha-sizing the serious threat posed to national security by the Vietnamese Com-munists, how could he have contained those who would have demanded the use of all available weaponry? Certainly, they would have joined the former head of the American Strategic Air Command, Gen. Curtis LeMay, who urged in 1964 that "we should bomb them into the Stone Age." Undersec-retary of State George Ball claimed that the administration feared the Right— "The Great Beast"—more than the Left. After all, Joseph McCarthy, who had shaken up American politics and especially the Democratic party, had departed from the scene barely more than a decade earlier.

Yet by not arousing Americans, Johnson made it difficult for them to sup-port what appeared to be an endless war. As George Ball had warned in the fall of 1964, and again in the summer of 1965, the public would tire of a long, inconclusive war in Vietnam. General MacArthur had offered Johnson—and Kennedy for that matter—similar advice. During the Korean War, a war that aroused very little political opposition, Americans began to demand the return of their boys by the middle of 1951. Ball predicted that this more un-popular war, whose origins were far less clear, would certainly produce even more opposition. Ball and MacArthur were correct.

Domestic factors indeed underlay the president's fateful speech to the nation on March 31, 1968. For one thing, the activities of the antiwar move-ment and other protest movements of the era had contributed to making the late sixties one of the most turbulent periods in American history. The anti-war movement in particular, strongest on elite college campuses, threatened to destroy the American establishment, as Johnson was told by his advisors both within and, especially, outside of the Washington Beltway. The coun-try was falling apart and the children of the establishment had become alien-ated from the system.

This instability, coupled with Johnson's reluctance to cut his Great Soci-ety programs or raise taxes, helped weaken the U.S. economy, a development that worried Wall Street in the late winter of 1968. As it had been for the French in 1954, although the United States had not been defeated on the ground and still had the physical resources to continue to fight in Vietnam, the establishment and much of the public demanded deescalation and some sort of face-saving withdrawal.

Johnson's March 31 decision was also the first major war-peace decision in American history to be affected by television. Most Americans found it difficult to believe that Tet was a communist defeat, which it ultimately was in the military sense, when they saw newsreel footage of Vietcong sappers inside the American embassy compound in Saigon. And many were sickened when photographers caught the chief of the Saigon police executing a prisoner on the streets of his city.

After the Tet Offensive, the most respected anchorperson on the air, Walter Cronkite, went to Vietnam to have a look for himself at the way things were. Upon his return, he told viewers, including Lyndon Johnson who watched the CBS News special on tape the next day, that things were not going well and that there was no end in sight. Johnson worried about the impact of Cronkite's analysis because of his special position in the country as a responsible and moderate journalist.

Some of Johnson's military advisors called for escalation and not deescalation in the wake of the U.S. and South Vietnamese victory in Tet. But their request for 206,000 more soldiers would have meant that Johnson would have had to call up the reserves. The reserves had become a refuge for many middle- and upper-class young people to escape being sent to Vietnam. He had resisted calling them up earlier in part because of the potential opposition to such an action from influential Americans. Had he dipped into the reserves earlier, the antiwar movement conceivably could have grown even more powerful as more than just politically impotent working-class parents would have borne the direct costs of the increasingly bloody war.

That movement posed a further personal problem for Johnson. For the first time in American history, a president found it virtually impossible to travel freely among his people. Everywhere Johnson went, antiwar picketers appeared to harass and insult him. His aides experienced similar treatment, with Secretary of Defense McNamara threatened with physical harm in the sanctity of Harvard Yard in November 1966. Impossible to measure, the omnipresence of picketers shouting, "Hey, hey, LBJ, how many kids did you kill today?" took an immense physical and emotional toll on the president and his family. They must have breathed a sigh of relief after the March 31, 1968, speech—their critics would no longer have him to kick around.

Both candidates in the 1968 campaign, Johnson's vice-president, Hubert H. Humphrey, and Republican Richard M. Nixon, contended that if elected they would end the war in Vietnam. Democrats, especially, were not convinced that Nixon, the old Cold Warrior, would beat such a hasty retreat from Southeast Asia. In a situation comparable to Senator Fulbright supporting the Gulf of Tonkin Resolution in 1964 because he feared the election of Barry Goldwater, the chief negotiator at the Paris peace talks, W. Averell Harriman, was so distressed at the prospect of a Nixon victory that he went beyond his instructions in an unsuccessful attempt to secure a settlement before election day.

Johnson was not entirely pleased with Humphrey's campaign. Nevertheless, he helped him on October 31, six days before the election, with the announcement of a complete bombing pause over North Vietnam in order to get the peace talks moving. This initiative originated from a suggestion from Moscow (which, as in 1960, did not want to see Nixon win) that North Vietnam would be open to new peace proposals.

Republican intermediaries secretly countered this "October surprise" by urging the South Vietnamese to resist any new peace moves until after the election of their friends in the Republican party. Most likely, Richard Nixon was not directly involved in this gambit. According to Republicans, such intervention was legitimate because of Johnson's allegedly cynical use of a national security issue to help elect Humphrey. (Johnson privately worried that what he considered to be a genuine diplomatic breakthrough would be perceived as a "cheap political trick.") Surely, Republicans contended, it was not coincidental that Johnson offered olive branches to the enemy on the eve of the election. What would they have said had they known about Moscow's role in the surprise package?

These contrasting initiatives were but the first of a series of real and rumored October surprises in the international sphere during election years. Presidents found it much easier to manipulate events there than in the less controllable domestic sphere. From 1968 through 1980, the concept of "October surprise" became so common that thereafter opponents and journalists alike made it difficult for a president to consider any foreign policy initiative during the last weeks of the campaign for fear of being accused of playing fast and loose with national security in order to be elected. We seem to have come full circle, with presidents virtually immobilized to do much in the international sphere as they approach election day, unless they obtain their opponents' support.

The second major case of a major Vietnam policy decision having been influenced by the powerful antiwar movement occurred during the Nixon administration. Upon taking office in 1969, the new president initiated a program of covert escalation, including the bombing of Cambodia, to force the Communists to adopt a more conciliatory position at the peace talks. He wanted to demonstrate to them that he could escalate without attracting the attention of the antiwar movement. Thus, the bombing, which was not a secret to the Cambodians or the North Vietnamese, was kept a secret from the American population and even from some of the military involved in the operation.

In July, Nixon sent communist leader Ho Chi Minh a secret ultimatum—be more forthcoming at Paris or face even more serious escalations. Within the White House, aides discussed a variety of escalatory "savage blows," which included the mining of Hanoi and Haiphong harbors and the bombing of the flood-control systems in the north.

As Washington and Hanoi considered their options, and after Nixon had failed to announce publicly a program to hasten an end to the war, antiwar leaders began planning a new type of demonstration for October 15, two weeks before the ultimatum deadline about which they knew nothing. This demonstration, the Moratorium, involved over 3 million Americans in over 200 cities participating in vigils and rallies to protest the pace at which Nixon was withdrawing from Vietnam. The numbers involved were so large, and the several millions of not just young people but "responsible" adults (including former Vietnam peace-talk negotiator W. Averell Harriman) who took part were so impressive, that Nixon had to take them into account when he permitted the November 1 deadline to pass without any action, even though Hanoi had not budged.

In fact, Nixon was so concerned about his deteriorating position on the homefront that he went to work on his Silent Majority speech of November 3, the most important speech of his presidency to that time, to rally the alleged majority of administration supporters against the antiwar crowds in the streets. He needed to mobilize those supporters before he was able to reescalate in Southeast Asia. The administration coupled the Silent Majority speech with a fierce attack, led by Vice-President Spiro T. Agnew, against the elite media, which the administration claimed was liberal and unpatriotic. Nixon and Agnew's Silent Majority and media offensive helped turn the tide of public opinion for a while and certainly affected the amount of coverage the television networks devoted to the Mobilization demonstration in Washington on November 15, the largest single-city antiwar demonstration to date.

But Nixon discovered he did not have a free hand to escalate in Southeast Asia when the nation erupted in protest after he sent American troops into Cambodia on April 30, 1970, just two weeks after the Moratorium formally closed up its offices in Washington. The invasion, and especially the killing by the Ohio National Guard of four students at Kent State University at a protest rally, sparked riots and burnings on hundreds of campuses and even the premature closing of some colleges until the fall. The domestic crisis, which followed on the heels of the invasion of Cambodia, forced Nixon to cut short the operation before it had accomplished all of its goals.

Aside from its impact on Johnson's March 31, 1968, decision and on Nixon's November 1, 1969, nondecision, the antiwar movement further influenced the war in at least one other important way. Vietnamese Communists counted upon opponents of the war in the United States to influence that country's policies. Thus, even though both Johnson and Nixon claimed repeatedly that American policy was not made in the streets by antiwar demonstrators, the fact that they knew that Hanoi took the movement into account in its own calculations certainly affected Washington's calculations.

The relative success of the antiwar movement, supported after 1968 by more and more prominent Americans, spelled the end of the bipartisan Cold War consensus. This development led to increased politicization in the foreign policy–making process in the 1970s and 1980s, which was marked by congressional muscle-flexing, the pervasiveness and aggressiveness of the electronic media, the weakness of the political parties, and the proliferation and power of well-funded interest groups.

Although the antiwar movement declined in influence after the spring of 1971, in part because fewer and fewer American soldiers were participating in the combat in Southeast Asia, the war did figure in the election of 1972. In the first place, the Democratic candidate, Sen. George McGovern (D-S.D.), was nominated in part because of rule changes in his party that were precipitated by the riots at the 1968 convention in Chicago when antiwar activists and others were excluded from the political process.

More important, as in the election of 1952, Republicans labeled their Democratic opponent with a negative alphabetic slogan—he was the AAA candidate, an alleged supporter of abortion, appeasement, and amnesty for draft dodgers. McGovern's greatest appeal, moreover, derived from his promise to end the war more quickly than Nixon. That promise lost its salience when Nixon's popular national security advisor, Henry Kissinger, announced on October 31, 1972, four years to the day from Johnson's October surprise, that he had an agreement with the Communists—"Peace is at hand." Hanoi had decided that it was better to accept a compromise agreement from Nixon before he was elected than to have to deal with him after an anticipated electoral victory. Like Johnson in 1968, Nixon worried that his genuine breakthrough might be perceived as a political ploy by critics.

A deal may have been struck with the North Vietnamese, but Kissinger did not have one with the South Vietnamese, who rejected the terms he had negotiated. Unlike the situation four years earlier, the administration was able to keep Saigon's rejection a secret. Only following the election did the president inform Americans that Kissinger's deal had come unglued because the *North* Vietnamese had reneged. This alleged reneging led to the bombing of Hanoi and Haiphong with B-52s for thirteen days in December in order to force the Communists back to the negotiating table. The time chosen for the devastating raids, the Christmas holiday season, was calculated. With students away from colleges for vacation and Congress in recess, antiwar critics could not organize meaningful protests. Before opposition could mobilize, the North Vietnamese agreed to return to the negotiating table and soon after signed the Paris Peace Accords.

America's longest war had a profound influence on the conduct of its foreign and domestic policies long after the last American left Saigon in the spring of 1975. For one thing, the military, which had found it difficult to fight a long unpopular war with draftees, shifted to all-volunteer forces. In an implicit tribute to the power of the antiwar movement, Richard Nixon had promised during the 1968 campaign to end the draft.

In addition, a myth developed around the notion that the media had helped to lose the war by ignoring military progress and by approving of the antiwar movement. That myth became so ingrained that even editors and journalists behaved quite differently—more "patriotically"—in later American military interventions.

Above all, Americans agreed with the slogan, "No More Vietnams," no more long, inconclusive wars. At the least, there would be no more such wars unless the decisionmakers were certain that the public would back the effort. Remembering the political situation in the homefront during the Vietnam War, later presidents thought twice about committing American forces to combat for an extended period of time.

The war's impact on the American economy further affected national strength and foreign and domestic policies well into the eighties. Defense spending had increased by about 2 percent of GNP over almost a ten-year period at a total of $150 billion. One may add to that the costs of inflation, payments on the debt, programs for veterans, and lost output from disabled veterans.

The Vietnam War was not the only international issue that involved domestic politics during Nixon's tenure in office. No president had ever been so concerned about the public-relations activities of his presidency. His extensive daily media analyses, wide use of privately commissioned public opinion polls, and record-setting ceremonial foreign travel attest to that concern. Convinced that diplomacy was part theater, Nixon played his role consummately with an eye to how his actions would appear on American television. He planned what historian Daniel Boorstin has called "pseudo-events." For example, on one occasion, Nixon orchestrated an unlikely triumphal greeting on a trip to Italy by arriving during rush hour so that citizens back home would think that the crowds of Romans on the streets were hailing his visit. David Gergen, one of Nixon's aides (and later an aide to presidents Reagan and Clinton), wrote,

> We had a rule in the Nixon administration that before any public event was put on his schedule, you had to know what the headline out of that event was going to be, what the picture was going to be, and what the lead paragraph would be. You had to think in those terms, and if you couldn't justify it, it didn't go on the schedule.

But that was all bread and circuses for public consumption. Nixon and Kissinger finessed democratic tradition by practicing the most secret—and deceitful—diplomacy of any president in this century. Both concluded that the only way that they could compete with the Soviets and the Chinese was to convince them the United States was capable of operating a Metternichean-style diplomacy shielded from the media, the public, and Congress.

Thus, during the 1971 war between India and Pakistan over the independence of Bangladesh, President Nixon publicly proclaimed neutrality while covertly supporting Pakistan. He had to keep his soon-to-be famous "tilt" secret because the majority of Americans were rooting for the poor people of Bangladesh, supported by India, who had been brutally suppressed by Pakistan. He felt, rightly so, that they would not understand the reasons of state behind his opposition to India. When Jack Anderson published a leak about the tilt, some in the White House toyed with the idea of assassinating the allegedly unpatriotic columnist.

Similarly, Nixon "shielded" the public from learning about the successful destabilization of the freely elected democratic socialist regime of Chile's Salvadore Allende. Shades of old Caribbean-basin dollar diplomacy, his operatives worked closely with the International Telephone and Telegraph Company and the Chilean opposition to rid that nation of a system that nationalized foreign enterprises and allegedly threatened to spread Socialism or even Communism beyond its borders.

On the other hand, the way that Nixon held his cards close to the vest made sense, even in a democracy. No doubt two of his 1972 successes, the Strategic Arms Limitation Treaty (SALT I) and the opening to the People's

Republic of China, were preceded by months of negotiations and meetings that were kept from the public, the media, and political opponents who might have killed those policies in the womb.

Nixon was not always successful in practicing his old-fashioned secret diplomacy. He suffered a major embarrassment in 1971 when the Supreme Court permitted the *New York Times* to publish the purloined *Pentagon Papers,* a classified history of America's involvement in the Vietnam War compiled by McNamara's Defense Department. His lawyers argued to no avail that the publication of the documents would make it impossible for the United States to do business in the world. No foreign government would ever again talk frankly to Washington for fear that its conversations would be published in the *New York Times.* The administration's argument for prior restraint failed, the *Pentagon Papers* were published—and the only ones embarrassed were American officials, mostly Democrats, who made a series of boneheaded decisions about which they had deceived the public over the years from 1945 through 1967.

Almost as soon as he was reelected in 1972, Nixon's administration began to unravel. The Watergate affair, which started with a simple break-in in June 1972 at Democratic party headquarters in Washington by a group working for the Committee to Reelect the President and ended with Nixon's resignation in August 1974, also had its foreign components. As the bill of particulars against the president developed through 1973, charges that he ordered the break-in of the office of the psychologist of *Pentagon Papers* leaker Daniel Ellsberg, sold ambassadorial appointments, and, especially, harassed and surveilled illegally thousands of alleged enemies in the antiwar movement contributed to his downfall. Indeed, the first such illegal activity began over a Vietnam War issue when a *New York Times* reporter wrote about the secret bombing of Cambodia in May 1969. This led the Nixon administration to request FBI wiretaps of those suspected of the leak, including four prominent reporters and members of Nixon's own NSC and White House staff. The president also relied on intelligence agencies to search for evidence, often unlawfully, as he maintained that antiwar protesters were "highly organized and highly skilled revolutionaries dedicated to the violent destruction of our democratic system."

Nixon also sought to capitalize on his public image as the nation's chief diplomat in his Watergate defense. When he chose Gerald R. Ford as the vice-president to replace the disgraced Spiro T. Agnew, he thought that the prospect of that inexperienced and insular congressman moving into the Oval Office would make Congress think twice about impeachment. As he rhetorically asked Nelson Rockefeller during a 1973 White House visit, "Can you imagine Jerry Ford sitting in this chair?"

On the other side of the equation, the pressures of the year and a half–long Watergate crisis, which involved domestic crimes and misdemeanors primarily, significantly affected the president's foreign policies. He was compelled to downplay détente with the Soviet Union in order to maintain conservative support in Congress, and during some crises, such as the Yom Kippur War in 1973, he may have been physically or emotionally unable to exert his authority in the White House.

Nixon's—and other presidents'—illegal use of the CIA and the FBI led to the Rockefeller and Church committees' investigations of American intelligence agencies in 1975. Because of those investigations, citizens learned for the first time of assassination plots against foreign leaders as well as innumerable violations of their rights to assemble, petition, and protest. The CIA, acting at times as a "rogue elephant," illegally engaged in domestic spying and wiretaps, covertly financed nongovernmental organizations like the National Student Association and the Congress for Cultural Freedom, and even secretly subsidized the publication of books and magazines. For its part, the FBI's COINTELPRO maintained an elaborate surveillance and harassment operation against the antiwar movement, particularly left-wing groups like the Students for a Democratic Society (SDS) and the Socialist Workers Party. The outrage produced by these revelations led to new congressional oversight legislation, including a measure mandating prior notice of Congress's special oversight committee for covert activities (strengthening the 1972 Case-Zablocki Act), and a change in the leadership of the CIA that affected all covert intelligence activities.

During the five years following these reforms, the Soviet Union allegedly made gains around the world from Angola to Nicaragua. Critics attributed many of those gains to the weakening of the CIA's covert arm by Pres. Jimmy Carter's reform-minded agency director. As one CIA agent complained about the allegedly naive president, "As smart as Carter is, he did believe in Mom, apple pie, and corner drugstore. And those things that are good in America are good everywhere else."

When Ronald Reagan ran for president in 1980, he vowed to restore the agency's former capabilities. He kept that campaign promise when CIA director William Casey illegally and extralegally revitalized cloak-and-dagger operations. Of Casey's ignoring or finessing congressional oversight, one committee member complained, "We are like mushrooms. They keep us in the dark and feed us a lot of manure." Of course, the head of the Senate

Intelligence Committee in the early Reagan years was the conservative Barry Goldwater, who was not especially curious about CIA covert operations. As a critic noted sardonically, with Goldwater in charge, "the fox suddenly found himself inside the henhouse."

Reagan was unable to alter another major reform that stemmed from the Vietnam War experience. In 1973, seeking to restore some of its constitutional authority, Congress passed the War Powers Resolution over the veto of the Watergate-emasculated Nixon. In order to tether Cold War presidents who had moved the United States into undeclared wars, the act compelled the president to inform Congress within forty-eight hours after committing troops to a war zone and also to ask for Congress's permission to keep them in that zone beyond a sixty-day period. Although presidents have sometimes violated the intent of the War Powers Resolution, as was the case with Ford in Cambodia in 1975 and Reagan in the invasion of Grenada in 1983 and the bombing of Libya in 1986, its very existence has helped to right the balance intended by the founders who constructed the American system of shared powers. Through 1990, the president made formal reports to Congress under the resolution twenty-one times. Only once did Congress invoke the resolution itself, in 1983 in Lebanon, and then decided to give the president eighteen months, if he needed it, to complete the operation.

Legal scholars suggest that the resolution may be unconstitutional. It has never been formally tested in court. During the 1980s, when several legislators sued to demand that the War Powers Resolution be invoked to deal with American military advisors in the civil war in El Salvador and later with the American reflagging operation in the Persian Gulf during the Iran-Iraq War, federal circuit courts rejected the suits, ruling that the issues raised were political and not juridical in nature.

The controversial resolution was the most important but by no means the only example of congressional restrictions on presidential authority enacted during the 1970s, or the growth of "codetermination" in foreign policy. During the Vietnam War, for example, in 1971, Congress repealed the Gulf of Tonkin Resolution and, under the Cooper-Church Amendment, stopped the flow of funds to support American troops in Laos and Thailand. Congress forced the president to stop bombing in Cambodia in the summer of 1973 and then refused his urgent requests in 1974 and 1975 for increased aid to South Vietnam and in 1975 for an American-supported faction in the Angolan civil war. On the latter issue, Pres. Gerald Ford wanted to intervene forcefully in the war in part to improve his foreign policy record in the upcoming presidential election. Indeed, his principal opponent during the 1976 presidential primaries, Ronald Reagan, attacked him for permitting Angola to "fall" to a Soviet-sponsored liberation movement.

Excoriated by Ford for lacking "guts," Congress exerted itself in other ways as well. As a precursor of the War Powers Act, the Case Act of 1972 compelled the president to tell Congress within sixty days about any international agreements he had signed. In addition, the Hughes-Ryan Amendment of 1974 represented the first significant exertion of congressional control over covert activities when the president was compelled to inform Congress when he used money for them and to undertake such activities only after issuing a "finding" that they were "important to the national security." Interestingly, the reporting provision of Hughes-Ryan gave members of Congress an informal veto in the sense that they could kill a covert program by leaking news about it to the press—which they occasionally did. Further, the Nelson-Bingham Act of 1974 placed controls on government arms sales over $25 million, the Foreign Assistance Act of 1976 contained provisions concerning the human rights activities of recipients, and in 1978 Congress placed controls on the export of nuclear materials. During the late 1970s, Congress was successful in killing administration arms deals with Turkey, Chile, Argentina, Libya, and Iraq, among other countries. In a related action, the 1985 Solarz Amendment to the Foreign Assistance Act cut off military and economic aid to nonnuclear nations that illegally imported nuclear materials. In the same year, the Pressler Amendment demanded that as a precondition for aid the president certify periodically that Pakistan did not possess nuclear technology.

Presidents did not oppose all of these acts, but they were initiated by Congress and certainly restricted the executive branch's freedom of action. A frustrated President Reagan complained in 1985, "We have to get to the point where we can run a foreign policy without a committee of 535 telling us what we can do." Reagan was exaggerating. When Congress demanded that he report to them every six months on progress on the abysmal human-rights record of the El Salvador military regime in the early eighties as a condition for U.S. aid, Reagan's aides lied and blithely certified progress. He and they knew there was little progress and suspected that the military brass in that war-torn country ordered the shocking murder of a group of nuns in December 1980. Similarly, in the late 1980s, the administration lied to Congress when it certified that Pakistan was not developing nuclear weapons. There are always ways to get around Congress, as we will see in the more famous Iran-Contra scandal.

The Jackson-Vanik Act of 1974, a restrictive act that presidents Nixon and

Ford strongly opposed, was not so easy to circumvent, however. It held trade legislation hostage to improvements in the Russians' willingness to permit large numbers of Jews to emigrate. From the presidents' point of view, Jackson-Vanik weakened the centerpiece of their foreign policy, détente with the Soviet Union. At first glance, this appeared to be another case of successful lobbying by Jewish-Americans. But the story was more complicated. To be sure, in 1964, Jews had formed the American (later National) Council on Soviet Jewry to pressure the Soviets to allow Jews to leave their country. But in this case, the impetus for the amendment came from Sen. Henry Jackson, who approached the council for assistance in popularizing the cause.

Jackson pushed hard for several reasons. For one thing, as a leading Democratic hard-liner, he used the linkage of Jewish immigration to trade policy to weaken détente. Here he was correct, since the Russians were furious at this interference in their domestic affairs. Richard Nixon pointed out testily that his quiet diplomacy without threat freed far more Jewish émigrés than Jackson's bill.

It is also likely that Jackson developed the bill to help his own presidential prospects. His anti-Soviet and especially pro-Jewish position certainly helped him with Jewish-American groups, who in the primary season of 1976 were influential in New York, New Jersey, Massachusetts, Florida, Pennsylvania, and California, six states that controlled 30 percent of the electoral votes. In his unsuccessful campaign for the president, more than 60 percent of the votes Jackson won in the New York primary came from Jewish-Americans.

Finally, Jackson represented a state with major defense industry contracts. The so-called Senator from Boeing came naturally to being a hard-liner. His state was severely shaken in the 1990s when, in the wake of the end of the Cold War, the Pentagon cut back dramatically on airplane procurement. Fundamentally, of course, Jackson was deeply suspicious of détente.

His ardent support for Israel was not shared by all Americans. The Yom Kippur War (1973), which involved an Egyptian-Syrian surprise attack on Israel, marked a major turning point in U.S. relations in the Middle East. For the first time, Arab members of the Organization of Petroleum Exporting Countries (OPEC) organized a successful boycott of friends of Israel, including the United States. At that point, Americans imported more than one-third of their oil, much of it from OPEC countries. The limited gasoline shortages all Americans experienced in the months after the war made some think about the price they were paying for their tacit alliance with Israel.

Making matters worse, OPEC raised world oil prices exponentially, dramatically affecting every nation's economy, including that of the United States. A loyal American ally, the shah of Iran, was among those most responsible within OPEC for the price rise. Although Nixon and Kissinger have denied it, there is evidence that they were not distressed with the shah's strategy because the rise in oil prices enabled the Iranian to purchase huge quantities of new American arms. His arms buildup permitted him to take his place as a major element in the Nixon Doctrine. That doctrine, relating to "No More Vietnams," envisaged American national security interests in crucial regions being defended by regional strongmen like the shah. By 1977, the shah had become the largest single purchaser of American arms.

Without admitting his approval of the 1973 price hikes, Kissinger unveiled an energy policy for the United States in 1975 that encouraged even higher oil prices. He reasoned that the higher the oil prices, the more Americans would develop expensive alternate sources of energy, and the less the nation could be held hostage by Middle Eastern oil producers and OPEC.

Jewish-Americans were not the only ethnic group that helped determine American policy in the Mediterranean. Greek-Americans figured prominently in American responses to the Cyprus crisis in 1974 when Congress adopted policies the president opposed. In 1974, Turkey invaded Cyprus after fighting broke out between Greek and Turkish Cypriots. Most observers blamed the Greeks for initiating the action. Turkey's partial occupation of the island-nation produced a strong reaction from the small Greek-American community, particularly the American Hellenic Educational Progressive Association (AHEPA) and the American Hellenic Institute (AHI). Since there were no comparable Turkish-American groups, Greek-Americans had a relatively easy time developing sympathy for their cause, which was aided immeasurably when democrats overthrew the military dictatorship in Athens. With the help of friendly congresspeople, including two prominent Greek-Americans, Congress passed an amendment to a foreign aid bill cutting off military aid to any nation not using that aid for self-defense. When Turkey, a key member of NATO along with Greece, became subject to that cutoff, it ordered the closing of American military installations. President Ford and Secretary of State Kissinger, who preferred to serve as mediators between their two allies, were distressed by the way NATO's strategic position had been undermined because of American ethnic politics and congressional codetermination of foreign policy.

On this issue and others during the period, members of Congress gained a measure of revenge against six years of Henry Kissinger's "Lone Ranger" diplomacy. Characteristic were the sentiments of Sen. Lloyd Bentsen (D-Tex.), who in 1975 described Kissinger's policy as "dangerously constricted and convoluted with an . . . emphasis on secret diplomacy, personal negotiations, and one-man authoritarianism." A State Department aide, responding to Congress's Cyprus initiatives, said he "was not surprised that Congress is beginning to assert itself once more. The only thing that troubles me is that it has gotten off to such a raucous beginning—which has a vindictive air about it."

With Congress playing an increasingly important role in foreign policy, foreign lobbyists swarmed through the halls and cloakrooms on Capitol Hill trying to influence legislation. This was not a new development, however, having begun with French agents during the Revolution. The differences between this manifestation and earlier manifestations of foreign lobbying were the pervasiveness and the quality and quantity of such activities.

As television-based election campaigns became more and more expensive, foreign lobbyists' lavish gifts were welcomed by congresspeople. In 1984, the 1,000 registered foreign lobbyists, often working with major public-relations firms, spent more money in Washington than the 7,000 acknowledged domestic lobbyists. Occasionally, their activities breached the law, as with the Koreagate influence-peddling scandal of the early 1970s, when Korean agents spent an average of $500,000 to $1,000,000 a year in cash and gifts to as many as 115 lawmakers on Capitol Hill.

The shah of Iran maintained a huge operation during the seventies, which included employing the wife of the influential senator Jacob Javits (R-N.Y.) to manage Iranian public relations in the United States. During the late 1980s, at least 125 former government officials were working for the government of Japan in Washington. In 1990, Kuwait paid a public relations firm $12 million to represent its interests in the United States, and Mexico prepared to spend as much as $50 million to support passage of NAFTA in 1993. A Mexican spokesperson commented on the need to lobby Congress and other groups, "When in Rome, do as the Romans." Ross Perot raised the issue of foreign lobbyists in the 1992 presidential campaign and then again when Bill Clinton appointed Ron Brown, who had previously worked for foreign interests, his secretary of commerce. That issue was obviously related not only to the costs of running campaigns but also to Congress's codetermination in foreign affairs.

CONGRESSIONAL CODETERMINATION had little to do with Jimmy Carter's record of nonintervention in pursuit of his diplomatic goals. Despite the fact that his administration was the first of the Cold War to keep the United States out of war or large-scale covert military interventions, the election of 1980 was one of those most influenced by issues relating to foreign affairs. And on most of those issues, the president was on the defensive.

Such an outcome irritated Carter because of the relative success that he claimed to have enjoyed in international relations. Not only did he keep the United States out of war but he also brought about the Camp David Treaty (1979), the first peace between Israel and one of its Arab neighbors. That treaty was the last step in a process that began in 1977 with a television journalist playing the important mediating role that American diplomats had long unsuccessfully pursued. Barbara Walters was central to the process when, in her extensive televised interview, Pres. Anwar Sadat of Egypt shocked the world—and a State Department taken completely unawares—by indicating a desire to go to Israel to seek peace. More and more, diplomacy was being conducted over public airwaves irrespective of the wishes or strategies of foreign offices around the world.

But his work as peacemaker in the Middle East was not enough to earn Carter the credit he so desperately sought for running an effective foreign policy. Nor was he helped by his vaunted shift away from the amoral *Realpolitik* of the Nixon-Kissinger years. Carter stressed human rights, albeit inconsistently, in an attempt to pursue a foreign policy that reflected American democratic values and institutions. However, his new State Department Bureau of Human Rights was caught between the nation's long-term rhetorical commitment to moral diplomacy and practical national security needs. For example, although Carter supported a vigorous policy of opposition to apartheid in South Africa, he did not support the call for a complete economic boycott because some American industries were dependent upon minerals they obtained from that country as well as their heavy investment in branch plants. In better economic times, Carter might have been willing to support such a boycott, but not during the late seventies. Similarly, he saw the oil-rich shah of Iran as presiding over an important "island of stability" in the Persian Gulf and helped Zaire's dictator suppress a secessionist revolt. On the other hand, his attacks on Soviet officials for their violations of human rights angered them and reinforced those in the United States who were opposed to the détente that his administration continued to pursue.

Carter also faced a crisis in Mexican-American relations concerning a flood of undocumented aliens during his tenure, with as many as 500,000 slipping across the porous borders in 1978 alone. On the West Coast and in the Southwest, Americans complained that the illegal immigrants took American jobs, drove down wages, and raised the costs of social services. Mexican leaders strongly opposed Carter's solution to the problem, which included amnesty for those already there and tighter border controls, mainly because he fashioned his program without consulting them. Not until 1986 did Mexico and the United States agree to a joint program, but undocumented aliens from Mexico and Central America continued to sneak into the country. The hostility expressed by Californians in particular to Mexican and other illegal aliens certainly affected Mexican-American relations. In the 1993 debate over NAFTA, proponents contended that by improving the Mexican economy the agreement would keep Mexicans south of the border. In a related vein that same year, Pres. Bill Clinton, among others, defended his intervention in Haitian domestic politics as one way of keeping unwanted Haitian illegal immigrants at home.

JIMMY CARTER inherited the revolt against détente that had begun in the Ford administration. In 1976, a bipartisan group of conservative and neoconservative politicians and intellectuals formed a new Committee on the Present Danger to combat the alleged softness in U.S. policy toward the Soviets. This committee was a successor to the one that had lobbied Congress to support the military programs called for in NSC 68. Pressures from antidétente intellectuals from the committee and the Republican Right led Gerald Ford to appoint a special extragovernmental panel known as Team B to present estimates of Soviet intentions and capabilities that challenged those of the allegedly pro-détente CIA.

Especially concerned about its country's approach to arms negotiations, the Committee on the Present Danger lobbied successfully against the SALT II agreements. Those arms limitation agreements, first drawn up during the Ford administration, were dead in the Senate even before the Soviet Union invaded Afghanistan in December 1979. Prior to the invasion, the Carter administration claimed to have discovered a brigade of Soviet soldiers secretly stationed in Cuba. The story about the brigade had first been brought to light by Democratic senator Frank Church, the head of the Foreign Relations Committee, who, running for reelection in his home state of Idaho, found himself under attack for appearing in a photograph with Fidel Castro.

The president helped to create a minicrisis over the issue—a tempest in a teapot since the brigade had been on the island since the early sixties—to prove to the growing number of critics in Congress and the Committee on the Present Danger that he, too, could get tough with the Russians. By 1979,

Carter realized that détente with the Soviet Union was unpopular and was becoming a potent issue for his political opponents. But if he thought that by acting tough on Cuba he could convince people to support the SALT agreement, he was sadly mistaken. The Cuban flap merely increased anti-détente sentiment in the country. The Russians themselves blamed the failure of the SALT II agreement entirely on American domestic politics.

Carter also took a beating for the Panama Canal treaties he negotiated. The president deserved high marks for such a statesmanlike and rational diplomatic act. Panama had been restive for a generation over control of the canal and the canal zone with severe riots breaking out during the Johnson years. The canal, which could easily be put out of commission by acts of terrorism, was no longer so important to U.S. or world trade in any event. But it was a highly emotional issue in which Carter appeared to be a weakling giving away historic American property. One could see the firestorm coming as early as 1974. When the Ford administration began negotiating with Panama, Sen. J. Strom Thurmond (R-S.C.) introduced a resolution in the Senate, supported by thirty-four of his colleagues, opposing any treaty. His action, backed by more than the one-third needed to defeat a treaty, helped convince Ford to break off negotiations.

When Carter submitted his treaties to Congress late in 1977, conservative political opposition rallied around the issue as liberals had once rallied around the antiwar and civil rights causes. The president of Panama, Omar Torrijos, even enlisted the support of one of his friends, conservative actor John Wayne, to work for the treaty's passage in the United States. Wayne failed to convince his friend Ronald Reagan to support the treaty. Reagan had stated in 1976, "We bought it. We paid for it. And we should keep it." The treaty made it through the Senate by two votes, only after Carter and the Panamanians reluctantly accepted a reservation that permitted unilateral American intervention in a crisis. One junior senator, Dennis DeConcini (D-N.M.), whose undecided vote was desperately needed by treaty supporters, forced that reservation on the administration. Despite the DeConcini clause, Sen. Orrin Hatch (R-Utah) saw fit to label the treaty as "the culmination of a pattern of appeasement and surrender." In an augury of things to come, to gain public support for the treaty Carter became the first president to appear on a radio call-in show.

In 1980, Ronald Reagan ran against Carter as the candidate who would restore American power and prestige in the world. He claimed that under the weak Democratic leader the United States had permitted Communism to expand in Central America and Africa. Moreover, from November 1979 through the campaigning season and beyond, Americans were held hostage in Tehran by young militants working for the fiercely anti-American Ayatollah Khomeini, who had emerged as the leading power in Iran after the overthrow of the shah earlier that year. The issue of the hostages in Tehran, placed on the top of America's agenda by constant media attention, was the main reason Carter launched a risky and ultimately disastrous rescue mission in April 1980. Carter's chief of staff, Hamilton Jordan, urged the action "to snatch our people up . . . [to] prove to the columnists and our political opponents that Carter was not an ineffective Chief Executive who was afraid to act." Carter himself explained that he had "to give expression to the anger of the American people. If they perceive me as firm and tough in voicing their rage, maybe we'll be able to control this thing." Carter's poll numbers against his main opposition within the Democratic party, Sen. Edward M. Kennedy (D-Mass.), rose during the early months of the crisis, proving again that the public tends to rally around a president in an international crisis, at least in its initial stages.

During the difficult campaign he waged against Kennedy for the Democratic nomination, Carter hinted that he was on the verge of achieving a diplomatic breakthrough on the morning of an important primary in Wisconsin. There was no diplomatic breakthrough. Of Carter's concern about reelection and the Iranian issue, Cyrus Vance, his secretary of state who resigned over the rescue mission and the president's general shift to the right, commented that "smart politics produce bad policies."

For Reagan and his supporters, the hostage issue demonstrated how feeble the powerful United States had become, unable to free its citizens held captive by a Third World nation. With the Republicans and television newscasts keeping the issue alive, Carter was fatally wounded by his inability to bring the hostages home. During the late summer and early fall, when the issue receded somewhat from the headlines, Carter began closing the gap in the opinion polls. But just days before the election, on November 4, 1980, newspapers and television stations ran special features on the one-year anniversary of the hostage-taking. When Carter saw those stories that reminded voters of his embarrassing foreign policy failure, he knew that he had no chance of overtaking Reagan at the polls. During the primary season, Carter's popular support had been boosted by the media's overriding interest in the drama in Tehran as the public rallied around the flag. In the long run, however, the media's concentration on the issue for so long a time ultimately harmed his chances in the general election.

The hostages were valuable to Iran only so long as they were an issue in the United States. Some observers hoped that the media would ignore them in much the same way that they hoped that the media would ignore the hostages in Lebanon during the mid-eighties. But there was no way for a democratic government to keep the stories out of the newspapers and from the air, especially when the hostage-takers in Iran in particular renewed interest every few days with mediagenic hate-America parades and a variety of rumors, intrigues, and trial balloons.

Carter's Iranian and Soviet policies were not the only diplomatic issues with which Reagan had to work. He also assailed the Democrats for giving the Panama Canal and the canal zone to the Panamanians, an issue that Republicans used successfully against several targeted Democratic senators, including Frank Church. Finally, Carter appeared to be a dupe of Fidel Castro when he had to accept 100,000 refugees in the Mariel boatlift, many of whom turned out to be criminals.

In this campaign, as in 1968, Republican operatives interfered with a Democratic president's diplomacy. At the least, they purloined or otherwise obtained classified government documents to make certain that Carter had no October surprises for them in terms of a sudden release of the hostages. Most likely, they were assisted in their illegal activities by friendly CIA officials who opposed the Carter restraints on the agency. Some intriguing but unsubstantiated evidence suggests as well that Republicans may have struck deals with Tehran not to release the hostages until Reagan was safely elected in exchange for arms they desperately needed for their war against Iraq that began in 1980.

However the Republicans may have interfered with Carter's Iranian diplomacy, Americans who voted for Reagan were motivated primarily by domestic issues. Although they certainly agreed with the Republican candidate that Carter was inept in the foreign realm, that issue took second place to double-digit inflation and high unemployment. Nonetheless, they eagerly looked forward to inauguration day when Ronald Reagan would begin to clean house at home and put the Ayatollahs of the world in their place.

SIX

An Emerging New World Order,
1980–1994

IRAN FIGURED PROMINENTLY in the most serious scandal of the Reagan administration, the Iran–Contra affair. Had it not been for the fact that the genial and detached president, according to Oliver North, "did not always know what he knew," the United States might have experienced its second impeachment hearing in little more than a decade.

The scandal began when Congress, through the 1984 Boland Amendment, prohibited the Reagan administration from providing military aid directly or indirectly to the Contras in their war against the Sandinista regime in Nicaragua. The administration had supported such aid against what some Americans considered a hostile communist government since 1981; however, the illegal mining of Nicaraguan harbors in 1984 by American operatives and their agents shocked many legislators who were also angered because the CIA had not told their oversight committee about the action. The Boland Amendment, drawn up in response to the mining operation, reflected the general opposition to military intervention in Nicaragua that obtained throughout the entire period.

At the same time, under pressure to liberate Americans taken hostage by Iran-backed terrorists in Lebanon during the early 1980s, the administration engaged in secret negotiations with Iranians in 1985 and 1986 to trade arms for hostages. Ronald Reagan took very personally the need to liberate the American hostages in Lebanon. He was harassed continually by a hostage support-group, led by Peggy Say, the sister of hostage Terry Anderson, who took every opportunity to publicize her cause to maintain the pressure on the president. As with the Iranian hostage affair of 1979–81, the media concentrated attention on the issue, which was kept on the front pages by the periodic release or capture of other hostages and the latest sensational rumors from Tehran and Beirut.

To some observers, this hostage story was not central to American national security interests. The numbers of hostages in Beirut were far fewer than those in Tehran, they were held by semi-independent terrorists and not a government, and most had placed themselves in harm's way by ignoring a State Department warning to leave civil war–torn Lebanon. But no matter what the administration said and did, the implications of this news story, which just would not go away, challenged Ronald Reagan's "macho" image. He had won the election in 1980 in part because he represented himself as a much tougher commander-in-chief than Jimmy Carter.

Although no Boland Amendment prohibited an arms-for-hostages transaction, the president and his aides had earlier taken a strong position against such a policy and even originated Operation Staunch, a worldwide arms embargo against the Iranians. Further, they were supposed to report arms sales of such a magnitude to Congress. When the complicated sale of arms to Iran for hostages in Lebanon produced "residuals" in the form of profit leftover from arms purchases, North channeled them to the Contras. During congressional hearings about the affair in 1987, he claimed that the Boland Amendment did not apply to the National Security Council, where he worked. Of course, Congress assumed that only the State and Defense departments and the CIA would have been authorized to make payments to the Contras. The NSC, which began as a simple liaison agency under Truman, had been transformed into a super-secret mini-CIA under Reagan to hide covert activities from congressional scrutiny. Since CIA Director William Casey died before he could testify, we may never know the extent of his alleged plans to create an "off-the-shelf" covert network that would perform functions denied to the CIA by federal statutes and congressional oversight.

With the assistance of the CIA as well, North had also raised money for the Contras from private American organizations and from American allies Saudi Arabia and Brunei. These voluntary contributions, he later claimed, did not violate the Boland Amendment, adding that even the residuals from the Iranian arms sales could be looked upon as a "contribution" from a third country (Iran!) to the Contras and thus did not constitute aid from the administration in violation of the Boland Amendment.

Nicaraguans voted the Sandinistas out of office in 1990 in an election arranged as part of the peace agreement that ended the civil war. They voted for the pro-American opposition in part because of the economic disruption, destruction, and horrors of the previous decade's war. According to North's and Reagan's supporters, had the administration not worked under the table to bypass Congress and even lied to the legislators, Communists would still be in power in Managua. As Attorney General Edwin Meese contended in 1985, repeating a theme that has echoed throughout this book, "It is the responsibility of the President to conduct foreign policy; limitations on that by Congress are improper as far as I am concerned." That statement came from the president's chief legal advisor and interpreter of the Constitution.

For his part, Secretary of State George Shultz worried about the impact of the Iran-Contra hearings, covered on the burgeoning Cable News Network (CNN), on the president's ability to engage in secret diplomacy with the Russians during 1987. Those hearings affected the Sandinistas as well. According to the U.S. ambassador to Nicaragua, Pres. Daniel Ortega and his colleagues did little each day except watch the hearings.

After the Iran-Contra affair blew up, Congress felt strong enough to involve itself directly in the peace process. Speaker of the House Jim Wright (D-Tex.) undertook several missions to Central America to offer his own suggestions about how the civil war in Nicaragua might end. At the start of his odyssey, he cooperated with the State Department, but according to Secretary Shultz he ultimately "spun out of control" and decided to go it alone. For a brief period, it appeared that the United States was operating two parallel foreign policies in the region, that of Jim Wright and that of Ronald Reagan. The State Department and the CIA were not pleased with the development but there was little they could do, aside from invoking the Logan Act, to restrain the speaker. After all, they could not stop private citizens Barbara Walters or Jesse Jackson from "negotiating" with foreign leaders, or did they even attempt several years earlier to stop several senators from "negotiating" terms of the Panama Canal Treaty with the Panamanian government.

Strong pressures from peace groups and from Congress also affected the Reagan administration's ability to do more to support the anticommunist regime in El Salvador in its war with communist insurgents. The president gave serious consideration to a more active U.S. military role in that civil war early in his presidency. One signal may have been the publication of a State Department White Paper in late February 1981 on "Communist Interference in El Salvador." Reagan's plans were affected by revelations of atrocities committed by the government the United States was backing. Despite the fact that his aides were able to bury information they had about the role played by leading figures in that government in the sensational murder of three nuns and a Catholic layworker, such heinous actions made it difficult for Americans to sympathize with the regime in San Salvador.

Reagan admitted that one of his "greatest frustrations" as president was his inability to convince Congress and the public of the importance of his Central American policy to national security. On this issue, like so many others in his presidency, a good deal of time and resources were spent trying to alter public opinion. One of his deputy press secretaries noted of his job, "The first, last and over-arching activity was public relations."

There were other, less legitimate ways to try to alter public opinion. Like Richard Nixon before him, Reagan went to the extreme of using the Internal Revenue Service to harass his foes. For example, the service challenged the tax-exempt status of the National Congress on Latin America (NACLA), which opposed his Central American policies. Although NACLA retained its status, the IRS investigation consumed much of its energies for a while. Despite activities such as these, and the popularity of the Great Communicator with a majority of Americans, Reagan could not obtain widespread support for his policies in Central America. From the mid-seventies through the early nineties, as part of the so-called Vietnam Syndrome, most Americans were far less interested in military interventions in the Third World than were the presidents, and certainly were fearful of getting mired in another guerrilla-style war.

To be sure, Reagan could have tried to risk intervention without the support of the majority of the public. But like Roosevelt and Johnson before him, domestic and not foreign policy issues were highest on his priority list. He, too, had a revolutionary legislative program, albeit one devoted to lessening and not increasing the government's role in society. He and his aides feared they would undercut support for that program by intervening more forcefully in Central America. This was another reason why they chose covert extralegal operations to pursue their goals in the region.

Of course, many Americans thrilled to Reagan's patriotic and tough speeches on other diplomatic issues and approved of his brief and safe invasion of Grenada in 1983. Despite his and Shultz's heated denials, that invasion may have been related in part to the political and personal embarrassment the president suffered when 241 Marines became victims of a terrorist's explosives in U.S. barracks in Lebanon. The Marines were part of a contingent of Western forces trying to keep the peace in Lebanon after Israel's 1982 invasion accelerated that country's drift toward violent anarchy.

Looking back, Shultz attributes the widespread popular support for the Grenada invasion, which, according to the military's own evaluations, was marred by terrible logistic errors and much unnecessary loss of life, to television images of liberated American medical students from Grenada kissing American soil as they landed in the United States. Television images did not always work against the U.S. government.

The victory in Grenada may have thrilled most Americans but not everyone was enthused about Reagan's intensification of the Cold War, symbolized by his use of the term "Evil Empire" to characterize the Soviet Union. Although those words frightened many Americans, according to the president's chief arms negotiator, Paul H. Nitze, they made many Russians ashamed because they knew the charge was true. Whatever the impact in the Soviet Union, in the United States a nuclear freeze movement, which enjoyed popularity throughout the country and in Congress in 1983, threatened to make foreign policy a key issue in the election of 1984. The Nuclear Weapons Freeze Campaign, a coalition that boasted over 10 million participants in over 6,000 local organizations, helped to alter the public agenda, if not attitudes, through its successful campaigns.

In 1983, the House passed a resolution in favor of a freeze of existing nuclear weapons at their then-current levels, the Catholic bishops issued a pastoral letter challenging the morality of nuclear deterrence, a book about nuclear winter, *The Fate of the Earth,* became a best-seller, and a widely seen television movie, *The Day After,* frightened Americans about the heating up of the Cold War. Secretary of State Shultz worried about how the film might affect public opinion on the delicate issue of installing Pershings, a new generation of intermediate-range missiles, in Western Europe. Indeed, he was so distressed that he appeared on television after the film in an attempt to limit the damage. He and his colleagues had already formed an Arms Control Information Working Group, which traveled the country, meeting with editors, civic groups, and college students and appearing on radio talk shows to contain the damage to their policies done by the Freeze.

Dovish pressures, as well as pressure from U.S. allies and his wife, Nancy, contributed to Reagan's decision to soften his rhetoric as the 1984 campaign began. Even though, as of 1984, he had been the first president since Hoover not to hold a summit with the Russians, he successfully finessed the issue in a campaign in which he routed the weak Democratic candidate, Walter Mondale.

The peace lobby, as well as most of the scientific community, strongly opposed the president's Strategic Defense Initiative (SDI), which it felt was not only provocative but a system that could only work in science-fiction movies. Interestingly, that lobby did not know that the Reagan administration had adopted SDI in part to recapture public support for their defense programs that had been weakened substantially by the freeze movement. Moreover, the peace lobby, as well as Congress, did not know at the time that the administration had not revealed the entire truth about the relative lack of success of early "Star Wars" tests. In an attempt to convince the Russians that SDI was viable and to convince Congress to continue funding the program, the Defense Department set up the tests in a way to suggest that significant progress had been made. However, even that information would not have helped Mondale in his futile campaign against the popular president. Although Mondale did not know it, the Soviet KGB and other agencies had tried to influence the election through information and disinformation campaigns that suggested that four more years of Reagan could jeopardize world peace.

Despite his landslide victory, Reagan's foreign policies were complicated by several developments on the homefront. During the 1970s and 1980s, new nationality groups appeared to exercise influence on American activities in the international sphere. Never a match for the American-Israeli Political Action Committee (AIPAC), the pro-Israeli lobby, the National Association of Arab-Americans (NAAA), founded in 1972, began to command attention in the media and Congress when arguing that the country was not even-handed in the Middle East and was spending far too much on aid to Israel. The Arab-American lobby did influence American attitudes toward Israel, which changed in the seventies and eighties, especially with the development of a new sensitivity toward the Palestinian problem and lingering concern about oil prices.

In 1975, one AIPAC official boasted, "We've never lost on a major issue." Three years later, Jimmy Carter pushed through Congress the sale of sixty F-15s to Saudi Arabia, a sale that led to the resignation of his chief liaison with the Jewish-American community. Then, in 1981, in a 52–48 vote, the Senate approved an agreement to sell Saudi Arabia AWACS planes and other equipment against which AIPAC had fought hard and long. Reagan complained about AIPAC, "I didn't like having representatives of a foreign country—*any* foreign country—trying to interfere with what I regarded as our domestic political process and the setting of our foreign policy." Sen. William Cohen (R-Maine), for one, claimed he voted for the AWACS sale against his better judgment because of the rise of anti-Israeli—and anti-Semitic—sentiment in the nation.

Most likely, the Reagan administration was aided by a deemphasis on the issue by the Israeli government in exchange for shared intelligence and even financial support for the Mossad, the Israeli secret service, from the CIA. In addition, between 1978 and 1980, the oil industry spent $4.5 million on the political campaigns of those friendly to its Middle East interests. As one oil lobbyist admitted candidly, "We came to a decision some time ago that the only way we could change the political fortunes of the petroleum industry was to change Congress."

Carter's and Reagan's victories over AIPAC suggested that there were limits to its fabled power, especially when a president wanted to contest that lobby. But AIPAC did reap some revenge. After the Carter administration took a position hostile to Israel in March 1980, members of the Jewish-American community helped Edward Kennedy defeat the president in a primary election in New York. Two years later, one of the senators who voted for the 1981 Saudi arms deal, Charles Percy (R-Ill.), the influential chair of the Senate Foreign Relations Committee, was defeated in his bid for reelection when Jewish-Americans worked vigorously for his pro-Israeli opponent, Paul Simon. In addition, after Israeli allies massacred Palestinians in refugee camps near Beirut that same year, the administration proved unable to "punish" Israel when it failed to convince Congress to reduce a supplementary aid bill to the Jewish state. Furthermore, in 1984, Reagan did not have the heart to contend with Israel's supporters in Congress when they fought against the sale of Stinger missiles to Saudi Arabia and Jordan.

During the Reagan and Bush administrations, some prominent politicians grumbled about AIPAC's influence. Bush's secretary of state, James Baker, allegedly referred to Jewish-Americans with an expletive when pointing out that they should be ignored since they did not vote for Bush in great numbers. In 1991, the president himself complained publicly about "1,000 lobbyists" who challenged his opposition to a $10-billion loan guarantee to Israel. Despite those lobbyists' alleged power, in the 1992 primary campaign Pat Buchanan challenged Bush for the Republican nomination arguing, among other things, against support for Israel, especially from what he labeled the "Amen corner" on Capitol Hill.

African-Americans also began to flex their muscles on foreign policy issues of interest to them. Beginning with the foundation of the Congressional Black Caucus in 1970 and TransAfrica Incorporated in 1978, African-Americans devoted special attention to South Africa. As with Arab-Americans and the Palestinian issue, they contributed information to the debate over American policy toward the white minority government. In 1986, supported by many allies in Congress, they helped push through a bill over the president's veto barring a wide variety of investments in that country. This was the first time since Richard Nixon's veto of the War Powers Resolution in 1973 that Congress overrode a presidential veto on a foreign policy matter. In a similar manner, Hispanic-Americans were successful in influencing proposed legislation on immigration reform. Spearheaded by the National Council of La Raza, which was founded in 1968, they helped defeat the Simpson-Mazzoli bill, which they felt was unfair to Mexican immigrants.

The role of such groups in the development of American foreign policy had not diminished, as some melting-pot theorists had earlier predicted, in part because assimilation had never been a complete process. Ethnic interest groups were alive and proliferating in the 1980s. Members of the oldest such group, the Irish-Americans, continued to offer support to the liberators of Northern Ireland from English rule. Violent rhetoric and even physical clashes marked the relationships between Hungarian- and Rumanian-Americans, Arab- and Jewish-Americans, and Serbian- and Croatian-Americans. Sen. Charles McC. Mathias (R-Md.) considered this to be a most unfortunate development: "Ethnic politics . . . have proven harmful to the national interest" and generate "fractious controversy and bitter recrimination." But there is little one can do about it. Daniel Patrick Moynihan, his Democratic colleague from New York, has long contended that ethnicity is one of the primordial features of humankind and continues to be a central factor in international relations, despite what Marxists and Realpoliticians have said and done.

New and increasingly effective nationality groups were not the only domestic pressures late twentieth–century presidents faced as they tried to construct their foreign policies. Despite the gradual warming of Soviet-American relations after Mikhail Gorbachev's accession to power in 1985, problems relating to the failings of the American economy impinged on both Reagan's and Bush's abilities to construct an American foreign policy based upon purely strategic considerations.

America's economic conflict with Japan in the eighties and into the nineties was an excellent example of an "intermestic" issue, one with international and domestic components. For over a decade, the U.S. automobile industry had been battered by Japanese competition. The main reason, despite administration and auto-executive complaints about an unlevel playing field, was the simple fact that Honda was making better cars than General Motors. Ronald Reagan and George Bush may have been free traders, but they could not ignore the clamor from their constituents to do something about Japanese automobiles. Economic conflict between Detroit and Tokyo, stemming primarily from the failure of the American automobile industries to compete, led to increasingly tense Japanese-American diplomatic relations. The popular media were full of stories of a coming economic war that could even lead to a shooting war. Many Americans took out their anxieties about Japanese competition on Japanese products—and people—in the United States and further complicated diplomatic relations. Visitors parked their Japanese-made cars at peril in the parking lot of national headquarters of the United Auto Workers in Detroit, and in one notorious case of mistaken identity, an autoworker killed a Chinese-American, Vincent Chin, because he thought he was a Japanese-American.

The United States did not come to the trade debate with Japan with entirely clean hands. On his January 1992 trip to Japan and Australia, Bush encountered Australian farmers who complained about subsidies to American farmers, which enabled them to undersell the Australians. Bush countered by pointing to subsidies the European Community awarded to their farmers as the reason for American price supports. Bush, like the Europeans, could not afford to alienate such an important sector of the economy and the electorate, even though he theoretically opposed all subsidies.

Those voters in the normally anticommunist farm belt were earlier enraged when Jimmy Carter embargoed wheat shipments to the Soviet Union to punish the Communists for invading Afghanistan in 1979. The United States had been selling wheat to the Soviet Union since 1963 when John Kennedy overcame spirited conservative opposition in Congress to promote the mutually beneficial trade. Conservatives adopted a different position in 1980 when fiercely anti-Soviet Ronald Reagan championed the farmers' cause in the election campaign, in another example of the complexities of intermestic politics. Reagan promised the farmers he would lift the embargo and he did.

Congress genuflected to agricultural interests in 1986 with the Bumpers Amendment to a Supplemental Emergency Appropriations bill that restricted foreign aid to nations that might use it to increase food production in sectors that competed with American farmers. The American Soybean

Association lobbied effectively for the amendment on behalf of its constituents. The Bumpers Amendment meant that the president could not work out certain aid agreements of benefit to recipients, and presumably to national security, because they might harm a small sector of the domestic economy.

In a comparable vein, one of the most popular and successful American initiatives of the Cold War was the Food for Peace program. On the surface, this program appeared to have been developed primarily to send American farm surpluses to friends who could not feed themselves. In reality, it had as much to do with the domestic economy as with foreign affairs. Legislators from farm states were strong proponents of the program since it enabled their constituents to dispose of surpluses that otherwise might have driven down agricultural prices.

A 1989 minicrisis highlighted the relationship between America's foreign and domestic food policies when Washington increased credits to the reforming Polish government to buy food. The Poles ultimately received less food for their credits because of the power of American farmers and unions who demanded that the food bought with American dollars be higher-priced American products sent on American vessels staffed by unionized crews.

Environmental politics was another intermestic issue that rose to prominence in the eighties. Most important in North America was the problem caused in Canadian-American relations by acid rain. Although both countries polluted one another's forests and lakes with acid rain, the bulk came from the United States to Canada. This issue was an unintended consequence of the lawful activities of American private enterprise. The solution, in terms of government-mandated sophisticated emission controls, turned out to be a costly one for companies and consumers alike. For many Canadians, it was the single most important issue in their relations with the United States.

Historically, Canada has generally been more willing than the United States to heed the warnings of environmentalists and conservationists. This reflects Canadian acceptance of greater government control over resources. As early as the 1890s conservationists, biologists, and even policymakers on both sides of the border were unable to create a plan for the conservation of fisheries in the Great Lakes because of the opposition of American fishing interests backed by legislatures in the Great Lake states.

The U.S. government also exercised little control over the relatively independent American banking system. Indeed, American banks were encouraged to loan money to Third World countries during the seventies and eighties. Many of the loans strapped those already struggling countries with huge foreign debts—or "debt bombs"—which affected their domestic stability when they tried to adhere to payment schedules and affected the solvency of the American banks when they defaulted. At the time, however, such loans appeared to be serving the interest of American foreign policymakers.

Not all Third World countries struggled during the period. Some in Asia, in particular within the ASEAN block, prospered to a point where they began to resemble Western European countries in terms of economic development. They did well in part because of the influx of capital into their relatively low-paying industries. As the United States lost control of its American-based multinational industries, those industries searched for the cheapest labor. This became a major issue of contention during the 1993 NAFTA debate, with the United States and Canada allegedly facing the exportation of millions of jobs to Mexico.

Many U.S. firms, including automobile companies, already had invested heavily in plants near the U.S. border in the *maquiladora* system. American unions and others feared that with NAFTA even more high-paying U.S. auto jobs would be transferred to Mexico, where wages were one-tenth or less of American wages. From the overall American perspective, NAFTA offered many benefits, including a more stable and prosperous Mexico, a decline in illegal immigrants because of that prosperity, and a growing market for American producers of industrial goods and foodstuffs. Autoworkers in the rust belt and elsewhere, influential in the Democratic party, were not convinced by the argument that in the long run more Americans would be helped by NAFTA than hurt by it. Throughout America's long history of tariff controversies, those who benefited from freer trade, often the majority of the consuming public, generally were less powerful than those who stood to lose by the opening of the American market to foreign competitors.

According to those who tried to convince legislators—and the public— to support NAFTA, Pres. Bill Clinton needed the bill not so much because of its effect on the United States and Mexico, but because he needed to appear to be in charge of economic policy as his negotiators worked on the far more sweeping GATT negotiations. Thus, the administration pulled out all stops in the House, "buying" votes through side deals with individual congresspersons who wanted to protect specific interests in their districts. With each vote bought for the greater political purpose of impressing the major economic powers, Clinton diluted NAFTA, much to the dismay of doctrinaire free-traders.

NAFTA, which Congress put on a "fast track" for presidents Bush and

Clinton, illustrated a trend in trade legislation that had been developing since the 1934 Reciprocal Trade Acts. From that point, Congress began to surrender a good deal of its control over such legislation because the political problems it posed were so intractable. Thus, according to economic historian I. M. Destler, legislators adopted "a pressure-diverting management system" that made the president increasingly more responsible for both the legislation and the negative political fallout it always produced.

Not all American industries suffered a decline in the seventies and eighties in competition with foreign producers. The independent and virtually unregulated American cultural "industry," which has long played a central role in U.S. foreign relations, flourished during the period. From the days since Washington sent "el Pato Donald" (Donald Duck) to Latin America during World War II to bolster support for the United States, the American film industry has dominated all others worldwide. In Latin America alone, for example, in 1969, 50 percent of all films shown in Chile and 70 percent of all films shown in Bolivia, Brazil, Paraguay, Peru, and Venezuela were made in the United States. In 1974, 84 percent of the television shows viewed by Guatemalans came from the United States and 50 percent of their world news came from United Press International and the Associated Press. By 1993, 80 percent of all box-office revenues in the world and one-half of all entertainment television programs involved American exports. In that year, the entertainment industry products constituted the second largest American export (jet engines were first). Even in France, which protected its film and television industries, 60 percent of all films and 50 percent of television fare shown in 1993 were made in America. That same year, revenues for the film industry reached $18 billion, of which 40 percent came from overseas sales. Concerned about the Americanization of their culture, France and several other European countries that wanted to protect their telecommunications industries made that issue one of the most difficult during the 1993 GATT negotiations.

By the early 1990s, the United States was exporting over 150,000 hours of television a week, CNN reached close to 100 countries, and MTV almost 200 million households. In many cases, CNN beat the CIA and other world-intelligence agencies to the news. As one State Department officer commented, "You can sit and watch things faster [on CNN] than you would get an official report." The United States had some inkling of the brave new electronic world to come when, in 1950, a wire service scooped the American ambassador in Seoul with the news that the North Koreans had invaded South Korea.

Sometimes American cultural penetration is resented. Because of economies of scale enjoyed by the U.S. film industry, once-thriving competitors in Canada and England have been weakened considerably. Aside from the economic impact of American cultural institutions, the messages in films laden with sex and crime do not always reflect well on the United States.

In general, except during World War II, the government has been both reluctant and unable to control the impact of American films, and culture in general, on other countries. The situation has become more complicated in recent years with the multinationalization of the communications industry. Nominally American companies have been taken over by megacorporations often dominated by foreign ownership. Moreover, it is in the economic interest of those corporations to present as international a product as possible so as not to appear too American. For example, in the 1980s, Ted Turner banned the use of the term "foreign country" on his 'round-the-clock CNN newscasts in order to make them appear more international and politically value-free.

A much more serious problem for American foreign relations was posed by the multinationalization of other vitally important segments of its economy. Although many "U.S." corporations are still based in the United States, like the movie studios and book-publishing companies, many are foreign-owned and others are loyal only to their stockholders, and thus owe little to the nation in which they are headquartered. They move workers and plants from country to country and make financial decisions without taking into account the needs of American economic or foreign policy. During the oil crisis of the 1970s, U.S.-based oil companies adopted policies on prices and production that were clearly not in the best interest of the United States—and there was precious little that the government could do about it.

On a few occasions, American corporations have independently assisted U.S. foreign policy when they developed enterprises for semi-charitable purposes in countries not very high on the State Department's foreign-aid list. For example, in the 1950s, the Rockefeller Foundation and the Kaiser Automobile Company sponsored separate industrial projects in Brazil that contributed to that country's economic development and political stability and thus supported U.S. foreign policy goals. But that was an exceptional case. Of course, one should not ignore the role of such private philanthropic institutions as the Rockefeller and Ford foundations and the Social Science Research Council, whose research programs, particularly in the Third World, often were influenced by the interests of American foreign policymakers. It would be hard to imagine one of those foundations funding a project developed by a group of Marxist college professors to assist Africans and Asians to nationalize private industries.

The multinationalization and internationalization of American businesses and the concomitant loss of control by and loyalty to Washington has become even more important in recent years as the amount of the gross national product (GNP) related to international trade has increased dramatically. For much of American history, less than 10 percent of the economy has involved foreign trade. As late as 1950, U.S. exports accounted for only 6.3 percent of its GNP and imports only 5.6 percent. By 1970, those figures had risen to 9.2 and 8.7 percent respectively and in 1990, they stood at 18.2 and 23.2 percent. Much of the imbalance in 1990 related to Japanese-American trade. In 1960, the United States sent $1.4 billion of goods to Japan and bought $1.1 billion. By 1990, American exports to Japan had risen to $48.6 billion while imports had skyrocketed to $89.7 billion.

With the end of the Cold War, trade policy began to replace security policy as the State Department's major concern. Early in his tenure in 1993, Secretary of State Warren Christopher told a gathering that his top priority was "American jobs." One could not imagine John Quincy Adams, Dean Acheson, or Henry Kissinger making such a statement. Not all U.S. leaders were pleased with this new thrust. A former ambassador warned that "we may be inadvertently conveying in our rhetoric that all of our problems are foreign economic problems and that people should not worry about Bulgaria or Albania or Russia because they are not creating jobs." Similarly, as the CIA faced huge budget cuts in the wake of the ending of the Cold War, it too began to emphasize its role in defending the American economy. The agency proclaimed that illegal industrial espionage, practiced even by U.S. allies in the new highly competitive international economy, would be an additional raison d'être.

The ability of the executive branch to alter trade and other international economic policies is complicated by the number of congressional committees involved in those issues. In the Senate, for example, at least sixteen permanent committees are interested in foreign and foreign economic policy issues. To be sure, the Armed Services Committee and Foreign Relations Committee are among those sixteen, but so too are the Committee on Agriculture, Nutrition, and Forestry, the Finance Committee, and the Committee on Commerce, Science, and Transportation. The intermestic activities of the latter three committees demonstrate how domestic considerations affect not only foreign economic policies, but foreign policies in general.

Several of the major events that accompanied the end of the Cold War illustrate intermestic politics as well. When the nations of Eastern Europe and the old Soviet Union moved toward capitalism and democracy, Americans cheered. They were less enthusiastic, however, when their new friends asked for billions of dollars in loans and credits to make it through the difficult transition to a free-market economy. As Republicans and Democrats approached the election of 1992 during a serious recession, they were nervous about offering the much-needed massive aid to foreigners while their own economy was in the doldrums. Some brave politicians, who contended that helping the former Communists to transform their system in 1992 could save billions in defense expenditures in the future, discovered that their reasonable message was not very popular.

As for defense cutbacks in the early 1990s, many observers assumed that once the Cold War was over, the United States would enjoy a huge "peace dividend" that would come with a downsizing of its military-industrial complex. That dividend had to wait, however, at least until the 1992 election because downsizing meant the closing of factories and bases, which had an enormous impact on local economies. Americans supported defense cuts in the abstract until they involved installations in their cities or counties. In 1990, defense industries still employed one in sixteen American workers, and 30 percent of all mathematicians and 25 percent of all physicists. Economists suggested that every cut in defense industries of $1 billion could lead to as many as 30,000 job losses.

George Bush's secretary of defense, Dick Cheney, not known as a Pentagon budget-slasher, did recommend the termination of several weapons systems, including the Midgetman mobile missile, the Osprey tilt-rotor plane, and the Grumman F-14 fighter. Congress rejected his cost-cutting program, with, for example, Thomas J. Downey, a liberal Democratic congressman from Long Island, the home of Grumman, explaining, "The significant job loss, the financial burdens placed on Grumman, and the rippling effect on smaller businesses threaten the future of the island." More important, during the election campaign of 1992, both major party candidates promised the maintenance of unneeded arms programs, including the Osprey that the Bush administration had earlier earmarked for extinction.

Even the simple reduction of armed-forces personnel threatened economic stability since it threw tens of thousands of young people on the job market during a time of high unemployment. Thus, the United States reached a position in the early 1990s where it had built up a massive military-industrial complex to fight an enemy that no longer existed. But that complex had become so important politically and economically that it could not be dismantled without creating a domestic tidal wave of opposition. Although of little solace to Americans, the Russians faced even more difficult problems. One of the reasons they dragged their feet in removing troops from Eastern Europe was because they had no homes or jobs for them.

FOREIGN POLICY SYMBOLS, if not foreign policy itself, figured prominently in the 1988 election. Both candidates, Republican George Bush and Democrat Michael Dukakis, tried to demonstrate that they were not "wimps." Dukakis, in particular, under the gun for appearing to be too peaceful a fellow to succeed Ronald Reagan, took a ride in a tank at a Michigan plant to demonstrate he was tough enough to command the American military. Unfortunately, the Massachusetts governor looked so silly in the tank that his well-publicized photo opportunity backfired. Bush was far more successful demonstrating that despite his preppy image he was a red-blooded American who would defend the nation against foreign enemies as well as domestic flag-burners. Moreover, he was helped by his impressive experience in foreign affairs, which included service as director of the CIA, head of the China mission, ambassador to the United Nations, and the vice-presidency, a record that stood in contrast to that of Dukakis, who had only been a governor.

Despite a dossier demonstrating his abilities to deal with the tough world of international politics, Bush still struck some observers as too timid during the first year of his presidency. Indeed, the "wimp" factor appeared again in early October 1989 when he failed to back a nearly successful coup to oust the year's Public International Enemy Number One, Gen. Manuel Noriega of Panama. The critical reaction to his inaction during the October coup—Sen. Jesse Helms (R-N.C.) referred to "a bunch of Keystone Kops"—may have helped convince Bush to launch the invasion of Panama in December in order to arrest its drug-running leader. Not surprisingly, while the Organization of American States was virtually unanimous in its condemnation of the United States' unilateral intervention, most Americans applauded the forceful and resolute manner in which the president had solved the Panamanian "crisis."

They were not so pleased to discover the once-friendly relationship between Noriega and the CIA. American agents had looked the other way at evidence of his drug dealing and the fact that Panama had become a major drug entrepôt because of the general's value as an intelligence source. This was not the first time American intelligence agents looked the other way when their "assets" dealt drugs. For example, in 1950, they sent money and arms to Corsican gangs in Marseilles to help their drug-running allies break communist-led strikes. Later, during the Vietnam War, the CIA supported the legendary Gen. Vang Pao and his mercenary Hmong army in Laos while turning a blind eye toward his heavy involvement in the drug trade. Critics allege that American airplanes were used in that trade. The vaunted "War on Drugs" became even more difficult to win when one part of the government winked at the importation of drugs into the United States that another part of the government was trying to stop.

Periodically during that War on Drugs, American officials bribed and pressured Latin Americans to stop drug cultivation in their countries. Peru and Bolivia even permitted American agents and military personnel to assist in crop substitution, aerial spraying, and, of course, law enforcement. But Latin Americans complained that the problem was not the growing of poppies on their farms or the supply; it was the demand, or the widespread use of drugs in the United States. They contended the drug war had to be won in the United States through better law enforcement, education, and treatment. Nevertheless, in 1992, Washington still spent $150 million on counternarcotics military aid to several Latin American countries.

Like presidents before him, Bush reacted aggressively to what he perceived to be extraconstitutional attempts by a Democratic-controlled Congress to limit his authority in the international sphere. For example, he vetoed a 1989 measure to extend Chinese students' visas in the wake of Beijing's Tiananmen Square massacre of pro-democracy dissidents because he "wanted to keep control of managing the foreign policy of this country as much as I can." Looking beyond the moral concerns of those on Capitol Hill to a day of reconciliation with Beijing, he did not want to irritate the Chinese government unduly. He also vetoed a 1989 foreign-aid appropriations bill with several congressional strings attached, a chemical weapons sanctions bill in 1990, and pocket-vetoed the fiscal year 1991 intelligence authorization bill, all of which, he charged, represented congressional usurpation of presidential authority in foreign policy making. With his wealth of experience in the tough and amoral international sphere, Bush jealously guarded his prerogatives against what he perceived to be amateurish and sentimental congressional encroachment.

His foreign policy expertise and contacts with leaders all over the world contributed to his relative success in the global crisis precipitated by Iraq's invasion of Kuwait in August 1990. During the first week of the crisis, he initiated a variety of actions as the nation's chief diplomat and commander-in-chief without congressional consultation. Quickly, however, he moved to bring Congress and the public on board. As during the Vietnam War, the homefront was a major factor in the president's ability to wage the political, and ultimately military, battles in the Gulf crisis of 1990–91. Learning from the failures of Johnson and Nixon during the Vietnam War, Bush made certain that he had the support of the population before he introduced escalatory policies. For example, although he did not request a declaration of war, he did ask Congress for approval to use force if necessary to remove Iraq from Kuwait. One advisor noted that "it will be easier to get the U.N. to agree than Congress." But he did get Congress to approve the use of force by votes of 53–47 in the Senate and 250–103 in the House.

Before the war started, American forces in Saudi Arabia were hampered by the fact that Congress had to approve all military expenditures for specific items that cost more than $200,000. When coalition leader Gen. H. Norman Schwarzkopf determined that those tight purse-strings were making it impossible to plan his offensive, he went to the Japanese embassy in Riyadh for the needed funds.

By this time, most Americans believed the myth that they had lost the war in Vietnam, in part because of weakness at home produced by the media, which allegedly supported antiwar positions. Despite the lack of evidence to support the myth, even those who ran the media believed it. Concerned about their negative image during the Gulf crisis, they undercovered dissenting activities and generally accepted the strict constraints placed upon them in combat areas. Seventy-nine percent of Americans polled approved of those censorship measures.

Of course, there was little that George Bush could do about the unprecedented global reach of CNN's services. During the late fall of 1990, CNN broadcast extensive coverage of the congressional hearings on the Gulf crisis. Many expert witnesses, including prominent American military leaders, told Congress—and viewers worldwide—that going to war with Iraq would be a terrible mistake. It is possible that Saddam Hussein, who saw or was informed about these debates, may have decided not to pull out of Kuwait because congressional testimony convinced him that Americans would not call his bluff. There were those who contended that the North Vietnamese had been similarly encouraged when they saw in newsreel footage and read in American media reports about dissent in the United States. Similarly, in 1994, Haiti's Gen. Raoul Cédras allegedly was emboldened to hang on to his power until the eleventh hour because of CNN coverage of overwhelming opposition in Congress and the public to Bill Clinton's threatened military intervention.

General Schwarzkopf is convinced that Saddam Hussein was watching his many press conferences on CNN during the crisis; the general thus tailored his comments to achieve the maximum possible effect in Baghdad. Television coverage of the war also caused problems with America's allies. Furious when cameras caught pictures of women dancing for the troops on sacred Saudi soil, a prince from the royal family told Schwarzkopf, "You must order them taken off the TV." The general could not censor the newscasts but he was able to convince the networks not to cover the covert Christmas and Hanukkah services for American forces in the Islamic nation. However, the general and the administration did not try to stop the Public Broadcasting System from running its popular "Civil War" series in September 1990, even though they feared its heart-rending depictions of that bloody conflict might make American citizens less supportive of the military buildup in Saudi Arabia.

By the 1980s, CNN became so adept at covering international affairs that it often "scooped" intelligence agencies. During the Gulf War, leading officials of the KGB in the Soviet Union were glued to CNN for their news while the American secretary of defense referred to its reports to support his arguments during press conferences. Similarly during the crisis, one American official noted that one way to get a message to the Russians was to make a public announcement since "diplomatic communications just can't keep up with CNN." Given its worldwide reach, the network had achieved the capability of helping to set the foreign affairs agenda for world leaders. As early as the late '70s, Carter aide Lloyd Cutler expressed dismay at how much of the timing and even substance of administration foreign policy was being affected by television news deadlines and schedules. He complained, "Whatever urgent but less televised problem may be on the White House agenda on any given morning, it is often put aside to consider and respond to the latest TV news bombshell in time for the next broadcast. In a very real sense, events that become TV lead stories now set the priorities for the policy-making agenda."

Independent international television networks, not easily controlled by host governments, continue to figure prominently in the main events of our time. No doubt the failure of the counterrevolutionaries to censor the international television services in Moscow in the summer of 1991 contributed to the success of Boris Yeltsin's defense of the revolution. And there is evidence that the American Broadcasting Network's special interest in Bosnia in 1992 kept the spotlight on the atrocity stories and even, according to a State Department official, saved one specific town in that civil war–torn republic.

Despite the increasing prominence of electronic journalism in international affairs, print journalists, sometimes assisted by the broadcast media, continued to play their historic roles. In Washington during the '80s, a new generation of Walter Lippmanns began to appear on television and in the newspapers and magazines to become major actors in the dialogue among the Fourth Estate, the administration, and the public. Referred to as the "punditocracy," they included such people as New York Times columnist William Safire, the syndicated McLaughlin Group, and the New Republic. A word about foreign policy in their columns or on television often created ripples in the international system. During the mid-sixties, Lyndon Johnson said that the editorials of his friend at the Washington Post were "worth two divisions in Vietnam." On the other hand, LBJ complained that the reports from Vietnam from AP correspondent Peter Arnett have "been more damaging than a whole battalion of Vietcong." In 1989, after the publication of several Safire columns on the relations between Libya and German poison-gas makers, German leader Helmut Kohl remarked that "this Safire fellow has done more damage to German-American relations than any other individual." A Safire column in early 1994 also figured prominently in Bobby Ray Inman's decision to withdraw his name from consideration as Pres. Bill Clinton's secretary of defense.

Memories of the Vietnam War affected more than just media relations in the Gulf War. Bush explained,

> If there must be war, we will not permit our troops to have their hands tied behind their backs, and I pledge to you there will not be any murky ending. . . . In our country I know that there are fears of another Vietnam. Let me assure you, should military action be required this will not be another Vietnam. This will not be a protracted, drawn-out war.

Bush felt he had to end the war immediately after the Iraqis had withdrawn from Kuwait, not only because of pressures from his international coalition but because he felt that any attempt to take Baghdad and throw Saddam Hussein from power would lead to a much longer war with many more casualties. Given the Vietnam—and Korean—War experiences, he feared a rapid diminution of his widespread popular support once the war dragged on for a while. Indeed, he did not aid the Kurds and Shiites, whom he had previously encouraged, in their postwar rebellions against Saddam in fear of that longer war, which would erode his high standing in the public opinion polls. General Schwarzkopf again points to the media as central in this situation. He wanted to continue the war at least one more day but claimed that television footage of his bloody mopping-up operations on what the networks labeled the "Highway of Death" made it impossible for President Bush to continue the war. It was also true that although the United States led the coalition, it was a coalition operating under the authority of the United Nations. Most of the members of that coalition were reluctant to extend ground operations to Baghdad.

At home, increasing American involvement in peacekeeping activities with the United Nations after the end of the Cold War gave rise to a new isolationism or unilateralism in which many Americans worried about surrendering sovereignty to international institutions. After American soldiers were killed in Somalia on another UN operation, the House of Representatives, in the fall of 1993, rejected an administration request for $30 million to help the world body train peacekeeping forces. One representative complained that "the administration is on the verge of moving United States foreign policy where the United Nations determines how and where operations are abroad." A month later, Senate Republicans unsuccessfully attempted to bar American forces from serving under UN command.

The fact that the Gulf War coalition did not depose Hussein made it more difficult for Bush to boast about his achievements in the war during the 1992 presidential campaign. One of his opponents, Bill Clinton, avoided military service in a controversial manner and even participated in the antiwar movement during the Vietnam War. Only a small percentage of the electorate claimed that Clinton's activities in the late sixties and early seventies affected their votes. It may well be that the 1992 election marked the beginning of the end of the Vietnam War as a volatile issue in American politics.

The dramatic fall in Bush's approval ratings as president from the dizzying heights they had reached in the aftermath of the Gulf War demonstrates how difficult it is to translate diplomatic or military success into electoral victory—unless the timing is perfect, as was the case of the missile crisis and the 1962 congressional elections. By the campaigning season in 1992, economic reverses had easily replaced diplomatic successes as the major interest of Americans.

The 1992 election was the first since 1940 in which foreign policy did not figure as an important issue. As in 1988, when he ran against Dukakis, Bush raised the experience issue. In addition, Clinton criticized the administration's policies in Bosnia and Haiti and then, when elected, in essence continued them. In fact, on the latter issue, when Clinton took office, Haitians resumed their attempts to emigrate to the United States, thinking that they would be more welcome by the new administration than the previous one. They were sadly mistaken. Ross Perot, a third-party candidate who received almost 20 percent of the popular vote in November 1992, devoted scant attention to foreign policy in his campaign, with the exception of opposing NAFTA and foreign lobbyists.

Like Woodrow Wilson who, eighty years earlier, expected to spend most of his time on domestic reform, Clinton discovered that the outside world intruded on his best-laid plans early in his administration. His programs soon became jeopardized in part because of the popularly held perception that he was a weak and indecisive leader when it came to formulating policies for Bosnia and especially for Somalia. The omnipresent electronic media, the same media that George Bush had excoriated for engaging in a love affair with the telegenic Arkansas governor in 1992, developed and reinforced the impression of the administration's incompetence through coverage of an apparently disastrous military engagement in Somalia. One wonders what would have happened to Woodrow Wilson had CNN been around to interview the elusive Pancho Villa as it interviewed the equally elusive Mohammad Farah Aidid, whose forces were responsible for the death of American soldiers in Mogadishu.

The loss of eighteen soldiers in Somalia produced a bipartisan call to terminate the American peacekeeping mission. Even though the United States now had an all-volunteer army, its citizens were reluctant to see even professional soldiers die in a crisis whose national security implications seemed remote. There was a time, before television, when great powers could send their forces to the Third World and suffer the loss of even hundreds of soldiers without raising much attention back home. This relatively new factor in modern diplomacy certainly made it difficult for the president of the United States, or for the leaders of England and France in Bosnia, and even Russia in Afghanistan, to project their power as they once did.

The ending of the Cold War apparently did not make the president's job in the international sphere any easier. And it certainly did not alter the complicated relationship between domestic and international politics. To take just one example of how the more things change the more they remain the same, in August 1994, Fidel Castro reappeared on the American political scene to make life difficult for Bill Clinton in much the same way that he made life difficult for Jimmy Carter in 1980. To resolve some of his own economic and political problems brought about by the end of the Cold War (and the end to Soviet subsidization of his feeble economy), the Cuban leader once again made it easier for dissidents to leave their homeland for the United States. Since 1966, Washington had permitted all Cubans who arrived in Florida to remain in the country without having to prove that they were political refugees. This policy worked well when the number of refugees who made it across the Florida Straits in makeshift vessels numbered a few hundred a year. But once Castro purposely opened the floodgates, as he did during the Mariel boatlift of 1980 and again in 1994, Floridians and others who had to take in hundreds and then thousands of boat people became concerned about the costs of serving as a refuge for anticommunists.

Looking back at the price Jimmy Carter paid in 1980, Bill Clinton confronted a myriad of cross-cutting domestic pressures. In the first place, most observers had given him relatively low marks in foreign affairs because of his indecisiveness, particularly on Haiti and Bosnia. Thus, he had to demonstrate that he could handle international crises with more dispatch and authority. In addition, Florida was an important state politically with the crucial 1994 congressional elections on the horizon. Most Floridians demanded an end to the open-door policy for Cuban immigrants and their Democratic governor, who was up for reelection, declared a state of emergency. On the other hand, leaders of the powerful Cuban-American community opposed any alteration in the Cuban immigration policy. Of course, that community always voted Republican because the GOP appeared to be more anti-Castro than the Democrats. Further, African-American politicians and pressure groups in the United States, among others, demanded to know why the mostly white Cubans were permitted entrance into the United States while darker hued Haitian refugees were being taken to detention centers in the Caribbean.

While all this was going on, the president tried to maneuver through a balking Congress two major domestic political programs, a crime bill and a health-care bill, before the fall elections. His actions or lack of them on the Cuban refugee matter affected popular and congressional impressions of his leadership skills and ability to defend American national security. Any further drop in his "presidential approval" ratings, because of ineptitude over Cuban policy, could have eroded support in Congress for his domestic agenda. Thus, the many domestic problems he faced during that difficult summer confounded any attempt by Clinton to view the Cuban issue in terms of narrow national security considerations.

Domestic politics also figured prominently in Clinton's Haitian policy that late summer and early fall. In the first place, the restoration to power of Jean Bertrand Aristide, the democratically elected president, was a major issue for the forty-member Congressional Black Caucus, a key group within the fast shrinking bloc of Clinton supporters. Intense pressure from that group, among others, had earlier compelled the president to tighten the economic embargo on Haiti, an action that led to an increased number of refugees who strained Florida's resources. Presumably U.S. national security interests in Haiti revolved around halting the flow of immigrants.

Further, although he claimed that the Constitution gave him the authority to invade the island in a police action, the president could not ask Congress to support his policy because he knew that such a request would be rejected. Even had Clinton presented his case in the most idealistic terms about the restoration of democracy in a near neighbor, most legislators, supported by the public opinion polls, did not want to lose one American life in a Haitian operation. Some even complained that Clinton was planning his own September or October surprise to achieve a foreign policy victory on the eve of the important congressional election. Of course, that accusation made little sense since the vast majority of the population opposed the invasion of Haiti.

Whether or not Clinton's Haitian policy revolved around idealistic principles, there is no doubt that his idealism took a battering when in 1994 he ignored his previous year's threat to China to improve its human rights record or face a cutoff of trade with the United States. In the end, he decided that China was more important to the American economy and to his North Korean policy than any abstract principles, especially considering that there was no way that the proud Beijing government was going to change its political system to accommodate an American president.

As Clinton prepared to do battle with a new Republican Congress in 1995, with the head of the Senate Foreign Relations Committee suggesting that he was unfit to be commander-in-chief, he faced a host of foreign policy problems with significant domestic components. Aside from a highly partisan Congress, he had to worry about textile producers in the South opposed to GATT, Cuban-Americans demanding the resettlement of refugees from detention camps, the military lobby decrying the slashing of the Pentagon budget, California voters adopting Proposition 187, a law that insulted the government of Mexico, and prying journalists who revealed every detail of his tortuous Bosnian diplomacy even before the ink dried on his latest internal position paper. Theodore Roosevelt, Woodrow Wilson, Franklin D. Roosevelt, and Richard Nixon, among other presidents, would not have been surprised by the difficulties Bill Clinton encountered as he tried to fashion a rational foreign policy in a democracy.

Democracy and Foreign Policy:
A Balance Sheet

FOR OVER TWO CENTURIES, American presidents have had to concern themselves with an unusually wide variety of domestic influences as they developed and conducted foreign policies. Whether those influences included the imminence of elections, partisan opposition from Congress, parochial economic considerations, or the lobbying of ethnic groups, presidents frequently found themselves constrained from pursuing policies they considered to be in the national interest. Of course, they themselves often cloaked their own partisan policies, directed toward their reelections, in the mantle of the national interest.

We have seen—from Washington's Farewell Address to John Adams's response to France's peace overtures in 1800, Madison's consideration of his options in the presidential election year of 1812 to a series of real and perceived "October surprises" since 1968—how electoral politics have influenced security policy decisions. To be sure, in all cases, candidates convinced themselves that their positions on those decisions had nothing to do with the upcoming elections. Indeed, there is little *documentary* evidence to demonstrate the contrary; few leaders would admit in public—or even to their diaries—that such self-interested motives lay behind their foreign policies.

In a similar vein, few senators or representatives would admit that their opposition to a presidential foreign policy was based upon anything but the most patriotic of motives. Nonetheless, partisanship lay behind Federalist opposition to Jefferson's Louisiana Purchase windfall, Democratic hostility toward McKinley's peace treaty with Spain, Republican rejection of Woodrow Wilson's League of Nations, and, more recently, that same party's refusal to approve GATT in the fall of 1994, even though it was originally a Reagan-Bush initiative, because it did not want to hand Bill Clinton a "victory" before the congressional elections.

The frequent success of parochial economic groups in attracting Washington's attention and ultimate support has been equally frustrating for those concerned about fashioning a rational foreign policy that reflects a truly national interest. One can begin, of course, with those encouraging the government to support formal and informal colonialism because of their needs for markets and raw materials. With disproportionate influence in Washington, the media, and even the churches, the interests of this informal group, which, not surprisingly, claimed to represent the best interests of all Americans in an early "trickle-down" theory, often led the United States into unnecessary international conflicts and wars in Latin America and Asia.

But one does not have to concentrate on promoters of the Open Door to find evidence of the impact of narrow economic interests on American foreign policy. For example, throughout the nineteenth century, the activities of New England fishermen embroiled the White House in unwanted controversies with London. Or similarly, one worries about the influence of a handful of New Panama Canal Company stockholders on the decision to choose Panama over Nicaragua for an isthmian canal, or of newspaper publishers interested in cheap newsprint during the debate over Canadian reciprocity in 1911, or of the American oil industry in affecting U.S. policy in the Middle East during the middle decades of the twentieth century.

In the latter case, the oil companies competed for influence with the Jewish-American lobby, in just one of the many examples of how ethnic groups helped to determine American policies. Throughout the nineteenth century, Irish-Americans proved to be a formidable obstacle to improved Anglo-American relations. And even in this century, as late as the 1980s, their support for the Irish Republican Army's rebellion in Northern Ireland contributed to an increase in tension in relations between London and Washington. Contrary to the expectations of melting-pot theorists, ethnic groups, now including Arab-Americans, African-Americans, and Greek-Americans, among others, continue to pressure leaders who appear to slight their original homelands' interests.

The problems posed by these domestic influences on foreign policymakers have been compounded by the free, partisan, and sometimes irresponsible media. From the leaking of the Jay Treaty to William Randolph Hearst's provocative activities prior to the Spanish-American War, to television's ability to generate interest in or sympathy for one civil war–racked nation or another, the media have often made it impossible for American diplomats to practice their craft with the cool rationality and sometimes necessary secrecy that characterize a sound foreign policy.

As we have seen, the central role of domestic politics in determining American foreign policy has changed little since Washington's day, and, if anything, has increased in potency and complexity. Writing in the 1830s, when the United States was a marginal player on the international scene, Alexis de Tocqueville was prescient when he worried about the ability of the unusual new nation to operate an effective diplomacy. Over a century later, surveying the history of American foreign policy, Walter Lippmann expressed similar concerns, concluding that "the people have imposed a veto upon the judgments of informed and responsible officials. They have compelled the governments, which usually knew what would have been wiser, or was necessary, or was more expedient to be too late with too little, or too long with too much." Dean Acheson agreed. After suffering withering political attacks when he was secretary of state, he feared that "the limitation imposed by democratic political practices makes it difficult to conduct our foreign affairs in the national interest."

But is the American diplomatic record, allegedly hobbled by democracy run rampant, really that bad? Although the United States did not always opt for the wisest foreign policy once it joined the major-power club at the turn of the century, it did survive its international crises and wars, while many other nations, which operated with fewer domestic constraints on their foreign policies, did not. Further, America's diplomatic friends and foes learned to live with its electoral cycles, nationalist campaign rhetoric, free-wheeling media, sensitive ethnic groups, and an independent legislative branch of government.

Obviously, the nation's impregnability until the 1960s contributed to its relative success, as did its unparalleled economic power and unusual political stability. It may be true as well that the need to cover all domestic bases in times of crisis made American foreign policy stronger because it generally was supported by most citizens. In the short run, states with undemocratic systems, and even those with democratic systems in which diplomats operated on longer leashes, appeared to have the advantage in diplomatic duels in which secrecy and dispatch were prime considerations. Such freedom, however, did not necessarily result in more rational policies than those produced by the cumbersome American system. In fact, that cumbersome system may have saved American leaders from making the sort of blunders committed by leaders in more autocratic states. Autocrats' abilities to move quickly and unilaterally have led them into dangerous crises and disastrous wars that might have been avoided in the United States. If war entries are one measure of diplomatic failure, American participation in eight big international wars over 200 years (1812, Mexican-American, Spanish-American, World War I, World War II, Korean, Vietnam, Gulf), when compared to double that amount from other major powers, makes the government's record appear to be praiseworthy. Yet, eight wars may be too many for a nation without large and menacing neighbors, and protected by vast oceans from other major military players in the international system. And of those eight, only World War II was precipitated by a direct attack on U.S. territory. Entry into the other seven, affected by domestic issues often unrelated to the issues that brought about the prewar crisis, may not all have been justified in terms of national security interests.

With the end of the Cold War and the elimination of the major-power enemy against whom most Americans would rally in a crisis, domestic influences may pose more problems for American foreign policymakers. Complicating matters is the dramatic increase in the number of democratic states in Eastern Europe, the former Soviet Union, and in Latin America, Africa, and Asia. They, too, will have to deal with more cumbersome political systems, often involving legislative-executive conflict, irredentist ethnic groups, local economic concerns, and periodic elections. Perhaps this development will level the playing field in the post–Cold War era but it also may bring into other nations' foreign policies the alleged irrational influences of parochial domestic interests. Thus, for example, as Americans tried to lead NATO and the United Nations on Bosnian policy in the spring of 1993, they had to worry about the political weakness of their putative democratic allies. Russia's Boris Yeltsin was concerned about his pro-Serbian population, Germany's Helmut Kohl, like many other European leaders on shaky ground because of a fragile economy, was bothered by pro-Croatian sentiment among Germans, and France's François Mitterand feared his faltering government might collapse if French soldiers in the UN peacekeeping force were killed because of bombing raids advocated by the United States.

Commenting on how foreign policy may be developed in the United States during the last few years of the twentieth century, Sen. Sam Nunn (D-Ga.) warned in 1993, "Today, the time element is not the same as it was during the cold war. There is the perception that there's more time for decision-making, more time for debate, and that inevitably means that Congress is going to be much more involved than in the past." Looking at congressional involvement during the 1970s and 1980s when the Cold War was on, one wonders what more involvement will mean. But as Louis Brandeis wrote in *Myers v U.S.* in 1926, the purpose of the separation of powers is "not to avoid friction but . . . to save the people from autocracy." Or as Warren Christopher contended in 1982, "we must accept the fact that American foreign policy making will never be as efficient as it is in undemocratic countries and that is not necessarily a bad thing."

It is true, however, that the democratic American foreign policy has not been especially erratic or volatile since the end of World War II when foreign affairs took center stage on the political scene. Despite what has been said during electoral campaigns about rollback and new frontiers, American foreign policies have been as consistent as in most other countries. For one thing, most of the nation's leaders come from the same class and background and tend to position themselves in the center of two parties that have not differed very much on principles of foreign policy. Moreover, for good or ill, the United States has developed a more or less permanent cadre of experts who show up continually in their parties' cabinets and National Security Councils. For example, 90 percent of George Bush's cabinet had served in high government positions in the past. As for those pernicious special interest groups that concern democratic theorists, they have generally been more effective on domestic issues than on international issues. And even on international issues, they tend to be strongest on economic policies that do not directly affect national security, except perhaps for election years when, as we have seen, candidates have often politicized such matters. In addition, for every group pushing in one direction, another group pushes in the other, as in the way doves have been generally balanced by hawks and Jewish-Americans by Arab-Americans now and the State Department's Arabists and their friends earlier.

Further, the constraints posed by increased congressional meddling in the future, along with interest and ethnic groups and lobbies, may not be as important as they once were since a "new world order," composed of increasingly more democratic states, may be more peaceful than the last, once the problems left over from the old order are resolved. A hopeful sign is that over the past 200 years, democratic states have rarely if ever engaged in war with one another.

As the outside world becomes less threatening, Americans may want to retreat again into a neoisolationism that will be attractive to those wanting to reduce government expenditures. During the early 1990s, politicians like Pat Buchanan were hailed by many citizens when they called for dispensing with most foreign aid programs, which amounted to only 1 percent of federal spending in 1992, and less involvement with the United Nations and other international bodies.

However Americans respond to such an approach to the international system, with the end of the Cold War, popular analyses of international problems have become less concerned with strategic realities than with moral and humanitarian issues. For example, both the Bush and Clinton administrations found it easier to send troops to Somalia, an area of marginal national security significance, than to the former Yugoslavia, a potential tinderbox for a broader European war, when Americans responded emotionally to starving Somalian children staring out at them from their television sets. Similarly, both administrations found themselves hamstrung by the MIA issue when they attempted to normalize relations with Vietnam, even though such a policy made a good deal of economic and political sense.

In cases like these and others we have examined, it appears that the American democratic system has not always produced the most rational and effective foreign policies. At least, that is what Tocqueville worried about in the 1830s and so-called realists like John Hay, Walter Lippmann, Dean Acheson, George F. Kennan, and Henry Kissinger have complained about ever since. If only U.S. diplomats could operate according to the principles of *Realpolitik* established by the Metternichs and the Bismarcks. On the other hand, as one examines the total American diplomatic experience, it is clear that presidents and aides like Acheson and Kissinger may have committed more blunders when they tried to operate secretly and in an undemocratic fashion than when they produced programs that were influenced by and acceptable to the wide variety of often insular groups outside the State Department, the Oval Office, and the National Security Council. Further, much of the time, even with a free press and obstreperous congresspersons, they were able to employ traditional diplomatic strategies that would have pleased the most cold-blooded realpolitician. Perhaps Tocqueville was not so prescient after all.

Bibliographic Essay

Introduction

IN THE BIBLIOGRAPHY for his article on "Politics and Foreign Policy" in Alexander DeConde, ed., *The Encyclopedia of Foreign Policy* (1978), Fred Harvey Harrington notes, "One can find pertinent material [on domestic politics] in almost every volume dealing with American diplomatic history, but there is an urgent need for an overall coverage of the topic from the beginning to the present." Harrington's analysis of the literature in the field is still accurate. Although political scientists have written texts and monographs on the subject, there is no single historical study of the way domestic politics have affected foreign policy throughout American history.

There are, of course, many related surveys that bear on the subject. Robert Dallek examines cultural themes and popular moods in *The American Style of Foreign Policy: Cultural Politics and Foreign Affairs* (1983). Michael Hunt concentrates on intellectual and cultural currents in *Ideology and U.S. Foreign Policy* (1987). Richard J. Barnet analyzes the positions taken by presidents and the public in *The Rockets' Red Glare: When America Goes to War, The Presidents and the People* (1990). One of the founders of modern American diplomatic history, Thomas A. Bailey, contributed *The Man in the Street: The Impact of American Public Opinion on Foreign Policy* (1948), an early pathbreaking study. For skeptical views about the public that Barnet, and to some degree Bailey, celebrate, Walter Lippmann, *Essays in the Public Philosophy* (1955), George F. Kennan, *American Diplomacy: 1900–1950* (1951), and Gabriel A. Almond, *The American People and Foreign Policy* (1950), serve as classic counterpoints.

Based upon research grounded in the experiences of foreign service officers in the 1950s and 1960s, Bernard C. Cohen's thoughtful *The Public's Impact on Foreign Policy* (1973) is enlightening. The best textbook in the field is political scientist Jerel A. Rosati's *The Politics of United States Foreign Policy* (1993). Although somewhat outdated, another work directed to political science students, Barry B. Hughes's *The Domestic Context of American Foreign Policy* (1978) remains useful. Political scientists are the chief contributors as well to Charles W. Kegley and Eugene R. Wittkopf, eds., *The Domestic Sources of American Foreign Policy: Insights and Evidence* (1988), a reader that contains several articles relevant to historians' concerns. See also David A. Deese, ed., *The New Politics of American Foreign Policy* (1994).

Among books on democratic theory, Kenneth N. Waltz's *Foreign Policy and Democratic Politics: The American and British Experience* (1967) is still thought-provoking. Another stimulating discussion can be found in Max Beloff, *Foreign Policy and the Democratic Process* (1955). Robert Strausz-Hupé's *Democracy and American Foreign Policy: Reflections on the Legacy of Alexis de Tocqueville* (1995), although too discursive and current policy–oriented, has some interesting things to say. For the inherent tension between Congress and the president over foreign-policy issues, Abraham D. Sofaer, *War, Foreign Affairs, and Constitutional Power: The Origins* (1976), and Henry Bartholomew Cox, *War, Foreign Affairs, and the Constitution, 1829–1901* (1984), are indispensable. Among other useful studies of the same issue are Louis Henkin, *Foreign Affairs and the U.S. Constitution* (1990), and the more popular survey by John Lehman, *The 200-Year-Old Battle between the President and Congress over How America Goes to War* (1992). See also Robert J. Spitzer, *President and Congress: Executive Hegemony at the Crossroads of American Government* (1993), an up-to-date text, and W. Taylor Reveley, *War Powers of the President and Congress* (1981), for an interesting legalistic approach. Cecil V. Crabb and Pat M. Holt focus on the recent period in *Invitation to Struggle: Congress, the President, and Foreign Policy* (1989).

Although his impressive study revolves primarily around domestic politics, Stephen Skowronek's *The Politics Presidents Make: Leadership from John Adams to George Bush* (1993) suggests an interesting analytical framework. Somewhat less theoretical is *Presidential Wars and American Democracy: Rally 'Round the Chief* (1993) by John T. Rourke. Forrest McDonald's chapter on the development of the presidential role in foreign policy in his important *The American Presidency: An Intellectual History* (1994) is a useful contribution to the debate. For a while in the 1960s and 1970s, Aaron Wildavsky's concept of "The Two Presidencies," *Transaction* 4 (1966), was very influential. Beginning with presidents after Eisenhower, Joseph G. Dawson Jr., ed., *Commander in Chief: Presidential Leadership in American Wars* (1993), is a companion volume to the earlier Ernest R. May, ed., *The Ultimate Decision: The President as Commander in Chief* (1960). William Quandt, who worked in several administrations as a Middle East expert, worries about the president's ability to conduct an effective foreign policy in "The Electoral Cycle and the Conduct of Foreign Policy," *Political Science Quarterly* 101 (1986). See also Barbara Kellerman and Ryan J. Barilleaux, *The President as World Leader* (1991), and Deepa Mary Ollapally, *Containing Conflict: Domestic Factors and U.S. Policymaking in the Third World* (1993), which deals with the Cold War era.

As for Congress, W. Stull Holt's *Treaties Defeated by the Senate: A Study of the Struggle between Presidents and Senators over the Conduct of Foreign Relations* (1933) covers the contentious issue to 1933. On a related matter, Loch K. Johnson examines *The Making of International Agreements: Congress Confronts the Executive* (1984). Still useful is Robert A. Dahl, *Congress and Foreign Policy* (1950). Although it covers only a limited number of post–World War II years, Warren A. Miller and Donald E. Stokes's influential article, "Constituency Influence in Congress," *American Political Science Review* 57 (1963), demonstrates that foreign-policy issues rarely excite local constituencies. Another article that traces congressional activity during the Cold War is James M. McCormick and Eugene R. Wittkopf, "Bipartisanship, Partisanship, and Ideology in Congressional-Executive Relations, 1947–1988," *Journal of Politics* 52 (1990).

The best survey of the role of ethnicity in America's diplomatic history is Alexander DeConde, *Ethnicity, Race, and American Foreign Policy: A History* (1992). It supplants Louis L. Gerson, *The Hyphenate in Recent American Politics and Diplomacy* (1964), which emphasizes the periods 1914–24 and 1933–56. Concentrating on post–World War II history, *Ethnicity and U.S. Foreign Policy* (1977), edited by Abdul Aziz Said, contains several valuable case studies. Ethnicity is sometimes related to sectionalism, a subject meticulously catalogued by Edward W. Chester in *Sectionalism, Politics, and American Diplomacy* (1975).

A sound and judicious history of peace activism in the United States is Charles Chatfield, *The American Peace Movement: Ideals and Activism* (1992). Helpful as well are Charles DeBenedetti, *The Peace Reform in American History* (1980), and Merle Curti's older classic, *Peace or War: The American Struggle, 1636–1936* (1936). Ron Pagnucco and Jackie Smith present a more theoretical approach in "The Peace Movement and Foreign Policy," *Peace and Change* 18 (1993). The most influential survey of economic influences on American foreign policy is William A. Williams, *The Tragedy of American Diplomacy* (1959).

Chapter One
Establishing a Tradition, 1789–1895

Frederick L. Marks's *Independence on Trial: Foreign Affairs and the Making of the Constitution* (1973) deals with the debates over the important constitutional issues that appear frequently throughout this and succeeding chapters. Felix Gilbert traces the philosophical underpinnings of early American foreign policy in *The Beginnings of American Foreign Policy To the Farewell Address* (1961). For how the Constitution was interpreted by Washington and Adams, Stanley Elkins and Eric McKitrick's magisterial *The Age of Federalism* (1993) is essential. Frank Reuter looks more specifically at foreign policy in *Trials and Triumphs: George Washington's Foreign Policy* (1983), while Paul A. Varg's survey, *Foreign Policies of the Founding Fathers* (1963), which ends with the War of 1812, pays a good deal of attention to domestic politics.

For the diplomacy that resolved the first Anglo-American crisis, Gerald

Combs, *The Jay Treaty: Political Battleground of the Founding Fathers* (1970), is important. Anglo-American relations improved in part because of the disruptions caused by Citizen Genêt whose exploits are recounted in *The Genêt Mission* (1973) by Harry Ammon. *The First Rapprochement: England and the United States, 1795–1805* (1955) is carefully described by Bradford Perkins. Alexander DeConde looks at Adams's diplomacy in *The Quasi-War: The Politics and Diplomacy of the Undeclared War with France, 1797–1801* (1966) and Jefferson's in *This Affair of Louisiana* (1976), a book that can be paired with Robert Tucker's and David C. Hendrickson's study of Jeffersonian expansionism, *Empire of Liberty: The Statecraft of Thomas Jefferson* (1990). See also, Doron S. Ben-Atar, *The Origins of Jeffersonian Commercial Policy and Diplomacy* (1993). Covering Adams, Jefferson, Madison, and Monroe, Doris A. Graber analyzes *Public Opinion, the President, and Foreign Policy: Four Case Studies from the Formative Years* (1968) in an imaginative manner, considering the lack of polling data for her period.

Of the many books on the War of 1812, those with a special sensitivity toward domestic politics are Roger H. Brown, *The Republic in Peril: 1812* (1969), Bradford Perkins, *Prologue to War: England and the United States, 1805–1812* (1961), and Ronald Hatzenbuehler and Robert C. Ive, *Congress Declares War: Rhetoric, Leadership, and Partisanship in the Early Republic* (1983).

As with his other books, the third volume in Bradford Perkins's fine trilogy, *Castlereagh and Adams: England and the United States, 1812–1823* (1964) pays careful attention to the relationship between economic and political currents and Republican diplomacy. Ernest R. May's *The Making of the Monroe Doctrine* (1975) also emphasizes domestic political variables, particularly the upcoming presidential election, on the positions taken by Monroe and his cabinet members as they cobbled together their Latin American policies.

For the conflict with England over British North American boundary problems and other issues, Wilbur D. Jones, *The American Problem in British Diplomacy: 1841–1861* (1974), Howard Jones, *To the Webster-Ashburton Treaty: A Study in Anglo-American Relations, 1783–1843* (1977), and Kenneth Stevens, *Border Diplomacy: The Caroline and McLeod Affairs in Anglo-American-Canadian Relations, 1837–1842* (1989), are helpful, as is John Belohlavek, *"Let the Eagle Soar": The Foreign Policy of Andrew Jackson* (1985), for Jacksonian diplomacy.

The preceding serve as a backdrop to the first great era of American expansion. Albert K. Weinberg's venerable *Manifest Destiny: A Study of Nationalist Expansion in American History* (1935) provides an exhaustive catalogue of arguments presented for expansion. Frederick Merk's elegant essay, *Manifest Destiny and Mission in American History* (1963), is far more readable. Norman Graebner stresses the desire for West Coast ports in his classic *Empire on the Pacific: A Study in American Continental Expansion* (1955), while *Diplomacy of Annexation: Texas, Oregon, and the Mexican War* (1973) by David M. Pletcher, more multicausal than Graebner, is the best single volume on the subject. Reginald Horsman takes another tack in his important *Race and Manifest Destiny: The Origins of American Racial Anglo-Saxonism* (1981). For the opponents of the Mexican War, see John H. Schroeder, *Mr. Polk's War: American Opposition and Dissent, 1846–1848* (1973). Although Civil War diplomacy was a sideshow for Lincoln and his advisors, their skill in managing the British relationship permitted them to concentrate on domestic battlefields. Norman Ferris looks at Secretary of State Seward's early activities in *Desperate Diplomacy: William H. Seward's Foreign Policy, 1861* (1976) and *The Trent Affair: A Diplomatic Crisis* (1977). Howard Jones examines domestic issues on both sides of the Atlantic in *Union in Peril: The Crisis over British Intervention in the Civil War* (1992), while Paul Crook, in *The North, the South, and the Powers, 1861–1865* (1974), covers a somewhat broader terrain. Tensions in Anglo-American relations affected the Canadian-American linkage, a subject handled admirably by Robin Winks in *Canada and the United States: The Civil War Years* (1960). For Irish-Americans' forays into Canada during the immediate postwar years, see Brian Jenkins, *The Fenians and Anglo-American Relations during Reconstruction* (1969). For the 1880s, David Pletcher, *The Awkward Years: American Foreign Relations under Garfield and Arthur* (1962), and Charles Callan Tansill, *Canadian-American Relations, 1875–1911* (1943), are dependable. Tom E. Terrill, *The Tariff, Politics, and American Foreign Policy, 1874–1901* (1974), demonstrates the importance of that seemingly prosaic issue.

Chapter Two
The Progressive Era, 1895–1920

In his seminal *The New Empire: An Interpretation of American Expansion, 1865–1898* (1964), Walter LaFeber stresses economic variables. Data to support his arguments can be found in Cleona Lewis, *America's Stake in International Investments* (1938), Mira Wilkins, *The Emergence of Multinational Enterprise: American Business abroad from the Colonial Era to 1914* (1970), and William Becker, *Dynamics of Business-Government Relations: Industry and Exports, 1893–1921* (1982). For other factors influencing the expansionists, David Healy, *U.S. Expansionism: The Imperialist Urge in the 1890s* (1970), is perceptive. America's entry into the Spanish-American War is described by John L. Offner, *An Unwanted War: The Diplomacy of the United States and Spain over Cuba, 1895–1898* (1992). After writing a solid traditional survey of the war in *Imperial Democracy: The Emergence of America as a Great Power* (1961), Ernest R. May returned to the subject employing a new paradigm that emphasizes elite opinion in *American Imperialism: A Speculative Essay* (1968). Charles Brown looks at the role of the press in his lively *The Correspondents' War: Journalists in the Spanish-American War* (1967), while Marcus H. Wilkerson attacks the issue in a more scholarly tome, *Public Opinion and the Spanish-American War: A Study in War Propaganda* (1932). On a related matter, Robert C. Hilderbrand's

Power and the People: Executive Management of Public Opinion in Foreign Affairs, 1897–1921 (1981), traces the development of what we now call spin control.

The opposition to expansion is evaluated by Robert L. Beisner in *Twelve against War: The Anti-Imperialists, 1898–1900* (1961), and Richard E. Welch in *Response to Imperialism: The United States and the Philippine-American War, 1899–1902* (1979). For the response of African-Americans, see Willard Gatewood, *Black Americans and the White Man's Burden, 1898–1903* (1975).

Covering a longer period are E. Berkeley Tompkins, *Anti-Imperialism in the United States: The Great Debate, 1899–1920* (1970), Sondra R. Herman, *Eleven against War: Studies in American Internationalist Thought, 1898–1921* (1969), David S. Patterson, *Toward a Warless World: The Travail of the American Peace Movement, 1887–1914* (1976), and John W. Chambers, *The Eagle and the Dove: The American Peace Movement and United States Foreign Policy, 1900–1922* (1976). Göran Rystad explains how expansion affected the 1900 election in *Ambiguous Imperialism: American Foreign Policy and Domestic Politics at the Turn of the Century* (1975).

Thomas J. McCormick concentrates on America's search for Asian markets to solve its economic problems in *China Market: America's Quest for Informal Empire* (1967). His arguments are supported by Charles S. Campbell's *Special Business Interests and the Open Door Policy* (1951). American religious leaders were also deeply involved in trying to influence China policy, as seen in James Reed, *The Missionary Mind and American East Asia Policy, 1911–1915* (1983). What Americans told one another about the Pacific is examined in Marilyn B. Young, *The Rhetoric of Empire: 1895–1901* (1968), and Jerry Israel, *Progressivism and the Open Door: America and China, 1905–1921* (1971). Useful for the way restrictive immigration laws affected Theodore Roosevelt's China policy is *Chinese Exclusion Versus the Open Door Policy, 1900–1906: Clashes over China Policy in the Roosevelt Era* (1976) by Delber McKee. TR's 1906 confrontation with racism in California is described by Thomas A. Bailey in *Theodore Roosevelt and the Japanese-American Crisis: An Account of the International Complications Arising from the Race Problem on the Pacific Coast* (1934) in his characteristic highly readable fashion.

For the tangled background of the Panama Canal affair, the prize-winning *The Path between the Seas: The Creation of the Panama Canal, 1870–1914* (1977) by David McCullough can be supplemented with Dwight C. Miner, *The Fight for the Panama Route* (1940). Looking at cultural factors in the United States and in Latin American nations, Richard H. Collin's *Theodore Roosevelt's Caribbean: The Panama Canal, the Monroe Doctrine, and the Latin American Context* (1990) offers a challenging new way to view American imperialism. Another monograph that emphasizes cultural factors in which the Panama Canal is just one issue is Bradford Perkins, *The Great Rapprochement: England and the United States, 1895–1914* (1968). That rapprochement affected and was affected by the ups and downs in Canadian-American relations, a subject explored in L. Ethan Ellis, *Reciprocity 1911: A Study in Canadian-American Relations* (1939).

For the forces pushing for a large American Navy, *The Navy League of the United States* (1962) by Armin Rappaport is the best source. The American Navy's legendary 'round-the-world trip is chronicled in the delightful *The Great White Fleet: Its Voyage Around the World, 1907–1909* (1965) by Robert A. Hart.

For American entry into World War I, Ernest R. May, *The World War and American Isolation* (1959), is a balanced study that pays attention to both domestic and international factors. Americans were ready to go on a crusade in 1917 in part because of the preparedness campaign about which John Patrick Finnegan writes in *Against the Specter of a Dragon: The Campaign for American Military Preparedness, 1914–1917* (1974). The homefront during the war is covered in an interesting fashion by David C. Kennedy, *Over Here: The First World War and American Society* (1980). Other relevant specialized studies are, for ethnic groups, Carl F. Wittke, *German-Americans and the World War* (1936), Frederick C. Luebke, *Bonds of Loyalty: German-Americans and World War I* (1974), and Francis M. Carroll, *American Opinion and the Irish Question, 1910–1923* (1978), and for the propaganda wars, Horace C. Peterson and Gilbert C. Fite, *Propaganda for War: 1917–1918* (1957), Stephen Vaughn, *Holding Fast the Inner Lines: Democracy, Nationalism, and the Committee on Public Information* (1980), and George Blakely, *Historians on the Home Front: American Propagandists and the Great War* (1970). Joel Spring deals with the issue of government propaganda efforts from World War I through the present in his useful synthesis, *Images of American Life: A History of Ideological Management in Schools, Movies, Radio, and Television* (1992).

An introduction to the arguments of those who opposed war entry is provided by Fred Giffin in *Six Who Protested: Radical Opposition to the First World War* (1977). Seward W. Livermore pays attention to partisan politics in *Politics Is Adjourned: Woodrow Wilson and the War Congress, 1916–1918* (1966), while John C. Vinson concentrates on the election of 1920 and the League of Nations issue in *Referendum for Isolation: The Defeat of Article X of the League of Nations Covenant* (1961). The fight over the League is the subject of Thomas A. Bailey's anti-Wilsonian *Woodrow Wilson and the Great Betrayal* (1945). More balanced on Wilson, if less lively, is Thomas Knock, *To End All Wars: Woodrow Wilson and the Quest for a New World Order* (1992). Aspects of Wilson's alleged "betrayal" are considered by Ralph A. Stone in *The Irreconcilables: The Fight against the League of Nations* (1970) and Herbert F. Margulies in *The Mild Reservationists and the League of Nations Controversy in the Senate* (1989).

Chapter Three
From War to War, 1920–1944

A good place to begin studying the twenties is Ralph B. Levering, *The Public and American Foreign Policy, 1918–1978* (1978), which offers a brief intelligent survey of public attitudes and interest groups. Selig Adler spends a good deal of time on the twenties and thirties in *The Isolationist Impulse: Its Twentieth Century Reaction* (1957). See also Thomas N. Guinsburg, *The Pursuit of Isolationism in the United States Senate from Versailles to Pearl Harbor* (1982). For the controversies that swirled around possible American entry into the World Court, Denna F. Fleming, *The United States and the World Court* (1945), retains its value. How the United States reacted to the Russian Revolution and the question of recognition are considered by Christopher Lasch, *The American Liberals and the Russian Revolution* (1962), for the early period and Peter Filene, *Americans and the Soviet Experiment, 1917–1933* (1967), for the twenties.

Although the apparently isolationist United States did not enter the World Court in the twenties or recognize the Soviet Union, its businesspeople were active abroad during the period. The intimate relationship between Washington and Wall Street is the subject of Carl Parrini's *Heir to Empire: United States Economic Diplomacy, 1916–1923* (1969). For American economic policy over a longer span see Joan Hoff Wilson, *American Business and Foreign Policy, 1920–1933* (1971), and Joseph Brandes, *Herbert Hoover and Economic Diplomacy: Department of Commerce Policy, 1921–1928* (1966). Alfred E. Eckes takes an interesting journey "Revisiting Smoot-Hawley," an unpublished paper that suggests we have misinterpreted the significance of that tariff. The role of American finance capital in postwar Europe is explored by Melvyn P. Leffler in *The Elusive Quest: America's Pursuit of French Security and European Stability, 1919–1933* (1979). Michael J. Hogan looks across the channel in *Informal Entente: The Private Structure of Cooperation in Anglo-American Economic Diplomacy* (1977). Emphasizing cultural relations, Frank Costigliola, *Awkward Dominion: American Political, Economic, and Cultural Relations with Europe, 1919–1933* (1984), serves as a companion piece to Leffler and Hogan. American diplomats, and especially American peace groups, were involved in the background of the Washington Conference and the Kellogg-Briand Pact. For those subjects, one must turn to John C. Vinson, *The Parchment Peace: The United States Senate and the Washington Conference, 1921–1922* (1955), and Robert Ferrell, *Peace in Their Time: The Origins of the Kellogg-Briand Pact* (1952).

Japanese-American relations were affected by American immigration laws during the period as can be seen in Roger Daniels, *The Politics of Prejudice, The Anti-Japanese Movement and the Struggle for Japanese Exclusion* (1962). For immigration laws in general, see Robert A. Divine, *American Immigration Policy, 1924–1952* (1957). Prohibition's impact on Canadian-American relations is considered in Peter C. Newman, *Bronfman Dynasty* (1979), and Richard N. Kottman, "Volstead Violated: Prohibition as a Factor in Canadian-American Relations," *Canadian Historical Review* 43 (1962).

With war in Europe and Asia coming closer to American shores, isolationism became an even more important issue in the thirties. Geoffrey S. Smith deals with the more extreme elements in that movement in *To Save a Nation: American 'Extremism,' The New Deal, and the Coming of World War II* (1992), while Wayne Cole and Manfred Jonas look at the issue from a broader perspective in *Roosevelt and the Isolationists: 1932–1945* (1983) and *Isolation in America, 1935–1941* (1967), respectively. In a sophisticated study of the way American peace groups have operated, Robert Kleidman compares the Emergency Peace Campaign of the 1930s with SANE and the Freeze in *Organizing for Peace: Neutrality, the Test Ban, and the Freeze* (1993). James C. Schneider's *Should America Go to War?: The Debate over Foreign Policy in Chicago, 1939–1941* (1989) is a valuable case study. Two groups that took opposite positions in the debate were America First and the Committee to Defend America by Aiding the Allies. Their activities are described in Wayne S. Cole, *America First: The Battle against Intervention, 1940–1941* (1953), Walter Johnson *The Battle against Isolation* (1944), and Mark Lincoln Chadwin, *The Warhawks: American Interventionists before Pearl Harbor* (1968). John Edward Wiltz, *In Search of Peace: The Senate Munitions Inquiry, 1934–1936* (1963), offers the best analysis of the Nye Committee. Isolationists, among others, opposed the institution of the draft, a subject studied by J. Garry Clifford and Samuel Spencer Jr. in *The First Peacetime Draft* (1986). George Q. Flynn's splendid survey, *The Draft, 1940–1973* (1993), which devotes space to the same issue, explores the impact of the Selective Service System on society as well as on the military.

Weaving his way between the isolationists and the interventionists was Franklin D. Roosevelt. Robert Dallek covers the president's approach to the world crisis in his impressive *Franklin D. Roosevelt and American Foreign Policy, 1932–1945* (1979). The Quarantine Speech is the subject of Travis Beal Jacobs, "Roosevelt's Quarantine Speech," *Historian* 24 (1962), which should be read with Dorothy Borg, *The United States and the Far Eastern Crisis of 1933–1939* (1964). Looking just at the war entry, Waldo Heinrich's *Threshold of War: Franklin D. Roosevelt and American Entry into World War II* (1988) examines a host of foreign and domestic variables that went into the president's decisionmaking. Lloyd C. Gardner concentrates on one variable in his thought-provoking *Economic Aspects of New Deal Diplomacy* (1964). A related study of value is Frederick C. Adams, *The Export-Import Bank and American Foreign Policy, 1933–1941* (1976).

For the remarkable story of American volunteers in the Spanish Civil War, Peter Carroll, *The Odyssey of the Abraham Lincoln Brigade* (1994), supplants Robert Rosenstone, *Crusade of the Left: The Lincoln Battalion in the Spanish Civil War* (1969), as the best of many accounts. As for Roosevelt's approach to that war, Richard P. Traina, *American Diplomacy and the Spanish Civil War* (1968), is a good place to begin, while how Americans reacted to that war is handled well in Allen Guttman, *The Wound in the Heart: America and the Spanish Civil War* (1962). Although the literature for the Italo-Ethiopian War is nowhere near as rich, Joseph E. Harris, *African-American Reactions to War in Ethiopia, 1935–1941* (1994), merits attention.

From 1940 through 1988, foreign policy was a key issue in every presidential election. The place to begin a study of those elections through 1972 is Robert A. Divine, *Foreign Policy and U.S. Presidential Elections*, 2 vols. (1974). During World War II, although partisan politics were muted, Democrats and Republicans still clashed occasionally over foreign policy, the subject of Richard Darilek, *Loyal Opposition in War: The Republican Party and the Politics of Foreign Policy from Pearl Harbor to Yalta* (1976), and Martin Melosi, *The Shadow of Pearl Harbor: Political Controversy Over the Surprise Attack, 1941–1946* (1977). Examining both the war years and the early Cold War years is the somewhat outdated H. Bradford Westerfield, *Foreign Policy and Party Politics: Pearl Harbor to Korea* (1955). For the way the government sold the war, Allan M. Winkler, *The Politics of Propaganda: The Office of War Information, 1942–1945* (1978), and Michael Leigh, *Mobilizing for Consent: Public Opinion and American Foreign Policy: 1937–1947* (1976), offer interesting perspectives. Part of that selling had to do with the Russian alliance of convenience that not all Americans accepted easily, as seen in Ralph Levering, *American Opinion and the Russian Alliance, 1939–1945* (1976), and Melvin Small, "How We Learned to Love the Russians: American Media and the Soviet Union During World War Two," *Historian* 36 (1974). Another selling job was needed to convince Americans to join a new international organization, a process described by Robert A. Divine in *Second Chance: The Triumph of Internationalism in America during World War II* (1967). Hollywood also contributed to the cause, as reflected in Clayton Koppes and Gregory Black, *Hollywood Goes to War: How Politics, Profits, and Propaganda Shaped World War II Movies* (1987).

For the way the Roosevelt administration, as well as the Jewish-American community, reacted to the Holocaust, see David S. Wyman, *The Abandonment of the Jews: America and the Holocaust, 1941–1945* (1984). Aaron Berman concentrates on the Jewish response and the relationship of the Holocaust to Israel in *Nazism, the Jews, and American Zionism* (1933–48). John W. Dower, in *War Without Mercy* (1986), sensitively surveys Japanese and American racism in the Pacific war and on their homefronts. Looking at the relationship in a broader fashion is Akira Iriye, *Power and Culture: The Japanese-American War, 1941–1945* (1981). Another issue dealing with American racism is analyzed by Fred W. Riggs in *Pressure on Congress: A Study of the Repeal of Chinese Exclusion* (1950).

For domestic economic influences on policymakers during World War II, see Lloyd C. Gardner, *Architects of Illusion: Men and Ideas in American Foreign Policy, 1941–1949* (1970). Richard Gardner, *Sterling-Dollar Diplomacy: Anglo-American Cooperation in the Reconstruction of Multilateral Trade* (1956), and Randall Bennett Woods, *A Changing of the Guard: Anglo-American Relations, 1941–1946* (1990), are key to understanding the complex economic relationship between the United States and England. Irvine H. Anderson, *Aramco, the United States and Saudi Arabia* (1981), Aaron David Miller, *Search for Security: Saudi Arabian Oil and American Foreign Policy, 1939–1948* (1980), and Michael Stoff, *Oil, War and American Secu-*

rity: The Search for a National Policy on Foreign Oil, 1941–1947 (1980), explain how oil became central in defining American policy in the Middle East.

Chapter Four
The Cold War's Darkest Days, 1944–1960

For the entire Cold War period, Thomas J. McCormick's provocative *America's Half-Century: United States Foreign Policy in the Cold War* (1989) explains American diplomacy in terms of the economy. A critical but more balanced view of the same period is H. W. Brands's often witty *The Devil We Knew: Americans and the Cold War* (1993), which like McCormick, does not ignore economics. Raymond A. Bauer, Ithiel de Sola Pool, and Lewis A. Dexter examine foreign trade in *American Business and Public Policy: The Politics of Foreign Trade* (1967). Other studies that deal with this issue are Fred Block, *The Origins of International Economic Disorder* (1977), Mira Wilkins, *The Maturing of Multinational Enterprise: American Business Abroad from 1914 to 1970* (1974), and especially for the importance of domestic interest groups, I. M. Destler, *American Trade Politics* (1992). Ronald W. Cox, *Power and Profits: U.S. Foreign Policy in Central America* (1994) examines the role of the business community behind shifting U.S. programs for Central America. For the origins of the foreign aid program, David Baldwin, *Economic Development and American Foreign Policy, 1943–1962* (1966), is solid, and for an insightful survey of the complicated relationship between business and government see Kim McQuaid, *Uneasy Partners: Big Business in American Politics, 1945–1990* (1994). Many of the founders of the containment program came from Wall Street or corporate backgrounds as evidenced in Walter Isaacson's and Evan Thomas's chatty *The Wise Men: Six Friends and the World They Made* (1986). Most were involved in the Council of Foreign Relations whose history is ably chronicled in Robert D. Schulzinger, *The Wise Men of Foreign Affairs: The History of the Council on Foreign Relations* (1984).

For the pernicious impact of the Cold War on American society, Edward Pessen offers a perspective written at the end of the period in *Losing Our Souls: The American Experience in the Cold War* (1993). Jack Snyder, *Myths of Empire: Domestic Politics and International Ambition* (1991), is a sophisticated study of the many ways domestic issues interacted with foreign issues during the Cold War. James G. Richter, "Perpetuating the Cold War: Domestic Sources of International Patterns of Behavior," *Political Science Quarterly* 107 (1992), compares domestic variables in the Soviet Union and the United States.

The drug trade was one interesting domestic issue that became very important for the United States in several foreign theaters. The best work in this realm is William O. Walker's *Drug Control in the Americas* (1989) and *Opium and Foreign Policy: The Anglo-American Search for Order in Asia, 1912–1954* (1991). See also Jonathan Kwitney, *Crimes of Patriots: A True Tale of Dope, Dirty Money, and the CIA* (1987).

John Prados's *Presidents' Secret Wars: CIA and Pentagon Covert Operations since World War II* (1986), which examines U.S. military interventions without the benefit of war declarations, and the same author's *Keepers of the Keys: A History of the National Security Council from Truman to Bush* (1991) are valuable. Important for understanding the conflict between the president and Congress during the period is Philip J. Briggs, *Making American Foreign Policy: President-Congress Relations from the Second World War to Vietnam* (1991). Samuel Kernell focuses more directly on the president in *Going Public: New Strategies of Presidential Leadership* (1992), with his chapter on the Truman Doctrine especially interesting. Paul Brace and Barbara Hinckley, *Follow the Leader: Opinion Polls and Modern Presidents* (1992), looks at both domestic and foreign policy issues. Most American media blindly followed Washington's line as demonstrated by James Aronson in *The Press and the Cold War* (1978). In *The Press and the Origins of the Cold War, 1944–1947* (1988), Louis Liebovich contends that the press played a more independent role in shaping anti-Soviet opinion. H. Schuyler Foster, the State Department's long-time public opinion analyst, explains how *Activism Replaces Isolationism: U.S. Public Attitudes, 1940–1975* (1976). A new interest group, defense intellectuals, played a role in defining the parameters of the Cold War as critiqued by Gregg F. Herken in *Counsels of War* (1987).

For the impact of the atomic bomb on American society, see Paul Boyer's imaginative *By the Dawn's Early Light: American Thought and Culture at the Dawn of the Atomic Age* (1985), and Allan M. Winkler, *Life under a Cloud: American Anxiety about the Bomb* (1993). That anxiety led some Americans to support ban-the-bomb and other disarmament groups. Their activities, as well as those of peaceniks worldwide, are catalogued in Lawrence Wittner's impressive *One World or None: A History of the World Nuclear Disarmament Movement through 1953* (1993). Wittner also wrote an earlier volume, *Rebels against War: The American Peace Movement: 1941–1970* (1974), which covers issues aside from the bomb. Robert A. Divine, *Blowing on the Wind: The Nuclear Test Ban Debate, 1954–1960* (1978), and Milton S. Katz, *Ban the Bomb: A History of SANE, the Committee for a Sane Nuclear Policy, 1957–1985* (1986), highlight the relative success of one peace lobby.

For the origins of the Cold War, the best place to begin is Melvyn P. Leffler's convincing *A Preponderance of Power: National Security, the Truman Administration, and the Cold War* (1992), which examines domestic and international factors. Supplementing Leffler are the influential John Lewis Gaddis, *The United States and the Origins of the Cold War, 1941–1947* (1972), Fraser Harbutt, *The Iron Curtain: Churchill, America, and the Origins of the Cold War* (1986), and Thomas G. Paterson, *On Every Front: The Making of the Cold War* (1979). Paterson's article, "Presidential Foreign Policy, Public Opinion and Congress: The Truman Years," in *Diplomatic History* 3 (1979), also merits attention. Walter LaFeber's related "American Policymakers, Public Opinion, and the Outbreak of the Cold War," in Yonosuke Nagai and Akira Iriye, eds., *The Origins of the Cold War in Asia* (1977), is an insightful essay.

Because he covers events at home and abroad, Robert J. Donovan's *Conflict and Crisis: The Presidency of Harry S Truman, 1945–1948* (1977) is valuable. So too is Dean Acheson's memoir, *Present at the Creation: My Years at the State Department* (1969). Advising Truman, and the other Democratic presidents through Carter, was Clark Clifford, a keen political observer who recounts his life and times in *Counsel to the President: A Memoir* (1991).

For the connection between domestic and foreign anticommunism, see Richard M. Freeland, *The Truman Doctrine and the Origins of McCarthyism: Foreign Policy, Domestic Politics, and Internal Security, 1946–1948* (1972), and Athan G. Theoharis, *Seeds of Repression: Harry S. Truman and the Origins of McCarthyism* (1971). Theoharis's *The Yalta Myths: An Issue in U.S. Politics, 1945–1955* (1970) traces how the Republicans made the "Y" word a winning political issue. Bennet Korvig goes beyond Yalta in *The Myth of Liberation: East-Central Europe in U.S. Diplomacy and Politics since 1941* (1973). David Caute, *The Great Fear: The Anti-Communist Purge under Truman and Eisenhower* (1978), is horrifying. Throughout the Cold War, but particularly during its early years, policymakers exaggerated the threat of the Soviet Union as seen in Robert H. Johnson, *Improbable Dangers: U.S. Conceptions of Threat in the Cold War and After* (1994).

The development of the Marshall Plan was intimately related to the needs of the American economy—and was sold as such—as is evidenced in Michael J. Hogan's brilliant *The Marshall Plan* (1987). In his provocative *Harry S Truman and the War Scare of 1948* (1993), Frank Kofsky contends that the Truman administration exaggerated Soviet threats in the wake of the Czech coup to sell funding for the Marshall Plan and rearmament programs on Capitol Hill. Helpful as well are Robert A. Pollard, *Economic Security and the Origins of the Cold War* (1987), and Alan S. Milward, *The Reconstruction of Western Europe, 1945–1951* (1984). All sectors of American society were enlisted in the struggle to keep the communists from taking over Western Europe with Anthony Carew, *Labor and the Marshall Plan: The Politics of Productivity and the Marketing of Management Science* (1987), detailing how American labor did its share. See also here Ronald Radosh, *American Labor and United States Foreign Policy* (1969).

Throughout the Cold War, American policies toward the state of Israel colored the nation's policies toward the entire Middle East and beyond. For an overview of those policies, with special attention to domestic issues, see the lively journalistic account by Dan Raviv and Yossi Melman, *Friends in Deed: Inside the U.S.-Israeli Alliance* (1994). Very useful as well is David Schoenbaum's even-handed *The United States and the State of Israel* (1993). Michael Cohen explains the origins of those policies in *Truman and Israel* (1990). An earlier volume by John Snetsinger, *Truman, the Jewish Vote, and the Creation of Israel* (1974), is still required reading on the subject. The battle over Zionism in the Truman administration is an important element in the tragic story of James M. Forrestal told by Townsend Hoopes and Douglas Brinkley in *Driven Patriot: The Life and Times of James Forrestal* (1992). Looking at this period, as well as the entire Cold War era, is Edward Tivnan, *The Lobby: Jewish Political Power and American Foreign Policy* (1987). Paula Stern shows how that lobby worked during a later period in *Water's Edge: Domestic Politics and the Making of American Foreign Policy* (1979). David Howard Goldberg offers an imaginative comparative perspective in *Foreign Policy and Ethnic Interest Groups: American and Canadian Jews Lobby for Israel* (1990). In her controversial study, *Israel and the American National Interest: A Critical Examination* (1986), Cheryl A. Rubenberg argues that American support for Israel was not always in the nation's best interest. On the other hand, in their sensational but useful *The Secret War against the Jews: The Shocking Story of Israel's Betrayal by the Western Powers* (1994), John Loftus and Mark Aarons contend that Western intelligence agencies, former Nazis, and the oil companies conspired against Israel from World War II to the Gulf War.

Another powerful lobby is described by Ross Y. Koen in *The China Lobby in American Politics* (1960), and by Stanley D. Bachrack in *The Committee of One Million: "China Lobby" Politics, 1953–1971* (1976). For China policy during the Truman presidency see June M. Grasso, *Harry Truman's Two-China Policy, 1948–1950* (1987). Leonard A. Kusnitz traces the role of public opinion in affecting that policy from the communist victory to U.S. recognition in *Public Opinion and Foreign Policy: America's China Policy, 1949–1979* (1984). A. J. Steele concentrates on American attitudes in *The American People and China* (1966). Where such images came from is delineated in the pathbreaking *Scratches on Our Minds: American Images of China and India* (1958) by Harold R. Isaacs.

A good introduction to the Korean War, which examines the domestic scene as well as international complications, is Burton I. Kaufman, *The Korean War: Challenges in Crisis, Credibility, and Command* (1986). Informative analyses of civil-military conflict over several key issues appear in D. Clayton James with Anne Sharp Wells, *Refighting the Last War: Command and Crisis in Korea, 1950–1953* (1993). Of course, the major issue was the conflict between the president and his commander-in-chief, about which John W. Spanier writes in *The Truman-MacArthur Controversy and the Korean War* (1965). Helpful here also is Ronald J. Caridi, *The Korean War and American Politics: The Republican Party as a Case Study* (1969).

The demographic background of isolationist opponents of the emerging bipartisan Cold War consensus in American politics is skillfully examined by political scientist Leroy N. Rieselbach in *The Roots of Isolationism: Congressional Voting and Presidential Leadership in Foreign Policy* (1966). Employing a more methodologically traditional approach is Justus Doenecke in *Not to the Swift: The Old Isolationists in the Cold War Era* (1979). Robert Taft's central role is analyzed in

Henry Berger, "Bipartisanship, Senator Taft, and the Truman Administration," *Political Science Quarterly* 90 (1975). Others who fell outside that consensus are described in *Cold War Critics: Alternatives to American Foreign Policy in the Truman Years* (1971), edited by Thomas G. Paterson.

The foreign policy of the Eisenhower administration is admirably surveyed by Stephen E. Ambrose in *Eisenhower* (1983). H. W. Brands looks at some of Ike's advisors in *Cold Warriors: Eisenhower's Generation and American Foreign Policy* (1988). For the relationship between his trade policies and foreign aid, Burton I. Kaufman, *Trade and Aid* (1982), is first-rate. See also Walt W. Rostow, *Eisenhower, Kennedy, and Foreign Aid: Domestic Issues in Congress and Government* (1985), and Robert J. McMahon, *The Cold War on the Periphery: The United States, India, and Pakistan* (1994). An intriguing look at how private enterprise may develop an independent foreign aid program is provided by Elizabeth Anne Cobbs, *The Rich Neighbor Policy: Rockefeller and Kaiser in Brazil* (1992). *The Influence of the Carnegie, Ford, and Rockefeller Foundations on American Foreign Policy* (1983) by Edward H. Berman covers a similar issue over a longer period.

Diane Kunz concentrates on one aspect of the complicated Suez Crisis, which occurred just weeks before the 1956 election, in *The Economic Diplomacy of the Suez Crisis* (1991). Broader views are available in Keith Kyle, *Suez* (1991), and Donald Neff, *Warriors at Suez: Eisenhower Takes America into the Middle East* (1981). See also Isaac Alteras, *Eisenhower and Israel: U.S.-Israeli Relations, 1953–1960* (1993). Eisenhower's calm handling of the *Sputnik* furor is the subject of Robert A. Divine, *The Sputnik Challenge* (1993). Michael Beschloss considers another Eisenhower crisis in *Mayday: Eisenhower, Khrushchev, and the U-2 Affair* (1986).

Chapter Five
The World Becomes More Complicated, 1960–1980

Both Michael Beschloss, *The Crisis Years: Kennedy and Khrushchev, 1960–1963* (1991), and Richard Reeves, *President Kennedy: Profile of Power* (1993), are excellent places to learn about this presidency and especially how the politically savvy people in the White House reacted to foreign crises. Cuba was the venue for several crises, beginning with *The Perfect Failure: Eisenhower, Kennedy, and the Bay of Pigs* (1987) by Trumbull Higgins. For the background of that affair, see Richard A. Welch, *Response to Revolution: The United States and the Cuban Revolution, 1959–1961* (1985).

Kennedy's—and the world's—greatest Cold War crisis, the Cuban missile crisis, especially the domestic setting, are considered by Richard Ned Lebow in "Domestic Politics and the Cuban Missile Crisis: The Traditional and the Revisionist Interpretations Reevaluated," *Diplomatic History* 14 (1990), and Fen Osler Hampson in "The Divided Decision-Maker: American Domestic Politics and the Cuban Crises," in Kegley and Wittkopf, eds., *The Domestic Sources of American Foreign Policy*. For the latest from the participants themselves, including Fidel Castro, *Cuba on the Brink: Castro, the Missile Crisis, and the Soviet Collapse* (1993), edited by James G. Blight, Bruce J. Allyn, and David A. Welch, is quite revealing.

How the media dealt with Kennedy's several crises is the subject of the fine interdisciplinary study by Montague Kern, Patricia Levering, and Ralph A. Levering, *The Kennedy Crisis: The Press, the Presidency, and Foreign Policy* (1985). Denise M. Bostdorff examines Kennedy's rhetoric during the missile crisis, as well as the crisis rhetoric of presidents who followed him, in her interesting *The Presidency and the Rhetoric of Foreign Crisis* (1994).

Concern about nuclear war after the missile crisis did lead to a lessening of Soviet-American tension, symbolized by the Partial Test Ban Treaty about which Glenn T. Seaborg writes in *Kennedy, Khrushchev, and the Test Ban* (1981). Seaborg, a distinguished scientist, wrote a sequel, *Stemming the Tide: Arms Control in the Johnson Years* (1987). Walter A. McDougall considers Kennedy's declaration of the space race in *The Heavens and the Earth: A Political History of the Space Age* (1985).

With the Kennedy administration, the media, particularly the electronic media, came to play an increasingly more important role in diplomacy. Patrick O'Heffernan's *Mass Media and American Foreign Policy: Insider Perspectives on Global Journalism and the Foreign Policy Process* (1991), while concentrating on the more recent period, is useful on this subject. Lloyd Cutler, a Carter aide, worries about this issue in "Foreign Policy on Deadline," *Foreign Policy* (Fall 1984).

American trade policies are analyzed in Thomas Zeiler, *American Trade Policies in the Sixties* (1992), which is important for the response to the Common Market, and John W. Evans, *The Kennedy Round in American Trade Policy* (1975). The domestic impact of international economic issues, especially the role of OPEC, are admirably examined in Hobart Rowen, *Self-Inflicted Wounds: From LBJ's Guns and Butter to Reagan's Voodoo Economics* (1994). Trade, defense, and even personal issues created an unpleasant climate for Canadian-American relations during the period as described in a delightful manner by Knowlton Nash in *Kennedy and Diefenbaker: Fear and Loathing across the Undefended Border* (1990).

The Vietnam War ultimately affected every sort of domestic political issue—and vice versa. David Levy's survey, *The Debate over Vietnam* (1991), is a good place to start. For the Kennedy years, John M. Newman, *JFK and Vietnam: Deception, Intrigue, and the Struggle for Power* (1992), suggests that the president could not move precipitously to extricate the United States from the war because of the 1964 election. Noam Chomsky disagrees in *Rethinking Camelot: JFK, the Vietnam War, and U.S. Political Culture* (1993). For Johnson's decision-making, Larry Berman's two volumes, *Planning a Tragedy: The Americanization of the War in Vietnam* (1982) and *Lyndon Johnson's War* (1989), and George Herring's *LBJ and Vietnam* (1994) are authoritative. For the way the president dealt with foreign policy in general, see H. W. Brands, *The Wages of Globalism: Lyndon Johnson and the Limits of American Power* (1995), which stresses the role of Congress and public opinion, and Paul Y. Hammond, *LBJ and the Presidential Management of Foreign Relations* (1992). Herbert Y. Schandler concentrates on 1968 in *The Unmaking of a President: Lyndon Johnson and Vietnam* (1977). The views of George Ball, one of the few doves in Johnson's entourage, are outlined in David L. Di Leo, *George Ball, Vietnam, and the Rethinking of Containment* (1991). Among other things, Ball contended that the American public would not support a long limited war in Vietnam, an argument reinforced in John E. Mueller, *War, Presidents, and Public Opinion* (1973).

The best book on the antiwar movement is Charles DeBenedetti with Charles Chatfield, *An American Ordeal: The Antiwar Movement of the Vietnam Era* (1990), which can be supplemented with Tom Wells, *The War Within: America's Battle over Vietnam* (1994). Melvin Small traces the influence of the movement on policymaking in *Johnson, Nixon, and the Doves* (1988). William C. Berman writes about the leading antiwar critic on Capitol Hill in *William Fulbright and the Vietnam War* (1988). The Vietnam-era draft, which led many into the antiwar movement, is analyzed by Lawrence Baskir and Peter Strauss in *Chance and Circumstance: The War, the Draft, and the Vietnam Generation* (1978). David A. Cortright looks at the decline in morale in the military in *Soldiers in Revolt: The American Military Today* (1975). The role of the media in affecting the public is the subject of Daniel C. Hallin, *The "Uncensored War:" The Media and Vietnam* (1986), which maintains that journalists did not present an unfavorable view of American policy in Southeast Asia. Clarence Wyatt, *Paper Soldiers: The American Press and the Vietnam War* (1993), agrees with Hallin. For a reporter's eye–view, which also contains fascinating material on the Persian Gulf War, see Peter Arnett, *Live from the Battlefield: 35 Years in the World's War Zones* (1994). Moving from the battlefields of Vietnam to the streets of the United States, Melvin Small supports both Wyatt and Hallin in *Covering Dissent: The Media and the Vietnam Antiwar Movement* (1994).

However one judges the media's impact on opinion, there is no doubt that the American Cold War consensus came apart over the war, as seen in Ole R. Holsti and James M. Rosenau, *American Leadership in World Affairs: Vietnam and the Breakdown of Consensus* (1984), a study based upon survey research. The Democratic Party convention in Chicago, which is described in a lively fashion by David Farber in *Chicago '68* (1988), reflected that split. For the election itself, Lewis L. Gould, *1968: The Election that Changed America* (1993), is worthwhile.

For Vietnam during the Nixon years, one must begin with the president's *RN: The Memoirs of Richard Nixon* (1978). More revealing, especially in demonstrating how much diplomatic activity related to public relations, is H. R. Haldeman, *The Haldeman Diaries: Inside the Nixon White House* (1994). Henry Kissinger's literate and perceptive—though clearly self-serving—memoirs *White House Years* (1979) and *Years of Upheaval* (1982) have earned a special place in the literature.

A fair but critical view of that highly significant statesman is Walter Isaacson, *Kissinger: A Biography* (1992). It was during the Nixon administration that the MIA issue developed as H. Bruce Franklin reveals in *M.I.A. or Mythology in America* (1992). One of the better of the many exposés that believe in the MIA "myth" is Mark Sauter and Jim Sanders, *The Men We Left Behind: Henry Kissinger, the Politics of Deceit, and the Tragic Fate of the POWs after the Vietnam War* (1993). Stanley I. Kutler's *The Wars of Watergate: The Last Crisis of Richard Nixon* (1990) is the best source for the relationship between Vietnam and Watergate. James Cannon's *Time and Chance: Gerald Ford's Appointment with History* (1994) explains how Nixon tried to use Ford to save his position.

The many crimes and misdemeanors that constituted Watergate led Congress to flex its muscles in foreign policy for the first time since the forties as seen in Thomas M. Franck and Edward Weisband, *Foreign Policy by Congress* (1979). One major issue in that area is the subject of John H. Sullivan, *The War Powers Resolution: A Special Study of the Committee on Foreign Relations* (1982). John Hart Ely offers amendments to that resolution in *War and Responsibility: Lessons of Vietnam and Its Aftermath* (1993). Another key issue is considered by Loch K. Johnson in *A Season of Inquiry: The Senate Intelligence Investigation* (1985). Dan Caldwell shows how members of Congress, who opposed the Nixon-Ford détente policies, helped to derail Soviet-American disarmament negotiations in *The Dynamics of Domestic Politics and Arms Control: The Salt II Treaty Ratification Debate* (1991). They were involved in intermestic politics, a concept explained in Ryan J. Barilleaux, "The President, 'Intermestic' Issues, and the Risks of Policy Leadership," in Kegley and Wittkopf, eds., *The Domestic Sources of Foreign Policy*. As Congress came to play a larger role in foreign affairs, foreign lobbyists descended in great numbers upon Capitol Hill as, for example, depicted in Pat Choate, *Agents of Influence: How Japan's Lobbyists in the United States Manipulate America's Political and Economic System* (1990). Lobbyists are among other key players in Hedrick Smith's insider's guide to life inside the Beltway, *The Power Game: How Washington Works* (1988).

For the importance of new ethnic lobbies in American foreign policy, Clifford Hackett, "Ethnic Politics in Congress: The Turkish Embargo Experience," and Herschelle Sullivan Challenor, "The Influence of Black Americans on U.S. Foreign Policy," both in Said, ed., *Ethnicity and U.S. Foreign Policy*, Paul Y. Watanabe, *Ethnic Groups, Congress, and Foreign Policy: The Politics of the Turkish Arms Embargo* (1984), and Robert E. Villareal and Philip Kelly, "Mexican-Americans as Participants in U.S.-Mexican Relations," *International Studies Notes* 9 (1982), are representative. Arthur M. Schlesinger Jr. bemoans the increasing strength of such groups in *The Disuniting of America: Reflections on a Multicultural Society* (1991). Terry Diebel looks at public opinion in general in his pamphlet, *Presidents, Public Opinion, and Power: The Nixon, Carter, and Reagan Years* (1987), while Bruce Russett pays attention to the nuclear issue in "Democracy, Public

Opinion, and Nuclear Weapons," in Philip E. Tetlock et al., eds., *Behavior, Society, and Nuclear War,* vol. 1 (1989). Russett also offers a powerful critique of defense spending during the last years of the Cold War in *Controlling the Sword: The Democratic Governance of National Security* (1990).

Thomas J. Noer shows how Pres. Gerald R. Ford's foreign policy was affected by the 1976 election campaign in "International Credibility and Political Survival: The Ford Administration's Intervention in Angola," *Presidential Studies Quarterly* 23 (1993). Jimmy Carter's foreign policies created serious political problems for him as he admits in his memoirs, *Keeping Faith: Memoirs of a President* (1982). His chief foreign policy advisors' memoirs, Secretary of State Cyrus Vance, *Hard Choices: Critical Years in American Foreign Policy* (1983), and National Security Advisor Zbigniew Brzezinski, *Power and Principle: Memoirs of the National Security Advisor, 1977–1981* (1983), are also worth examining. A generally sympathetic view of Carter's foreign policy is offered by John Dumbrell, *The Carter Presidency: A Reevaluation* (1993). J. Michael Hogan, *The Panama Canal in American Politics* (1986), and George D. Moffett III, *The Limits of Victory: The Ratification of the Panama Canal Treaties* (1985), discuss one of Carter's most difficult political problems. In addition, his attempt to move from the Nixon-Kissinger *Realpolitik* to a policy that stressed human rights was also controversial as seen in Gaddis Smith, *Morality, Reason, and Power: American Diplomacy in the Carter Years* (1986). Also emphasizing the human rights thrust is Timothy P. Maga, *The World of Jimmy Carter: U.S. Foreign Policy, 1977–1981* (1994). Taking a critical view of such policies from the Right is Josh Muravchik, *The Uncertain Crusade: Jimmy Carter and the Dilemmas of Human Rights Policy* (1986), and from the Left, Michael T. Klare and Cynthia Arnson, *Supplying Repression: U.S. Support for Authoritarian Regimes Abroad* (1981).

Carter's greatest foreign policy problem during the 1980 election was the hostage crisis in Iran, the background of which is traced in Gary Sick, *All Fall Down: America's Tragic Encounter with Iran* (1985). Although they should be read with a grain of salt, Robert Parry, *Trick or Treason: The October Surprise Mystery* (1993), and Gary Sick, *October Surprise: American Hostages in Iran and the Election of Ronald Reagan* (1991), explore the possibilities of Republican collusion with the Iranians to help elect Ronald Reagan.

Chapter Six
An Emerging New World Order, 1980–1994

George Schulz's memoirs, *Turmoil and Triumph: My Years as Secretary of State* (1993), while nowhere as literate or gossipy as Kissinger's, are the best source for Reagan-era diplomacy. Useful as well are Alexander M. Haig Jr.'s frank account of his brief tenure as secretary of state, *Caveat: Realism, Reagan, and Foreign Pol-*

icy (1984), and Lou Cannon's readable and perceptive, *President Reagan: The Role of a Lifetime* (1991). For a favorable assessment of the peace movement's impact on Reagan, see David Cortright, *Peace Works: The Citizen's Role in Ending the Cold War* (1993).

The administration's complicated and controversial Central American policies are ably handled by Thomas Carothers, *In the Name of Democracy: U.S. Policy toward Latin America in the Reagan Years* (1992), and Cynthia J. Arnson, *Crossroads: Congress, the Reagan Administration, and Central America* (1989). These studies should be supplemented with Walter LaFeber, *Inevitable Revolutions: The United States in Central America* (1993). Of the many books on the sensational Iran-Contra scandal, the best is Theodore Draper, *A Very Thin Line: The Iran-Contra Affairs* (1991). Although it is undocumented, Bob Woodward's somewhat breathless *Veil: The Secret Wars of the CIA, 1981–1987* (1987) also merits attention.

Canadian-American relations took central stage for a time during the Reagan years with the dispute over acid rain ably handled by Jurgen Schmidt and Hilliard Roderick in *Acid Rain and Friendly Neighbors: The Policy Dispute between Canada and the United States* (1985). For an interesting glimpse at early attempts to establish a joint conservation policy, see Margaret Beattie Bogue, "To Save the Fish: Canada, the United States, the Great Lakes, and the Joint Commission of 1892," *Journal of American History* 79 (1993). Canadian-American relations improved after the completion of the controversial Free Trade Treaty, which is discussed in Jeffrey J. Scott and Murray G. Smith, eds., *The Canada–United States Free Trade Agreement: The Global Impact* (1988).

For Soviet-American relations during the Bush years, Michael R. Beschloss and Strobe Talbott obtained unparalleled access to the Kremlin for their *At the Highest Levels: The Inside Story of the End of the Cold War* (1993), a book that explores domestic issues that both leaders faced. Much of the opinion about those issues was influenced by a new electronic "punditocracy," whose increasing power worried Eric Alterman in *Sound and Fury: The Washington Punditocracy and the Collapse of American Politics* (1992), and Robert Parry, in *Fooling America: How Washington Insiders Twist the Truth and Manufacture the Conventional Wisdom* (1992).

Concerns about the media and how the Gulf War would play at home appear frequently in H. Norman Schwarzkopf, *It Doesn't Take a Hero* (1992), and Rick Atkinson's *Crusade: The Untold Story of the Persian Gulf War* (1993). For media coverage itself, no war has produced so many analyses of the subject in such a brief period of time. Philip M. Taylor, *War and the Media: Propaganda and Persuasion in the Gulf War* (1992), Robert E. Denton Jr., ed., *The Media and the Persian Gulf War* (1993), W. Lance Bennett and David L. Paletz, eds., *Taken by Storm: The Media, Public Opinion, and U.S. Foreign Policy in the Gulf War* (1994), and Thomas A. McCain and Leonard Shyles, eds., *The 1000 Hour War: Communication in the Gulf* (1993), look at what the world saw, how the journalists performed, and administration spin control.

A useful collection of articles that cover constitutional questions raised by the war is Marcia Lynn Whicker, James P. Pfiffner, and Raymond A. Moore, eds., *The Presidency and the Persian Gulf War* (1993). American covert support for Saddam Hussein's military buildup, as well as the nature of the contemporary international arms trade, are the subjects of Alan Friedman, *Spider's Web: The Secret History of How the White House Illegally Armed Iraq* (1993). On arms transfers in general, Michael T. Klare's critique, *American Arms Supermarket* (1984), is helpful. A former head of the Joint Chiefs, Admiral William J. Crowe Jr. has interesting things to say about the defense establishment in the eighties and nineties, particularly its relationship to the media and Congress, in *The Line of Fire: From Washington to the Gulf, the Politics and Battles of the New Military* (1993). For the tangled history of the Strategic Defense Initiative, whose development was influenced by domestic politics, see Donald R. Baucom, *The Origins of SDI, 1944–1983* (1992).

Among contemporary foreign economic issues is the fierce global competition that Martin Tolchin and Susan J. Tolchin claim the United States was losing in the nineties in *Selling Our Security: The Erosion of America's Assets* (1992). See also here, Chris C. Carvounis, *The United States and the Trade Deficit of the 1980s* (1987), and Lester C. Thurow, *Head to Head: The Coming Economic Battle among Japan, Europe, and America* (1992). Aid questions are ably explored in Paul B. Thompson, *The Ethics of Aid and Trade: U.S. Food Policy, Foreign Competition, and the Social Contract* (1992).

A useful early look at Clinton's foreign policy can be found in Elizabeth Drew, *On the Edge: The Clinton Presidency* (1994). Her discussion of the domestic policy currents swirling about the Bosnian and NAFTA issues are especially enlightening.

On the difficulty that contemporary presidents face in trying to project American military power, see the provocative article by Edward N. Luttwak, "Where Are all the Great Powers? At Home with the Kids," *Foreign Affairs* (July–August 1994).

Conclusion

Supporting the notion that the "people" in a democracy generally select wise and prudent foreign policies, particularly during the period since World War II, are Miroslav Nincic, *Democracy and Foreign Policy: The Fallacy of Political Realism* (1992), and Benjamin I. Page and Robert Y. Shapiro, *The Rational Public: Fifty Years of Trends in Americans' Policy Preferences* (1992).

William J. Dixon examines another aspect of the problem in "Democracy and the Management of International Conflict," *Journal of Conflict Resolution* 37 (1993). "Democracy and Foreign Policy: Community and Constraint," a special issue of the *Journal of Conflict Resolution* 35 (1991), features articles from a social-science perspective. Nils Petter Gleditsch offers a useful summary of the debate over the relationship between democratic nations and peace in "Democracy and Peace," *Journal of Peace Research* 29 (1992). Melvin Small is not so certain about the wisdom of American entry into war in *Was War Necessary: National Security and U.S. Entry into War, 1812–1950* (1980). A decade before he became secretary of state, Warren Christopher addressed the question of the relative inefficiency of foreign policymaking in a democracy in "Ceasefire between the Branches: A Compact in Foreign Affairs," *Foreign Affairs* 60 (1982). Robert W. McElroy makes a good case for the salutary role of morality in democratic foreign policies in *Morality and American Foreign Policy: The Role of Ethics in International Affairs* (1992).

The astounding influence of television on contemporary international politics is highlighted in Michael J. O'Neill, *The Roar of the Crowd: How Television and People Power Are Changing the World* (1993), which contends that with all its faults, television has served to democratize foreign policy throughout the entire international system. Noam Chomsky and Edward S. Herman are not as sanguine in *Manufacturing Consent: The Political Economy of the Mass Media* (1988).

For an interesting approach to local politics and foreign policy in the future, see the Stanley Foundation's conference reports, "Global Changes and Domestic Transformations: Southern California's Emerging Role" (1993) and "Shaping American Global Policy: The Growing Impact of Societal Relations" (1993).

Index

Brandeis, Louis, 169
Brezhnev, Leonid, 89
Briand, Aristide, 57
Bricker Amendment, 101–2
Brown, Ron, 135
Brunei, 142
Bryan, William Jennings, 30–32, 42, 44
Buchanan, James, 17
Buchanan, Pat, 147, 170
Bumpers Amendment, 149
Bundy, McGeorge, 108–9
Burlingame Treaty, 23
Bush, George, 148–49; AIPAC, 147; cabinet, 169; in elections, 58, 156, 161; Gulf War, 85, 157–61; policies, 149, 155, 157, 166, 170
Butler, Nicholas Murray, 57

Calhoun, John C., 13, 18
Cambodia, 124–26, 131
Camp David Accords, 136
Canada, 9, 18–19, 102–3, 151, 153, 166; political system, xvi, 41; and U.S., 14–15, 21–22, 59, 150
Captive Nations Week, 96
Carnegie, Andrew, 40
Caroline, 14, 15
Carter, Jimmy, 142, 162; AIPAC, 146–47; CIA, 130, 140; in elections, 105–6, 136, 138–40; Iranian hostage crisis, 112, 139–40; Panama Canal treaties, 138, 140, 143; policies, 136–38, 140, 149
Case-Zablocki Act, 130, 132
Casey, William, 130, 142
Castro, Fidel, 105, 111, 113, 137, 140, 162–63
Catholic church, 54, 68, 145
Cédras, Raoul, 158
Chaco War, 65
Chambers, Whittaker, 88
Cheney, Dick, 155
Chesapeake, 10
Chiang Kai-shek, 93
Chicago Democratic Convention, 126
Chicago Tribune, 56
Chile, 59, 128, 132
China, 32, 73, 82, 88, 92, 106, 156, 164; and American missionaries, 23–24; civil war, 65, 86, 93; Korean War, 94, 97; market, 32–33, 37, 41; Nixon, 128–29; and U.S., 33, 35, 54–55, 75, 157
China Lobby, 54, 92–93, 97
Chinese Exclusion Act, 34–35
Christian Council on Palestine, 78
Christopher, Warren, 154, 169
Church, Frank, 137, 140; and Church Committee, 130
Churchill, Winston, 74, 83

CIA, 137, 142–43, 147, 152; drug policy, 156–57; economy, defense of, 154; interventions, 97–98, 113, 141; Mafia, 113; and presidents, 91, 97, 118, 130, 140
CIO, 78
Citizens' Committee to Repeal Chinese Exclusion, 75
Civil War, 19–21, 122
Clark, Grenville, 70
Clark Amendment, 117
Clay, Henry, 13, 19
Clayton, Will, 84
Clayton-Bulwer Treaty, 33
Cleveland, Grover: in elections, 22–23; policies, 27–28, 30
Clifford, Clark, 87, 91
Clinton, Bill, 57, 128, 135, 151, 158, 160; in elections, 161, 164; policies, 64, 151–52, 161–64, 170
CNN, 143, 152–53, 158–60
Cohen, William, 147
Colombia, 34
Committee for the Marshall Plan, 86
Committee on Public Information (Creel Committee), 47
Committee on the Present Danger: 1951, 92; 1976, 137
Committee to Defend America by Aiding the Allies, 70
Common Market, 117–18, 149
Communist party, 68
communists, 88, 90; in State Department, 81–82, 93, 95
Confederate States of America, 19–21
Congress for Cultural Freedom, 130
Congressional Black Caucus, 148, 163
Constitution, 2, 5, 38; executive-legislative relations, xvi, 48–49, 65; treaties, xvii, 2, 16; war declarations, 93
Containment policy, 84–87
Coolidge, Calvin, 57–58
Cooper-Church Amendment, 131
Corwin, Edward S., xvi
Coughlin, Charles E., 56, 69
Council of African Affairs, 67–68
Council on Foreign Relations, 57, 75, 92
Cousins, Norman, 115
Cox, James, 51
Creole, 15
Croatia, 168
Croatian-Americans, 148
Cronkite, Walter, 123
Cuba, 17, 26–28, 105–6, 111, 137, 140; and Carter, 137, 162; and Clinton, 162–63; junta, 29–30; missile crisis, 112–14, 161
Cuban-Americans, 163–64

Index

Index

BOOKS IN THE SERIES

Library of Congress Cataloging-in-Publication Data

Small, Melvin.
   Democracy and diplomacy : the impact of domestic politics on U.S.
foreign policy, 1789–1994 / Melvin Small.
        p.   cm. — (The American moment)
   Includes index.
   ISBN 0-8018-5177-7 (alk. paper). — ISBN 0-8018-5178-5 (pbk. : alk.
paper)
   1. United States—Foreign relations.   2. United States—Politics and
government.   3. United States—Foreign relations—20th century.
4. United States—Politics and government—20th century.   I. Title.
II. Series.
E183.7.S515   1996
327.73—dc20   95-8962
                                                            CIP